The Other Side of the Painting

Wendy Rodrigue

University of Louisiana at Lafayette Press
2013

ISBN 978-1-935754-26-8

Printed in Canada.

Library of Congress Cataloging-in-Publication Data:

Rodrigue, Wendy Wolfe.
  [Musings of an artist's wife. Selections]
  The other side of the painting / Wendy Rodrigue.
     pages cm
  ISBN 978-1-935754-26-8 (hardcover)
  1. Rodrigue, George--Blogs. 2. Rodrigue, Wendy Wolfe--
Blogs. I. Title.
  ND237.R69R63 2013
  759.13--dc23
                                   2013024859

For Mignon
who named herself after a French actress

Contents

Chapter 4

A Woolf Inspires a Wolfe

Chapter 5

It's like I'm gonna get a stick stuck in my eye, and I can't wait to get it 'cause it's good for me

Chapter 6

We Emerged Into the Sunlight Dizzy and Disoriented

Chapter 7

Treat Your Painting Like a Jewel

Chapter 8

"A Maiden Who Waited and Wandered"

Chapter 9

More than a French Legend, More than a Dog

Chapter 10

I'm Thinking about the Road

Chapter 11

Breathe In "Who" Breathe Out "Dat"

Chapter 12

Lucky Dog

Foreword

This book might be one in a series by Professor Wendy Wolfe, adored teacher in ivy-covered halls, whose art criticisms are used as texts nationwide because they make painters and their work so accessible to eager students of art.

That could have happened, as we can see in a few of the essays in this collection. Back in the 1970s, Wendy was a wide-eyed sugar-whip of a girl who fell in love with Picasso because, she figures, her teachers reasoned that he was more accessible to young students than the lofty Abstract Expressionism of the day. This same girl, age ten, went with her mother on a ten-dollar budget to stand in line for twelve hours in cold and sleet to see the *Treasures of Tutankhamun*. Having traveled all the way from Fort Walton Beach to New Orleans, she can pinpoint that day as the moment she set out on a course of love for Art History.

Never having wavered, Wendy went to graduate school in Art History at Tulane. And throughout this book she makes dead-on allusions to Robert Motherwell, de Kooning, Warhol, and Donald Judd as if she were naming Baskin-Robbins flavors. Her citations of such writers as Alexander Pope and Virginia Woolf (and even John Kennedy Toole) blend seamlessly in with her own words, reflecting a scholar's quiet storehouse of sharp ideas.

We don't know exactly how chance dealt her out of using her academic's critical eye in the larger world of art historians.

This book was *not* written by Professor Wendy Wolfe. It was written by Wendy Rodrigue, who has given us a chance to look at the work of a single artist in a different way than any other critic could. Along the line, she married George Rodrigue. We learn where, we learn when, but why and how are part of the romantic mystery.

Wendy does not live in the ivory tower of a university. She lives with George in the Marigny of New Orleans and in the seascape of Carmel Valley, California. They travel across the heat of Texas. They take unexpected detours together for medical reasons. So we are given a chance to see George Rodrigue 3-D through her stereoscope—his life, his words, even his 2-D works—and then, through Wendy's prism we see colors that even George cannot find on his palette.

We ricochet dizzily among George, Blue Dog, Jolie Blonde, and, occasionally, Wendy, and keep saying to ourselves, "Wow, who knew that just by looking at those paintings!" George's evolution as an artist can't be given away right here. But the reader comes to know the young George well, bedridden at nine with polio, dealing with technical skill as an undergraduate at the University of Southwestern Louisiana, grappling with Pop Art at the Art Center College of Design in Los Angeles, and being drawn inexorably back to the culture and oaks of southwest Louisiana. His struggles to find his own way to paint nudes would be amusing, if not for the chemical effects of the paints necessary for painting female flesh. As for Blue Dog and Jolie Blonde, not a syllable will be leaked here.

His business history, too, plays to the voyeur in any reader: it's hard to believe today's George once sold Cajun paintings out of the trunk of his car. It is stories like this—and stories about his early triumphs of idea over technique—that make George Rodrigue more humanly and lovingly accessible than any artist could be.

This book is the result of blog posts dating back to late 2009. In what may be the linchpin of this collection of essays, "A Gallery of His Own," Wendy shares a rare private moment. It is after George and his son Jacques have spent nine months doing construction on the property now occupied by the Rodrigue Gallery. Wendy has been left out of the process. "You are doing something far more important with your blog," George says to her. "You're setting the story straight. That's where I need you."

It's more complicated than that. But Wendy helps us see how.

–Patty Friedmann

Acknowledgments

Thank you . . .

. . . to my husband George Rodrigue, who spent months on this book's layout and cover design, and who insists, despite my objections, that this project is mine alone. That said, he also requests a personal acknowledgment: to Dr. Maurice W. DuQuesnay, Associate Professor of English at the University of Louisiana at Lafayette.

. . . to the New Yorkers and the Irish, the agents and the editors: Roz Cole, Jack Lamplough, Emer Ferguson, and Sandy Gilbert. In twenty years, I've learned everything I know about books and, more important, about writing for the public, from these four. Thanks to them, I held to my own voice, edited with compulsion, and worked up enough confidence to see this through.

. . . to the Rodrigue Gallery Staff, who treats our business like their own. It's because of them that George and I have the time and resources to paint, to write, and to live.

. . . to the George Rodrigue Foundation of the Arts Staff, who makes us look good through their tireless work for Louisiana's youth and the arts in education.

. . . to UL Press, especially James D. Wilson, who stroked my ego when he tracked me down at the 2011 Louisiana Book Festival in Baton Rouge and insisted on a book.

. . . to Jim Davis of the State Library of Louisiana, who gives America's readers the Louisiana Book Festival, an annual free family event and a terrific venue for authors and publishers to stalk one another.

. . . to my friends and mentors: Dr. Coleen Grissom, English professor and former Vice President of Student Affairs at Trinity University; John Bullard, Director Emeritus of the New Orleans Museum of Art; and Dr. Chris Cenac, author of *Eyes of an Eagle: Jean-Pierre Canac, Patriarch: An Illustrated History of Early Houma-Terrebonne*.

. . . to Patty Friedmann, Tabitha Soren, David Lummis, and Debra Shriver, who contributed their encouragement and endorsements not only for this book, but also, long before, to Wendy Wolfe.

. . . to André Rodrigue, Jacques Rodrigue, and Mallory Page Chastant, who are not my children, but who are, always, my family.

. . . to the city of Houston, Methodist Hospital, and Doctors Preti, Teh, Haykal, and Bryan, because they saved George's life.

. . . and to my sister Heather, because she saved mine.

Introduction

My mom, an artist, talked me into my first Art History class, a sweeping journey from cave paintings to the start of the Renaissance. Previously, I avoided it, thinking I preferred self-discovery through my mother's books. Yet from day one, I sat lost in another time and world. I imagined the hand that held the brush, something I still do, even with George's paintings, even after I watched him apply the paint.

Somehow imagining the artist puts me in that place, those circumstances, as close as I would ever come to inside his head. It's been my obsession as long as I can remember—to understand how others think and feel, why they do the things they do, and that somewhere, somehow it's all rooted in good (. . . at which point George gives me the Hitler speech).

Simultaneous to early Art History, I took "Shakespeare's Comedies and Histories," also in the mid-1980s at Trinity University in San Antonio, Texas, interweaving in my mind the stories, historical figures, language, and art. In the library I discovered the media room where, in those pre-internet days, I watched the BBC Television Shakespeare, further enlivening not just history, but another's spirit, whether Shakespeare's, the character's, or the actor's, so that I might satisfy a small bit of my curiosity and learn *who they are* and *how they tick*.

Maybe it's empathy, but I think it's more. It's an indefensible obsession, something that drives George crazy, as I chase down a rude waiter not to tell him off or kill him with kindness, the southern way, which was never my way, but rather to honestly find out if we've had a misunderstanding, if we offended him, or if a thoughtful word just might help a problem that has nothing to do with us at all. I lose sleep over these unsolved muddles, replaying conversations and missed opportunities in my mind.

And I believe that all of it makes me capable of better understanding the artist, any artist, so that even a concrete sandwich is someone's personal expression. I may not relate to it or want it within my collection, but I respect it as coming from within someone else (. . . again from George the Hitler speech, this time combined with the crappy art speech).

George shakes his head over my elation at the recent find of Richard III's burial site and skeleton. I've watched the videos repeatedly of the dig and DNA discovery, imagining not that I'm the English king, but that I'm the archaeologist, enchanted by such a find. I imagine that the hand holding the tools is my hand, brushing away the dirt, carefully, revealing delicate finger bones, eye sockets, and teeth.

Suddenly Art History, Shakespeare, History, and Science coalesce into one magnificent, meaningful skeletal vignette. I run first to the internet and, dying of curiosity, to my mother's books and my college books and to Shakespeare, blending it in my mind as it has in England on a university's lab table.

I believe in integrating the arts into every aspect of education and as much as possible into daily life. This is why Louisiana A+ Schools (and similar programs in other states) is so exciting, along with a widespread move towards education awareness in museums. This is also why 100 percent of my proceeds from this book, as well as related lectures and exhibitions, benefit the programs of the George Rodrigue Foundation of the Arts, including art supplies for schools, college scholarships, and art camps.

I grew up in the artistic, near-theatrical bubble of Mignon, and today, more than twenty years since my last Art History class, I live in the environs of culturally rich New Orleans and naturally beautiful Carmel Valley, California. Every aspect of my daily life blends with the arts. My blog, *Musings of an Artist's Wife*, allows me to observe and reminisce on paper, with posts lasting indefinitely, unlike a magazine that may end up in the trash or on the bottom of the bathroom pile.

My husband, George Rodrigue, is an artistic embodiment. For him, as he creates and makes decisions, the art always comes first. He refers to me often as an artist too. But I'm uncomfortable with this title. On school visits, you won't find me painting with the kids. Instead I move through, admiring their work, envying a freedom of line unknown to me. I paint nothing. I draw nothing. Faced with a blank canvas, I feel only anxiety. Yet George wanted to subtitle this book, *The Story of Two Artists*, a title so uncomfortable that I barked my rejection without letting him explain.

More than "artist," the word "marketing" chills me, reducing my writing to a sales strategy. From the beginning, these Musings, whether in my blog, a magazine, or book, are based on one simple concept: sharing. Within my essays are my life's interests. My hope is that what I find intriguing, most of which involves George Rodrigue, and all of which, thanks to the filter placed on me by my mother years ago, involves the arts, will inspire others, because, ultimately, the joy of my self-expression, whether through writing or public speaking, lies in that challenge.

Chapter 1

I First Loved Picasso

Before I loved George, I loved his art. And before
George's art, I loved Picasso . . . and Klimt and Pollock
and Rodin . . . .

I First Loved Picasso

*It took me a whole lifetime to learn how to draw like
a child again.* –Pablo Picasso

As a kid, sometime around age twelve, I discovered my
mother's art books. She protected her prized tomes within plastic covers, locked behind the glass doors of a large,
bright yellow wooden bookcase. Her collection included
overviews of the Renaissance, Ancient Greece, and Lost
Worlds, as well as da Vinci, Rembrandt, Rubens, Dürer,
and Michelangelo—all massive books she purchased while
an art student at Louisiana State University around 1960.

Art books are expensive, and in those days her family,
an overnight success story in the 1950s oil industry, had
the money to support the whims they understood, such
as fashion and cars (in my mother's case, the latest Cadillac convertible annually), as well as the whims they never
understood—her Fine Arts major and her art book collec-

tion.

By the time my sister and I appeared, the money was gone, the dresses relegated to a costume closet, and the cars long sold. But the art books remained, and remain, protected and precious. Among them is a boxed set of linen-covered monographs of Modern Masters. These include Klee, Kandinsky, Dali, Braque, and my favorite, Picasso.

Pablo Picasso died in France in the spring of 1973. I was a young child, but I recall my mother showing me his work and talking about this creative genius. Her hero-worship affected me, and the artist rose even higher on that pedestal when my elementary school art teachers chose him for our studies. Looking back, they probably found Picasso more accessible to young students than the lofty Abstract Expressionism of the day, as typified by artists like Motherwell and de Kooning. Pop Art, as far as I can tell, was either not yet understood or not yet taken seriously enough to be worthy of the classroom.

Ironically, a decade earlier, as George Rodrigue studied art at the University of Southwestern Louisiana in Lafayette and the Art Center College of Design in Los Angeles, he too faced the lingering academic art of the day—Abstract Expressionism. Yet it was Pop Art, a movement dismissed by his teachers, which made the biggest impression.

When I reached high school and later studied Art History in college, I recall Picasso practically vilified in academic circles. There was talk that he hadn't done anything worthy of study since Cubism or *Guernica* and that he "lost his touch" as an old man, floundering between grotesque figures and half-hearted revisits of his earlier styles.

Rather than discourage me, these criticisms made me curious, and I poured through my mother's books searching for answers, training my eye, I thought, to see the master's downfall in his artwork.

Yet I saw brilliance.

I returned repeatedly to his simplest images, such as a drawing of a bull or face, and I wondered: *Why should this picture be in a book? Why should he call it finished? What does it mean?*

And finally, *Why is it that I would give up all my worldly possessions to own a simple Picasso drawing when even I, who can't so much as draw a daisy, could produce a fair copy?*

It was during this time that art took on specific meanings for me. I became an art snob in my circle-of-one. I gained freedom of thought, and I dared to look at art in my own way.

Little did I know that I was training for my future life with an artist, not only to study his work (in appreciation of what George has done in the past, for the projects currently on his easel, and for his unwillingness to retrace old ground); but also to face both the obvious insults ("my eight-year-old kid could paint that!") as well as the disguised ones ("Rodrigue is a brilliant businessman, a marketing genius!")

Picasso's life—the Blue Period, Cubism, the African paintings, and so much more—is inside his simplest works. Had he painted them all at age nineteen, they would mean nothing. But at age ninety, spanning a lifetime, they mean everything. The fact that he painted some in a matter of minutes or that second grade students everywhere can duplicate his simplest abstracted designs is irrelevant.

I asked George about Picasso, and he pulled a well-worn book, *Goodbye Picasso*, (David Douglas Duncan, Grosset & Dunlap, 1974) from the shelf and turned to a bookmarked page:

"I remember how messy his house was, and I was so impressed."

He also describes an assignment at the Art Center College of Design in which he was to create a painting in the style of an old master. George chose a guitar and collage à la Picasso (pictured at the top of this essay).

I've insisted for years that George is Picasso in many classrooms—not the same artist or talent, but a similar inspiration to my 1970s school year recollections. It's familiar and unsettling, as though I'll see "Rodrigue" not on a shiny new book, but on the worn-out titles and plastic-covered jackets of my mother's collection. It's the same eerie feeling I had at the New Orleans Museum of Art during their Rodrigue retrospective of 2008. Their memorabilia room held George's boots, jewelry, clothing, and other personal items normally worn, without fanfare, on his person.

Unsurprisingly, as George grows older the critics admire his early works, the pieces they denounced not only as he painted them, but for thirty years following. Like Picasso's *Les Demoiselles d'Avignon*, reviled in its day and now considered his masterpiece, George's first review, "Painter Makes Bayou Country Dreary, Monotonous Place" (Baton Rouge *Advocate*), derides the same paintings that today attract the region's academic elite.

I compare here the two artist's situations, not their actual artwork. One coveted the world's approval, while the other hoped for the approval of his artistic peers in his home state.

And yet repeatedly I hear from teachers and students that George is the only living artist on their syllabus. They study his Blue Dog paintings alongside Monet's *Water Lilies*, Van Gogh's *Self-portraits*, and da Vinci's *Mona Lisa*. Just as my teachers found Picasso more accessible to young students than the Abstract Expressionists, today's teachers may choose Rodrigue over conceptual, installation, and "intellectual" artists for the same reason.

Like Picasso, George reinvents himself. Most artists hope for one unique series of work discernible as their own. And yet Picasso and Rodrigue accomplished this multiple times. They both recognized the importance of a unique idea.

This is the only comparison I make between Picasso and Rodrigue, and it in no way links their actual artwork. To go further would be presumptuous on my part and invite criticism the likes of which I am unfit to fight. I merely draw the connection between Picasso's unwitting participation in my discovery of art as a child and what I know for a fact to be George's similar role in classrooms today.

George, although confident in his art, is uncomfortable with any comparison to the Masters. This doesn't deter him, however, from hoping for, one day, a respected and linked artistic legacy.

Rodrigue on Monet

In 1993 George and I visited Paris. We recently were dating, and I relished this artist-at-my-fingertips. Today I take that access for granted, and I remind myself that not everyone enjoys an expert guide while visiting a museum or watching *Frida* or browsing an art book. Back then I pinched myself daily, and I held questions at the ready, lest the relationship crumble without warning.

Our first stop was a small museum located in the Tuileries Gardens. Claude Monet chose Musée de l'Orangerie to house his *Water Lilies*. I admit even now that it wasn't high on my list. I was young, and university art class cynicism rolled around in my head. My roommate slept on Monet bed sheets, and another friend hung Monet posters matching her coverlet. Yet another coveted her Monet beach towel.

Never mind the museum shop, in the college bookstore I saw placemats, coffee cups, t-shirts, neckties, and umbrellas. The commercialism, in my mind, canceled any hope of meaning. Was it possible to toss everybody's favorite artist and his pretty, decorative kitsch aside and see these paintings with fresh eyes?

Something terrible happened to me, and I remained

clueless. Although, thankfully, the affliction seemed to come and go, I had, for the most part, lost my ability to see.

At the Musée de l'Orangerie, George and I walked into a smallish room with four or five enormous mural-type paintings. The canvases just fit the space, and, along with the walls, they curved, so that we formed the pupil of an eye as we sat on the single bench at the room's center. We were the only visitors.

At first glance I was unimpressed and saw only wallpaper. We sat in silence until I burst:

"What do you see? I mean, I get it—he painted the reflections, the light, the impression left on the water. And yes, it's beautiful. But what does it say? What's the big deal?"

And with that, George shared Claude Monet. He explained that Monet paved the way for all of the art following him, for Abstract Expressionism, Surrealism, Pop, and even the art of Rodrigue himself. He made me see that before Monet no one painted a landscape, or in this case a pond of water lilies, without a horizon line. There was no foreground or background. There were no boundaries framing a subject or narrative. There was only reflection.

Monet painted what he saw, not what he imagined. He painted without the influence of the rules of art or opinions of others, even if the result was something unrecognizable, a mere ghost of the tangible thing. Today, the abstract and imaginary are almost common. But when Monet painted the light reflecting from the pond and lilies, he broke new ground.

For three hours we discussed these paintings. I fell in love with them, and the appreciation grew in me for what Monet had accomplished, for the creative genius behind his innovation, for the shock he gave the art community of his day, and for the gift he left the world.

On the way out, we stopped in the museum shop

where I bought a Monet desk calendar and umbrella.

I've seen many Monets at many museums since, but none that matched the l'Orangerie paintings. George and I visited the Museum of Modern Art in New York and their collection of large-scale Monet *Water Lilies*. These too curve slightly, and the museum's exhibition echoes the l'Orangerie, displayed on curved walls in a single room with a center bench.

The crowds competed with my memories, and my hopes dashed of recreating that momentous afternoon sixteen years ago. I realized, however, that had I been alone, it still wouldn't be the same.

Something's not right, I thought, a bit anxious as shoulders rubbed mine.

"But these aren't the same paintings!" explained George later. "Monet saved the best for France."

And so he did. Don't get me wrong; it was still an important exhibition and worth the visit. However, in truth, the old wallpaper feelings haunted me. I hung in there and stayed longer, at one point closing my eyes. Within a room full of people, I pictured the aging Monet tending his gardens. I imagined his vision, and, after opening my eyes, *I saw clearly*. Like a dragonfly (a reference from the *New York Times* review), my eyes darted from here to there over the colors and in and out of the depths, until I soaked it all in at once.

It wasn't the philosophical and wholly memorable experience of the l'Orangerie, but the denouement came nonetheless: it is perfectly acceptable and even desirable to appreciate a beautiful painting.

American Artists in Paris

Every time I paint a portrait, I lose a friend.
–John Singer Sargent

As I dove through my mother's art books into the history of John Singer Sargent (1856-1925) and his scandalous portrait, *Madame X*, I found more than I expected, and I wandered into irresistible tangents both foreign and familiar.

Although born abroad, Sargent claimed his American heritage from his parents, defining his background by his roots, lest their nomadic lifestyle leave him homeless. Rather than formal schooling, they educated him through the eclectic experiences of travel, settling nowhere for more than a few months. Sargent, the great American portrait painter, was in his early twenties when he visited America for the first time.

I expected a Louisiana connection within the background of Sargent's most famous subject, Virginie Amélie

Avegno Gautreau, known in her portrait as *Madame X*, who lived as a child both at Parlange Plantation (built 1750) in New Roads and at 927 Toulouse Street in the French Quarter. I anticipated romance, the story of an artist and his muse, but found instead mere rumor.

To my surprise, it was a personal analogy that distracted me as I read. I learned that the American Sargent first caught the art world's attention when he won an Honorable Mention at the Salon in Paris in 1879 for his portrait of his mentor, artist Carolus-Duran. The award, steeped in European tradition and pomposity, is a rare honor for an American, even today.

I know this award firsthand, because it hangs on the wall of George's studio, and he speaks of it with reverence. He begins his story with his artist-friend Jean Pierre Serrier, a Frenchman who entered the Salon (est. 1725) annually for twenty years without hanging in the exhibition. In 1974 George removed from its stretcher sticks *The Class of Marie Courregé*, his painting of his mother's 1918 Mount Carmel Academy (New Iberia, Louisiana) school class, and shipped it, rolled in a tube, to Serrier in Paris. The artist stood in line for his friend with the now framed canvas, just as Sargent did with *Madame X* ninety years previous, with hopes of acceptance for exhibition.

In the case of both Sargent and Rodrigue, the American triumphs shocked the public and press, specifically the French newspaper *Le Figaro*, which wrote of Sargent, "No American has ever painted with such quiet mastery," and of Rodrigue, "America's Rousseau."

Each year the French Government presents five awards chosen from thousands of exhibitors: first and second place, and three honorable mentions. In Rodrigue's case, they shipped the certificate to Louisiana Governor Edwin Edwards, who presented the award on France's behalf. As with Sargent, the win guaranteed Rodrigue wall space in the following year's Salon, when he entered his

The Other Side of the Painting

Jolie Blonde of 1974.

John Singer Sargent continued his annual Salon entries throughout most of his life, often causing a stir at the well-attended societal affair and at least once, with *Madame X*, a scandal. Yet he was not the first to shock the high-minded audience.

Although the Parisian elite expected nudes, they related them to allegorical figures, mentally separating these subjects from their sexual allure. It was Edouard Manet who broke this bias with his portrait of a prostitute, *Olympia* (1863), accepted for exhibition in the Salon in 1865. The painting, dominated more by its subject's inviting gaze than her nudity, offended the Parisians as vulgar. The exception was Manet's friend, novelist Emile Zola, who predicted correctly, "It will endure as the characteristic expression of his talent, as the highest mark of his power."

Sargent's faux pas proved just as scandalous, yet his *Madame X* wore an evening gown. It was the thin strap falling from French society's darling Amélie Gautreau's shoulder that offended viewers, as though she were undressing for the public. This caused her such humiliation that she spent the rest of her life trying to quiet the gossip and upstage the memory, posing for several unmemorable portraits with hopes of once again enchanting her peers.

Sargent faced not only the public's hatred, but also that of Madame Gautreau, who refused to purchase the painting and nearly broke him financially. As with Manet and Zola, it was an author who defended Sargent, his friend Henry James, who wrote that he saw "each work that [Sargent] provides in a light of its own," and that he did not "turn off successive portraits according to some well-tried receipt which has proved useful in the case of their predecessors."

A compromised *Portrait of Amélie Gautreau*, now with two secure straps on her shoulders, remained hidden for more than thirty years in Sargent's studio, as he worked to repair his reputation as a portrait artist, catering to the upper class families of England and the American Northeast. Indeed, Sargent became that rare phenomenon, an artist both critically acclaimed and financially successful throughout most of his life. For years, in fact, he felt trapped by his portraiture and the demands of his patrons and tried unsuccessfully to break away.*

The Metropolitan Museum of Art in New York purchased the painting of Amélie Gautreau from the artist in 1916, the year following her death, accepting Sargent's condition that they separate the painting from its subject, renaming it *Madame X*. Far from a scandal today, many consider it his masterpiece, arguably the most famous painting in America's greatest museum.

In New Orleans, George's Salon award hangs in his studio, inspiring his work today and reminding him that the Parisians understood his art long before his American contemporaries. Like Sargent and Manet, he belongs in the story of Art History.

As far as I know, Sargent never visited Louisiana; however, the spirit of Amélie Gautreau lives on, not as Madame X, but as the young girl who once lived here and the stunning woman she became, immortalized not with another painting, but with the New Orleans Uptown restaurant that bears her name.

* "Such grave and distinguished portraits as those by Sargent strive, like the heads of medieval statuary, to read a soul into the human visage, and appear not merely to offer a depiction of their subjects but to render a judgment upon them." John Updike, *Still Looking: Essays on American Art*, (Alfred A. Knopf, 2005).

My Favorite Painting

George's *Loup-garou* is my favorite painting.

I first saw it on a Sunday afternoon in 1991, a day that changed my life. I walked into the Rodrigue Gallery in the French Quarter to visit a friend, the gallery manager. At the time, I worked at Ann Taylor while attending graduate school at Tulane University, and I worried as my college job morphed into my future. If I didn't take a chance, I might lose the art world.

That day I sought advice regarding museum work. My undergraduate studies at Trinity University in San Antonio, Texas, focused on the Northern Renaissance; Contemporary and Modern Art were far from my mind.

In 1991 I knew nothing of George Rodrigue or his art. I'd never been to Lafayette nor visited his gallery in the French Quarter.

Stepping through the Rodrigue Gallery door, I stared at the far wall and a 6 x 4 foot canvas. Without thinking, I touched it. I was stunned by the power in this painting, by the idea of some hand applying and blending the goopy paint, by an artist making something all about, and yet not the least bit about, one strong shape.

I learned later that this was George's first painting of the Blue Dog by itself, removed from the Cajun background. I didn't recognize it as a dog.

"What is it?" I whispered to my friend.

"It's the Blue Dog," he said.

Within a week I left Ann Taylor and graduate school and worked full-time with the *Loup-garou* in the Rodrigue Gallery.

Within six months I moved to California, my first visit to the West Coast, where I spent six years at the Rodrigue Gallery in Carmel-by-the-Sea. I called my friend,

"Send me the *Loup-garou*."

"No way. Too expensive to ship."

I asked until he agreed, and the painting hung at my desk for two years until my co-worker Sandra sold it. At $50,000 it was our biggest sale to date in Carmel. The gallery's success, however, did not assuage my disappointment, and in 1997 when George and I married, I still talked about it.

In 2002 George shocked me with the *Loup-garou*, returned by some negotiation still unknown to me, and the painting hung in our home for the first time. As I write this, I exchange a stare with my painting. I'm as confused and weak-kneed as I was twenty years ago.

Great paintings take on a life of their own, beyond the artist's intent or the owner's collection, or even, perhaps George's most frustrating battle, some collective assumption about them. The greatest works of art pose questions long after the artist's death. Consider Degas's *Yellow Ballerina*, Picasso's *Les Demoiselles d'Avignon*, and Monet's *Water*

Lilies.

The reason the Blue Dog lasts is not because it's a dog. I like dogs, but I've never had one, nor am I a "dog person." The Blue Dog lasts because it's painted and designed well, because it's rooted in twenty-five years of Cajun paintings, because no matter how long we wait, it won't explain itself, and because, most important, it is painted by George Rodrigue.

I'm not talking about George's appealing manner or his artistic intent or commentary. I'm talking about something far more complex, expressed from his soul and unique to him: his style.

Jackson Pollock at 100

"Pollock" is a colossal word in art. Automatically it brings to mind the abstract drip-paintings of a disturbed, passionate alcoholic who drizzled paint in layers as he circled huge canvases.

Despite his enduring fame, Jackson Pollock (1912-1956) created his most defining works in only four years. Prior to 1947, he searched for a direction, often changing course. After 1950, he battled the emotions and demands accompanying art-world fame, leading to acute alcoholism and, in 1956 at age forty-four, his death. Yet in this short period, he altered the definition of art, some thought irrevocably, abandoning the most basic canons—the easel for the floor and the brushstroke for the drip.

Within five years after his death, Pollock, thanks to a major spread in *LIFE* magazine and a retrospective at New York's Museum of Modern Art, was mythic. According to George, his teachers at the Art Center College of Design in Los Angeles (1964-1967) spoke with reverence about Pollock and the "death of easel painting":

> The teachers were ten to fifteen years older than the students, and they had vivid recollections of the drip

painting phenomenon. When I first arrived, I recall one teacher stating that following Pollock, he thought for a while that no artist again would walk up to a canvas on an easel and use a brush.

Yet by the time George reached art school in 1964, the students and teachers returned to easels. Even Pollock tried to move on in the early 1950s, but his agent and the critics wouldn't have it, and the work was ill-received.

Without studying Pollock, his art at first may appear simplistic, even child-like. Yet his paintings include a formula. Generally he dripped the darkest colors first and ended with white. He moved with both the drips and splashes in a deliberate pattern, resulting in canvases resembling shiny marble surfaces.

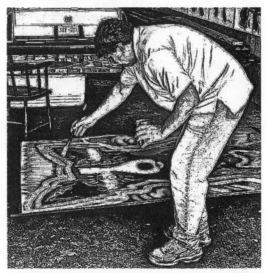

Years later, other artists apply paint using this same technique. George drips on the floor, on chrome pieces over Blue Dogs.

"Is this a tribute to Pollock?" I asked.

"I don't dare go that far," he explained. "Rather, I drip

paint on both the background and the dog as a way of blending, of transitioning from the dog to the chrome, in the same way Hunt Slonem (George's friend) unifies his shapes and images with lines and cross-hatches."

Sadly, Jackson Pollock suffered a short career dictated, perhaps near-bullied, by the art elite. This Abstract Expressionist, an American artist born in Cody, Wyoming, could not know his lasting contribution to the art world. Today, his legacy enriches museum collections such as our own New Orleans Museum of Art.

The Muse

For several years a pair of great horned owls sat each morning at the edge of our pond-like pool in Carmel, California, and watched the sunrise. I squinted at their silhouettes, side-by-side, stronger as reflections in the water than the hazy outline of their bodies against the valley. Occasionally I opened the door for a photo, but each time they spread their wings at the noise, landing separated in the branches of our lace oaks or on the peeks of our modern, oversized cabin, sending me running between windows for another glimpse.

My cousin Timber Wolfe, perhaps influenced by his name, reminded me recently that the great horned owls eat the bunnies, small foxes, and birds that also call this place home.

"The owls are predators," he said.

Yet my romantic sentiment persevered, even after yesterday's related incident, when a hawk sent a covey of quail from our fountain to the bushes, where they stood like statues for so long that even I abandoned the wait.

George, who paints all night and sleeps until noon, missed the owls for years.

"Take a picture!" he said, frustrated with my failure as a nature photographer.

This summer we went weeks without owls. But it was foggy, and I assumed they chose a clearer vista. One morning, however, the "hooo-hooo" called for an hour or more, waking George. We scanned the water's edge, the branches, and the roof in vain, seeking the source of the sad cry.

I recalled the owls this week as we watched *Bride of the Wind* (2001), a movie about muses, artists, and love affairs. It was twenty years ago that a similar movie, *Impromptu*, reflected, in a way, the impromptu shift in my life's course. I returned from Vienna only three years before, and it was there that I contemplated Gustav Klimt's *Adam and Eve* (1916), a painting I visited dozens of times while musing my destiny.

Impromptu (1991), based on the real life love affairs and friendships of author George Sand (a woman who posed as a man so that she would be taken seriously as a writer) with composers Frederic Chopin and Franz Liszt, poet Alfred de Musset, and artist Eugene Delacroix, inspired the hopeful muse within me, as though I were again thirteen, imagining that my knight climbed my hair towards my tower prison.

The year of *Impromptu* was also the year I risked change, abandoning graduate school for a job at the Rodrigue Gallery of New Orleans. It was the year I met George, the year my life changed forever.

I spent much of 1991 and 1992 reading the complete works of George Sand, as I listened to Chopin's preludes and etudes, immersing myself in this real-life fairytale. Similarly, I relate to the artists in *Bride of the Wind*, a movie based on the true story of Alma Mahler and her love affairs with composer Gustav Mahler, architect Walter Gropius, and artist Oskar Kokoschka. She lived in that same inspired world, the one that transported me as a college student, through *Adam and Eve*, to fin de siécle Vienna.

> How was I twisted magically, since from a hazy world, prospecting her, a small white bird summoned me, AL-LOS, ALLOS, whom I never came across. Since in an instant swiftly she transformed herself into my being, like a back door. Suffer, ears, Strive, you eyes, to spot her! I into the indigent summer night, which faded and cries from a rift in the earth.*

In 1988 my Viennese professor teaching Austrian Art and Architecture claimed to have had a long-running affair with Kokoschka. During her classes I struggled to retain the academic lessons while daydreaming about the romantic ones. It was this notion of "the lover of a great artist" that intrigued me. What on earth must it feel like to be a muse, to affect a creative soul in such a way that their personal expression involves you and remains as such forever?

I leave that question unanswered here, not because I don't know the answer, but because it confounds me, and I am left with pure emotion and no words.

This morning George joined me in the bedroom after painting all night. We stood at the window and watched the sunrise.

"There's only one owl," I whispered.

"Maybe they split up," he said.

But we both knew better.

---

* From the poem, "Allos Maker" (an anagram from the names Alma and Oskar, meaning "Happiness is otherwise"), by Oskar Kokoschka, 1913.

Indiscretion

All good art is an indiscretion.
–Tennessee Williams, *Memoirs*

It was my mom who explained the artistic nude to me, as perfected by Peter Paul Rubens. We flipped often through her Northern Renaissance tomes, pausing on pages of rosy-cheeked, fleshy women and discussing the notion of beauty.

"You see, Wendy, I'm a Rubenesque nude. I was born at the wrong time, that's all," explained my mother, as I considered the shapeless stick that was my adolescent frame.

The nude ideal today, unless your name is Botero, is anything but fleshy in a society so inundated with the skeletal female form that to post an example here would be redundant.

Wendy Rodrigue

However, since the beginning of art history the ample woman sends artists running to their easels or chisels, recalling the rotund *Venus of Willendorf* (22,000 B.C.), the ancient subject of the first day of my first college Art History class and, since her discovery in 1908, a source of endless debate:

She's a symbol of motherhood! Fertility personified! A typical female beauty! A child's toy! Grotesque! A goddess!

It was another fleshy female, as portrayed by Gustav Klimt in his unfinished painting *Adam and Eve* (1916), that lured me dozens of times over eight months in 1988 to the museum at the Belvedere Palace in Vienna, Austria. I saw something in this near life-size work that transported me to another time or, rather, another person, connecting me to something beyond paint on canvas, including a female ideal transcending the latest issue of *Vogue*. In this painting I sensed a connection between artist and model, a zone so intriguing that I wondered if it might be my destiny.

Soon afterward I met George, a modern artist clinging to classical ideals of beauty. Early in our relationship, my internal muse swooned when he observed,

"You remind me of a Valadié painting."

George's ideal lies somewhere between the skeletal and fleshy. He dislikes bones, preferring not quite the Rubenesque curves, but nonetheless the opportunity for longer, rounded strokes and broad areas of shape. Lucky for me.

Several years ago George gave me a 1936 lithograph by the Surrealist René Magritte of his friend, poet Paul Eluard (who was first married, incidentally, to Salvador Dali's famous model and wife, Gala). It hangs in my office for inspiration, along with a photograph of Tennessee Williams and a postcard of Klimt's *Adam and Eve*. This indiscreet image shows Eluard standing over a nude and faceless female. The poet scrawls one word across her torso:

"Écrire."

Chapter 2

His Heart Called Him Home

Following art school, unlike his classmates who pursued careers in New York, George Rodrigue returned home and painted Louisiana.

"Rodrigue" with Pronunciation

The name "Rodrigue" is a common one in Cajun country. However, outside the southern part of his home state, George Rodrigue endures mispronunciations and misspellings on a regular basis.

Most of the time, people say or spell the name "Rodriguez." A close second is "Rodrique" (with a *q* in place of the *g*). And above all, the most popular mispronunciation is "Rod-ree-gay."

People like George's mother (adamantly "French" as opposed to "Cajun") pronounce the name "Row (as in 'row your boat')-dreeg." And George, Cajun through and through, pronounces his name "Rod-reeg."

The name, I'm told, originated in Portugal and began as "Rodrigues" (pronounced "Row-dreegsh," rolling the first *R*). It probably changed, although no one knows for sure, in the mid seventeenth century when Jeanne

Rodrigues, born in Portugal, married Anne LeRoy, born in Paris, France, altering the name by dropping the *s* to sound more French in the Acadian community of Beauport, Canada, where they made their home.

By 1755 and the Grand Dérangement, the name Rodrigue existed for at least one hundred years. George's Aunt Bertha spent much of her adult life, long before the internet, researching the Rodrigue genealogy. The Courregé side (her father's name), was easy, because they knew that their father relocated to New Iberia, Louisiana, directly from France. His thirteen children used this heritage to call themselves the more elegant "French," as opposed to what they perceived as the more primitive "Cajun."

George's mother, Marie Courregé, (pronounced "Cour-a-zhay" in Louisiana, although in France it's closer to "Cour-rezh") was more Rodrigue than Courregé, especially once she married. Her mother was a Rodrigue, meaning that George's parents were first cousins.

According to Aunt Bertha, four Rodrigue brothers entered New Orleans in 1755. She suspected but could not confirm that they came from Canada. The brothers settled in the southeastern part of the state, in Lafourche Parish, specifically in and around the town of Chackbay, Louisiana. Today the town holds an annual Rodrigue reunion attracting three to four thousand people.

In 1972 George received a letter from a Canadian professor asking about the Rodrigue name. He discovered George in an art magazine as a painter of Cajun folk life. The professor filled in the puzzle, having traced the Rodrigue name from Portugal to Beauport, Canada. He knew of four Rodrigue brothers leaving Canada in 1755 but knew no further. George introduced him to Aunt Bertha, and they connected the dots.

George is proud of his name and his Cajun heritage. He named his sons, André Rodrigue and Jacques Rodrigue, after their Canadian ancestors. Throughout his career, he uses his name as both a symbol and an interesting graphic element. This is especially true of his Louisiana commemorative posters, when he enhances the border text with a large and bold signature.

With the *Blue Dog* series, specifically the original silkscreens, in numerous cases George incorporates his name as a design element with the Blue Dog for attention. The name is so important within his art that the second most asked question we receive (following "What's the story of the Blue Dog?") is "How do you pronounce Rodrigue?"

And so there you have it, the name Rodrigue (pronounced "Rod-reeg"), with a bit of genealogical *lagniappe* included.

How Baby George
Became an Artist

George grew up an only child in New Iberia, Louisiana, a small town in the heart of Cajun country. His father, George Sr., was a bricklayer by trade. In addition, as the youngest of thirteen children, Big George, as he was known, took on family businesses as his siblings died. And since George's mother, Marie Courregé Rodrigue, was the youngest of eleven children, the couple inherited several businesses from her side as well, eventually running a bar, trailer park, and Rodrigue's Portable Concrete Burial Vaults.

Big George designed and fabricated brick boilers for sugar mills throughout south Louisiana and Texas. He was a contractor who built houses, including the duplex where Baby George, as the family called him, was born in 1944, located on West Main Street in New Iberia, the old Highway 90 Spanish Trail running from New Orleans to Santa Fe. In 1951 Big George completed a family home on St. Peter Street where Baby George spent his youth. His mother remained in the house for fifty-seven years, and George still owns it, unable to part with his father's edifice.

New Iberia in the 1950s was an interesting mix of people. The large Cajun population blended with the Lebanese, Italians, African Americans, and descendants of the area's original Spanish settlers (hence, the town *New* Iberia, named after the Iberian Peninsula in Spain.) The town still boasts a primarily Catholic community, largely rooted in the descendants of the 1755 Grand Dérangement when British troops displaced some twenty-five thousand French people in Nova Scotia who refused to pledge allegiance to King George of England and the Protestant faith. George's family is descended on his father's side from four brothers who migrated into south Louisiana from Canada during this time. His mother's father, Jean Courregé, however, came to Louisiana directly from France in 1860.

George remembers clicking rosary beads as a small boy on his grandmother's front porch with his mother's oldest sister, Tante Magitte (1881-1970) as they recited together the Catholic prayer in French. Although he grasped a basic understanding, he did not grow up speaking French, and his parents discouraged the language at home. Beginning in the 1930s there had been a concerted effort to eliminate the French language in Louisiana schools.

George's parents spoke a Cajun dialect and remained self-conscious about what they considered an inferior form of the language. They hoped he would learn the correct French in school, because pride increased in Louisiana's French heritage during this time. However, those courses did not exist until George's senior year of high school, by which time he lost interest.

1950s New Iberia was not an art mecca. There were

no museums or art galleries, and no art classes in school or art books in the library. No paintings hung on the walls at the Rodrigue house or in the homes of their friends.

But George set his course as an artist at age nine when he remained bedridden for months with polio. To pass the time, his mother brought him modeling clay and a 1950s invention, paint-by-number. At age twelve, fully recovered, he studied with Mrs. Ella Fontenot Keane, the only artist known to his family, and in six months of Saturday morning classes, he completed three paintings, all still in his possession: a fruit still-life, a country road, and two quail in a corn patch.

Following Mrs. Keane, George continued his education with correspondence courses through an art instruction school in Minneapolis, Minnesota. When the school's southern sales representative called in person on the Rodrigue house with the news that George was accepted, he noted George with surprise, admitting that at age thirteen, he was their youngest student to date.

At age fourteen, George saw his first art exhibition. The actor Vincent Price teamed with Sears Roebuck, primarily known as a tire store, and traveled the country with an art show that promoted Sears's expanding efforts as a department store. George's parents drove him the seventy miles to Baton Rouge, where Sears and Price presented the show, offering original paintings and prints for sale.

George saw only one additional art show in the following five years, a western exhibition at Compton La-Bauve's Jewelry Store in downtown New Iberia featuring artist Joe Grandee, a cover illustrator for *True West Magazine*. According to George, when Grandee admitted to Mr. and Mrs. Rodrigue that he had not attended college,

"That's when the trouble started!"

George's parents, who encouraged his art, thought of it as a hobby and did not understand his career goals. They insisted he work for the Southern Pacific Railroad

Company like Uncle Albert or with the South Central Bell Telephone Company like Aunt Ruby. In a compromise, he enrolled at the University of Southwestern Louisiana in Lafayette for Fine Art Studies and Commercial Illustration, followed by the Art Center College of Design in Los Angeles.

Established in 1900, the University of Southwestern Louisiana (now the University of Louisiana at Lafayette) is the second largest university in the state and, most important, boasts an art department. George enrolled in 1962. He had no interest in pursuing a degree, however he wanted formal training in the fine arts. He describes these college years as a stepping-stone. Abstract Expressionism was the academic art of the day, but he had little interest in non-representational art.

While at USL, George realized that his strength lie not with his technical ability but in his ideas. He witnessed others, even his professors, struggling with originality, something natural for George throughout his life. His most important accomplishment at USL was the creation of his design book in Professor Calvin Harlan's class. Upon its completion, however, George felt saturated with the school's curriculum, and after only four semesters, he moved on, using his design book as a reference.

Accepted as an undergraduate at the Art Center College of Design Graduate School, George followed his calling, traveling from New Iberia to Los Angeles by train, soon replaced by his Corvair, filled in its unusual front trunk with his art books, protected and precious on the three-day drive. Fifty years later those same books remain an important source of reference, stored within his studio's bookcase.

It was his years at Art Center that gave George the fundamental skills needed to pursue a career as an artist. Known for its instruction in graphic illustration, advertising design, and automotive design, Art Center showed

George a new world. In addition to the fundamentals of art, he studied design of all kinds, including mock album covers for movie soundtracks, photography, including dark room development and printing, short films, brochures for fictitious American cities, and illustrations for refrigerators and ovens.

"What kind of woman do you picture opening a refrigerator door?" stated one assignment, so dated that even George shudders, for my benefit, as he recalls the class.

As much as school, the L.A. art scene supplied additional education. In 1962 Andy Warhol shocked the art world with his exhibition of Campbell's Soup Cans at the Ferus Gallery. His Brillo Boxes, Coca-Cola bottles, Marilyn Monroes, and Elvis Presleys debuted in regular exhibitions until the gallery closed in 1966. Although derided by his professors, Pop Art, specifically the idea of taking something from the popular culture and reinserting it into that same culture as a piece of art, fascinated George and his peers.

After intense studies with abstract artist Lorser Feitelson (1898-1978) at Art Center, George had already focused on hard edges. Pop Art, however, added repetitive imagery. In a strange way it was both abstract and representational. These qualities remain with George today, whether in his stylized oak or his iconic Blue Dog. Unlike the original Pop artists, however, George invented his most famous image *as a piece of art*. From the beginning, the Blue Dog existed only as he imagines it.

Art school affected George in many ways, none of which included a degree. USL inspired the design book leading him to Los Angeles. And at Art Center he studied for the first time with professional artists, mastering Hard Edge painting, Color Field painting, and figure drawing. But it was the 1960s Pop Art phenomenon combined with the long drives home, that affected him most. It was California that elucidated for George, albeit unwittingly, the unique state of Louisiana, and it was the big skies of Texas that illuminated the small, hopeful space beneath the Evangeline oak.

While his peers followed the art world to New York, Rodrigue followed his heart and culture home to Louisiana.

The Artist's Mother

"Aren't you happy?" asked my uncle of Marie Rodrigue on the night of my engagement to her son. "You're going to have a daughter-in-law!"

"I had one," she replied, her face deadpan. "It didn't work out."

When she died in 2008 at age 103, George's mother still wanted to "go home" to New Iberia. She wanted her car back, to remove her grandsons' hats and cut their hair, to lengthen my skirts and overcook my Thanksgiving turkey, to visit long-dead friends and family and, most important, to see her son get a real job, "with the telephone company," she said, as she worried about his pension:

"When will you realize that nobody's gonna buy those pictures?"

She was tough, "solid," as George used to say, with

legs like tree stumps (her description, not mine), and the closest she came to happiness was in worrying about it. At age ninety-two she called us in Carmel, California, as it stormed at our house in Lafayette, Louisiana, concerned about the rising water in the front yard. We heard the phone drop and an "Umph," amidst the thunder and rain, as she slipped on the front porch, her solid body rolling into the flower bed unharmed.

"Where are the sandbags?!" she hollered, recovering the phone as she lay trapped beneath an azalea bush.

Like most of her generation, the Depression hovered over Marie Rodrigue's decisions, threatening to return at any moment. However, she lived with another experience just as powerful. It was a Sunday morning in 1927, and like all of New Iberia, twenty-two-year-old Marie Courregé knew that the water was coming. Weeks before, the Mississippi River over-topped the levees for hundreds of miles above Acadiana. Marie parked her Model T Ford at the edge of the floodplain, just east of New Iberia, where the river ran for thousands of years, and where the land descends toward St. Martinville. She heard the water before she saw it, and for the rest of her life she recounted the story, her hands moving with the memory.

"The water was rollin'," she said, her arms twirling and her eyes wide. "I jumped in the car and drove to the church, the river rising on the wheels of daddy's car. 'It's coming!' I screamed in the middle of the sermon, and the people ran from the church and left town."

Marie Rodrigue, a devout Catholic, proud to be "French" as opposed to "Cajun," was an odd and some would say charming mixture of funny and mean. "She has no filter," George said in response to her biting comments. If it entered her head, it came out of her mouth, and like most families, maybe all families, it was those closest to her that felt the sting.

"George, you're full of shit," she said on more than

one occasion. And eventually I was too.

We learned to lie and tell her what she wanted to hear, that the new clothes were the dry cleaning, that I scraped the insides of the pumpkins for the pies, that we sold paintings on our vacations, that her savings paid for her living expenses, that our dinner guests left twenty dollars at the door, and that if she would wear a new suit instead of her shroud to our wedding, I would, "I swear, on the day you die, let the sleeves out again so that someone else can wear it."

George, an only child, tried to please her, and perhaps that is the best that can be said of their relationship. He loved her deeply and lied daily to his mother, because he wanted her happiness. I know for a fact that she bragged about George to others, yet she existed on another plane from her son, unable to acknowledge his accomplishments where it mattered most, to his face. Fortunately, her wit softened the blow.

"She didn't think she was funny," says George, "but she had a dry, cynical humor that cut to the chase real fast."

Immune to criticism from a young age, George is confident in his artwork and in life's decisions. In the years I've known him, he coveted only his mother's approval. Yet, in one of life's ironies, the harder he tried, the less likely her praise. The saving grace, both at that time and now, as we reminisce about Marie, is the left field humor in her retorts.

"Well, did he have anything good to say?" she asked, after we gave her a rosary and a signed proclamation from the Pope.

She wore step-ins instead of panties, passed a good time with her visiting relatives, went ridin' in the afternoons, had the *en vie* for chicken stew, and, unable to grasp the concept of reruns, marveled at how good Ed Sullivan looks for his age.

An insomniac, she roamed the house at night, checking doors and the refrigerator, one time locking me out in my nightgown at 5:30 a.m. as I picked blackberries in the backyard for a pie. (Thank you again, George Parker, our neighbor, for your discretion and the use of your bathrobe and phone.)

For no reason at all, she stood barefoot on a railroad tie in our driveway and bellowed the French National Anthem as George and I planted bamboo around our greenhouse. Another time she and her niece Berta Lou yelled like Janes throughout the evening during a Tarzan marathon, feasting on Doritos and red wine, as George, the boys, and I stared from the next room.

In the two years she lived with us, she expected "dinner" on the table each day at noon, shortcuts not allowed. I apologize here publicly to my stepsons for thinking that they finished off the cakes in the night, leaving me panicked nearly seven days a week for a new homemade dessert. It was the incessant roach problem that alerted me to the truth, when I found cakes and cokes stored beneath Marie's bed, hidden, she explained, "from all those kids . . . and from Dickie [Hebert]!"

On the road, George called her daily to reassure her that he was working. He often recounts the time some friends from California heard her on speakerphone after he explained that someone bought a painting for $50,000.

"She got real quiet and then said, 'How much?' So I repeated it slowly. She paused again before she got mad: 'For one of your pictures? George, you give those poor people's money back right now!'

"She was more worried about those 'poor people' than she was about me."

Without question, Marie softened with age. She forgot André's long hair and Jacques's girlfriends. She forgot that she hated Christmas. And she forgot me altogether. Unfortunately for George, she remembered that he took her car and that she wanted to go home. In her own way, a

Mother's way, she loved her son, and she reminisced until the end about his childhood studio in the attic and the way the other mothers cooed at him in the carriage.

While in her early nineties, Marie and George visited his father's grave in New Iberia, where a cousin left fresh flowers for what would have been his one-hundredth birthday.

"Those hussies," she snapped, "they're still after him!"

And she never visited him again.

For better or worse, Marie lived her later years (her last forty, according to George) in the past. Admittedly, the repeated conversations brought tears to my eyes.

"George, let's visit Lona," she said, dressed and ready for the ride.

"Lona's dead," he replied.

"Oh yes? Where's Caspa?"

"Dead."

"Well then, let's call Romain . . . ."

But they were all dead. Finally we lied about that too and spoke of ghosts as though they lived. We explained that they would visit her next week, as we grabbed a chance, a fleeting chance, to make her happy.

The Artist's Father

George rarely speaks of his father. I've written about his construction and tomb business, as well as peripheral facts regarding his Cajun heritage. Yet even when pressed, I struggled pulling personal information about Big George from his son.

George fights these memories, and he stares in the distance and speaks slowly, obviously distressed by my questions. I strain to hear him over the music in his studio, but he protests as I move to lower the volume. Johnny Cash and "Luther Sang the Boogie," he explains, help him with the past.

"Mama called him Daddy and everybody called me Baby George. To the town he was 'Big George,' not only because we shared a name, but also because he was strong, with huge hands. One cousin remembers him lifting the backend of a Model T Ford. He was also the pitcher for the New Iberia baseball team.

"He quit school in the sixth grade to work with his father, also a bricklayer. He was what they called a Master Mason, because he built fireplaces and designed brick boilers for the sugar mills. My daddy made his reputation on being an artist in his own right. He and my mama traveled throughout south Louisiana on bricklaying jobs for twenty years before settling again in New Iberia. He built the wishing well in our backyard because my mama wanted one. He built her a brick house because she wanted a brick house. He then built her a den off of the back because she wanted that too.

"My daddy surprised her when a master carpenter designed a fancy roof for the wishing well. She screamed about the money and they fought for days. But she got it anyway and everyone, including her, enjoyed it. We had tadpoles and two frogs, and then we let them go. We tried out goldfish, perch, and all sorts of minnows.

(Author's note: It's because of the well, I believe, that George will never sell this house. He painted it many times, sometimes with Evangeline peering into the water.)

"I was thirteen when my daddy got sick. At the hospital in Lafayette they said he would die, but when I woke the next morning, they said he would live. My mama sat in the waiting room clicking her rosary beads. She thought it was a miracle.

"His illness changed him, and he wasn't the same for ten years, until he died in 1967. He never saw me become an artist, but he saw me paint as a kid in my studio in the attic."

"But George, I pressed, what was he like as a person? Tell me about his personality, his beliefs. What kind of man do you remember?"

He sat quiet for a long time, his mind elsewhere.

"I didn't understand who he was when I was thirteen, but my older cousins told me about him.

"They said that when the street fair came to town, he knocked the bottles from the shelves with three balls. He won so many prizes that they banned him from the fair. But he changed his clothes and hat and returned, disguised, to play again. That was long before I was born.

"I was a pitcher for a while in the Boy Scouts. My daddy was the umpire, so naturally I never walked a player. I remember one time when I lost control and threw the ball straight in the air. The catcher caught it and someone in the stands yelled,

'Well Ump, don't you think that's a strike?'"

"Tell me that story again about when you went fishing."

"After his surgery, he couldn't work and mostly sat bored in the house. So we went fishing. We found all kinds of places in south Louisiana, some private, some paid, and some on the levee."

"What did you talk about?"

"It was important to him that I never pick up a brick. I like to draw plans, but he forbid me to be an architect. He hated them. 'They only know how to draw on paper,' he said, 'and not how to build, not how to make it a reality.'

"I was spoiled as an only child, but he had two sisters, Aunt Pauline and Aunt Evelyn, and they spoiled him. When they died, we inherited their husband's businesses, which he tried to run—rent houses, bars, and trailer parks. Eventually my parents sold everything, unable to keep it up."

"Anything else, George?"

"My daddy left fireplaces, houses, and walkways, all things people still use, and I guess that's his legacy. He built my uncle's house, my cousin's house, and two houses for us.

"I watched him build complex steps and structures, and in a way he helped me understand design. He never finished school, but he kept a book of figures. His work involved a lot of math, and I assume he taught himself. He died too young, and he got sick before I really got to know him or before he got to know me."

New Iberia, 1950
Fort Walton Beach, 1975

I try and, honestly, fail to imagine 1950s New Iberia, Louisiana. I've stared at this photograph for hours, a six-year-old George dressed as a cowboy on Christmas morning, an only child surrounded by symbols of the time: a Radio Flyer red wagon; promotional Coca-Cola Santa Clauses (in multiples because his dad traded them on a brick-laying job); a dartboard featuring Little Black Sambo, a bigotry so culturally ingrained that no one in young George's world even thought about it; and a photograph on the fireplace mantle of cousin Nootsie, a fighter pilot shot down during World War II.

I see the fireplace bricks George's father laid ever-so-straight with his bare hands, and I wonder at the Christmas ornaments, heirlooms of school projects, world travels, and craft fairs in my own childhood, still hanging on our tree today. Yet by the time George and I married in 1997, the Rodrigue family long ago wrote off their ornaments as junk, disappearing within George's mother's Depression-influenced memory. I asked her, a woman who had not decorated a tree in forty-seven years, "Where do I find your boxes of ornaments?"

"I threw those out years ago," she explained, her mild dementia drifting in and out, "when I turned the attic into a studio for George. Daddy installed a window unit, our first air conditioner, and I listened to its whirring while George painted." (A rather endearing end to the ornaments, I must admit . . .)

. . . at which point she twirled her hands in a disco move, the same gesture she made each time she talked about the floodwaters of 1927 rolling into New Iberia.

If you ask George he'll tell you that he had a happy childhood. He might point out, while laughing, that this Christmas, 1950, was the last time he received a gift from Santa or his parents. According to his mother, his father went overboard and gave him enough gifts at age six to last a lifetime. It was also the last year the family would "waste money" on a tree.

For me, the strongest image in the holiday photograph is of a lone boy, an only child, who, despite dozens of nearby cousins, spent Christmas with a Coca-Cola Santa, Little Black Sambo, a father well into his fifties and a mother getting close.

I also see a boy blissfully lost in his imagination, a cowboy enthralled with the Lone Ranger Radio Show, and a growing obsession with 1950s memorabilia that continues today.

At the time of this Christmas photograph, Earl Long was governor of Louisiana. Our politics, not unlike today, were full of both personal and public drama. Segregation was the norm in this small southern town, and young

George grew up with both his parents' and society's pervasive racism, an ugly reality he probably didn't consider until he served with the National Guard during the Selma to Montgomery marches of 1965.

The young George in this photograph could not know of the polio outbreaks and the resulting panic around the corner. (Today he says that the outbreaks were nothing new, but that television made it appear so, because everyone saw the ill children and the iron lungs for the first time). He could not know that three years after this Christmas of 1950, he too would contract polio, a disease that ultimately led to his discovery of art when his mother brought him paint-by-number sets and modeling clay to cure his boredom.

I look at this Christmas photograph of Baby George, as his family called him, and I think about my own childhood, about how I still feel like a young girl, as though it all happened last month. And yet, just recently, as I read a Nancy Drew book aloud to my godchild, I found myself horrified at the racial slurs prevalent throughout the series I adored as a child. Apologizing to her mother for my insensitive reading choice, I altered the text as I read, with hopes of sheltering today's child from something I brushed over without notice some thirty-five years ago.

I still feel young, and yet I wince at *Mad Men*, unable to face the treatment of women in the workplace and at home in the 1960s. I can't see the show without remembering my mother, newly divorced, holding my sister in one arm and my hand with the other, turned away in tears and humiliated from Sears, the only department store in 1973 Fort Walton Beach, Florida, because divorced women had no credit.

Finally, I see in this photograph an odd mix of a typical postcard-like Ozzie-and-Harriet American scene with a sad story of the times: a cousin lost to war, a mother wounded by the Great Depression, a country and culture steeped in racism. I see the reason why George grumbles, only for a moment, each year as I unpack the decorations, until, like me, he's transformed by the twinkling lights, eggnog, and Elvis as we sit together in our living room, recalling with sentimental nostalgia the holidays past while treasuring every moment of the current Christmas season.

The Family Table

In 1950 George drew and colored a turkey for his parents. On the back he wrote in a surprisingly elegant child's script:

For Mother and Dad on Thanksgiving:
1. Visits to chapel. 9
2. Prayers in school. 40
3. Decades of rosary. 27
George Rodrigue
2nd Grade

To fit the picture in a frame, George's mother folded back the question mark, so that when I removed the paper for a photograph, I was the first person to see this curiosity in years and perhaps the first ever to contemplate it. I immediately thought of George Emerson's question mark drawn on the back of a painting in E.M. Forster's *A Room With a View* (1908), a statement he flipped towards the wall, hiding it from others. As a result, both Georges' *why's* remained significant to them alone, and Rodrigue's tiny framed art, for six decades, showed only a turkey staring at a partially hidden and therefore barely discernible ax.

I asked George about the picture. His *Isn't it obvious?* expression amused me, as his face morphed into that of a precocious six-year-old child relating to a doomed and confused turkey, while already questioning the Catholic rote.

"I remember sitting on the porch in my grandmother's cane chair rocking in a trance, clicking the rosary beads and mumbling as I mimicked Tante 'Git. If she, the oldest of eleven children, felt this process important, then I did too."

Years later, George remains respectful of both the religion and the tradition, even as it remains, still, somewhat elusive. Recently, during the Catholic funeral of his cousin Donald LaBauve in New Iberia, Louisiana, I whispered during the sermon,

"What do you think of this? The words! The meanings! What does this have to do with Donald?"

George shook his head gently, his eyes watering.

"Nothing. He's on a tangent . . ."

. . . as the priest explained God's power to heal the sick and raise the dead.

Donald LaBauve lived to age ninety. As George's Boy Scout troop leader, he was a father figure to the young artist, especially after George Sr. became ill in 1958 and, according to his son, "was never the same." One of thirteen children, George's father died in 1967, only months following the Thanksgiving photograph below.

An only child, a young man in his early twenties, recently returned from art school in Los Angeles, sits at a table with his aging parents, a father ill and drifting away,

The Other Side of the Painting

and a mother consumed with her husband's care.

Somewhere in New Iberia, at the time of this photograph, are hundreds of relatives, twenty-three aunts and uncles, plus their spouses, children, and grandchildren, none of whom George recalls ever sharing a meal, at their table or his parents'.

"It was a different time," he explained. "And there were just too many of them."

As George and I enjoy holiday meals today with a crowd of family and friends, I view this 1960s family scene with irony. George, however, views it with melancholy, recalling days gone by but not necessarily missed.

The Art of the Trade

Most people find George hopelessly appealing. It's something about that Cajun accent combined with a Snagglepuss laugh and a down-to-earth demeanor that reels in both friends and strangers alike.

This is a handy character trait in his business. For years George sold his art himself, either on the road from the trunk of his car or from his gallery in Lafayette. Even today, although our capable staff handles the transactions, on occasion he still turns on the charm to close a sale, enchanting patrons and skeptics as he describes his art.

Although he avoids trading in recent years, early on it was a regular part of his business. Oftentimes this was because the potential buyer had no more money than George. If they loved the painting and offered something interesting, the barter was complete.

George tells a story of a young man who visited his gallery on Lafayette's Pinhook Road during the 1970s. He remembers these early clients because they were scarce, sometimes only two or three per month. This shoe salesman from Yazoo City, Mississippi, traveled through town regularly, stopping in for a dose of charismatic Cajun and haunting black trees. Eventually the two struck a deal. George gave him a painting and received in return, over the next three years, thirty pairs of shoes. Several years later in a similar scenario, he traded a newly completed painting for a set of shiny chrome rims.

Although I haven't seen much of this Wild West-type bartering in person, one incident does stand out regarding another artist. George and I admired his paintings, and he seemed flattered with the attention, as he followed George's career for years. We offered him a trade in exchange for one of his large canvases. However, when George delivered his own large-scale painting, the artist exclaimed,

"But you can't give me the same size! Your paintings bring more money than mine!"

To which George replied,

"But we'll enjoy yours just as much. Size for size; it's only fair."

On one occasion, George so enjoyed a trade that he painted the transaction. Rodney Fontenot, known as the Ragin' Cajun, was an antiques dealer from the tiny town of Ville Platte, Louisiana, specializing in architectural elements such as plantation shutters, fences, and flooring. George first met Rodney in the 1970s at his junk shop located off a then-questionable section of Magazine Street in New Orleans. The two Cajuns hit it off, and the Ragin' Cajun became George's source for architectural and knick-knack oddities. This included an old Coca-Cola icebox, perfect for storing paint. Strapped for cash, he offered a painting in exchange. A few years later he recorded the transaction in another painting, pictured above.

The image became moderately famous, joining a collection of twenty Rodrigue paintings in the highly successful Lafayette Junior League Cookbook, *Talk About Good II*, published in 1979.

Up and down on his luck, Rodney Fontenot moved his junk shop from New Orleans to Opelousas, then Lafayette, and finally home to Ville Platte. Periodically, he traveled the country in a gutted motor home in search of antiques.

"George, you still lookin' for a fence?" he called one day from a small town in North Carolina.

Rodney returned to Lafayette towing a mangled fence on a beat-up trailer. Turns out the Ragin' Cajun negotiated his purchase from the crooked caretaker of a graveyard, who also loaned him a trailer, complete with missing rear lights. Late that night as Rodney returned to Ville Platte, an 18-wheeler ran over the load. According to George,

"We renegotiated the price."

Other Ragin' Cajun acquisitions include an original 1950s barber's chair and a Coca-Cola machine sporting a "7-cents" sticker. George lost the barber's chair in a fire, but the coke machine remains on view in his Lafayette warehouse, a reminder of long lost friends, creative negotiations, and good ol' days.

Museums and Critics:
An Early History

I'm a survivor. –George Rodrigue, 2011

In 1969 the Art Center for Southwestern Louisiana held George's first solo museum exhibition. Located in Lafayette at the University of Southwestern Louisiana, the museum, also known as the Pink Palace, existed within a Mississippi River-style plantation, surrounded by huge columns and designed by architect A. Hays Town.

"USL offered to show my work," says George, "because of the notoriety from my first show, held earlier that year at Christopher's Antiques in New Iberia. I had painted full time for less than a year, and it all happened so fast that I mistakenly thought that fame and fortune were around the corner."

Despite his somewhat caustic recollection, a young

George did experience a rush of attention for a few years in the early 1970s. Most significant, the Louisiana State Art Commission sponsored a large Rodrigue exhibition at the Louisiana State Museum in the Old State Capitol in Baton Rouge in 1970.

"The director first told me that they book shows three years ahead and that I was wasting my time in trying. But two months later he called and explained that the scheduled exhibition fell through. Did I still have seventy framed oak tree paintings available?

"This was my biggest break yet, because I might be reviewed in the newspaper by the Baton Rouge art critic. As the state capitol's paper, *The Morning Advocate* was widely read and held tremendous influence across Louisiana. I waited anxiously every week for an article about my show."

George framed his landscape paintings in large gold antique frames, most of which he found in junk shops and flea markets. To this date, just prior to his *Aioli Dinner*, he had painted only two figures, small imaginary portraits, *Cajun Man* and *Cajun Woman*.

To his surprise, he opened the *Advocate* one Sunday to find his first ever newspaper article, a half page review with images. The headlines nearly destroyed this dedicated artist: "Painter Makes Bayou Country Dreary, Monotonous Place."

Art critic Anne Price derided both the artist and his art with her public opinion, words committed to George's memory today:

> The total effect is repetitious and monotonous, with all of the scenes similar, the treatment never varying . . . His paintings are flat and drab rather than teeming with life. His bayou country is a shadowy, depressing place with none of the life and color that pulses there. Even his few portraits are somber affairs, and his people give the impression that life is hard and serious

business. One feels that the artist takes Acadiana much too seriously, and perhaps himself as well.

George also memorized her fail-safe, written as though she knew her criticism might miss the mark:

> He shows some competence as a painter, particularly in his use of light . . . but he repeats the same theme and technique in virtually every painting. The ability is there, plus the obvious dedication to his subject, and he may well develop into a first class painter . . .

I was amused to find online a rather charming photograph of an elderly Anne Price, a woman I always imagined an ogre, along with a 2006 *Advocate* story of her sixty-one years at the paper. She and George never met, and yet at this point, I believe he would smile and shake her hand. She had a profound and lasting effect on him. The experience gave him self-confidence, and in twenty years, I have yet to see George rattled by negative remarks or criticism. Professionally, this resulting self-confidence helped him soar as an artist, barking at the canons and societal pressure of contemporary art, and rejecting outside advice in both his art and business.

In some ways George has defended himself for forty years against Price's analysis. In a 1974 article by Camilla Hunt Cole for *Art in America* he says, "I am not attempting to represent literally any one scene but to evoke a mood and stimulate imagination," a comment easily applied to his entire *oeuvre*, from *Landscapes* to *Cajuns*, as well as his later series: *Blue Dogs*, *Hurricanes*, and *Bodies*.

> Rodrigue's paintings are exciting because they are innovative. They appeal to the intellect as well as to the imagination. Moreover, he has succeeded in capturing the very essence of southwest Louisiana, its land and its people. In his paintings he reveals to us not what Acadiana looks like but what it is."
> —Camilla Hunt Cole for *Art in America*, 1974

Following the Baton Rouge show, Beaumont Art Museum Director Claude Kennard, as if rooting for the underdog, admired George's large-scale landscapes, described just months earlier by Price as "overly grandiose" and "the least stimulating" of all his works. The one-man exhibition premiered at the Beaumont Art Museum, now known as the Art Museum of Southeast Texas, to rave reviews in August of 1971.

> George Rodrigue's vision, abstract and severely linear in its inception, takes form first as a line-drawing, then through an obsession with major and basic forms, developing into an elemental landscape statement, austere and sober, limited in color but rich in range of hues, validly restrictive to the nature of the landscape of Lafayette Parish and surrounding areas in south Louisiana and southeast Texas. Human and architectural features emerge in terms of the dusky world of pervasive subtropical shade where white is exotic and sky minimal.
> —Claude L. Kennard, Director of the Beaumont Art Museum, 1971

Later that year, Alberta Collier, art critic for the New Orleans *Times-Picayune*, further redeemed the young artist, whom she described as

> . . . a romantic who loves the countryside where he grew up; he paints the bayous, the simple Acadian cabins and the moss-hung oaks with the love of the true native. His landscapes are not executed in a style he picked up from the past, but in a manner which has something of Louisiana Art Nouveau, something of the direct conceptions of William Aiken Walker, but more of Rodrigue himself.

For George, his crowning achievement during these early years occurred in 1974. Accepted as one of four thousand entrants in the prestigious Salon in Paris, he was the only American honored, receiving an Honorable Mention for his painting *The Class of Marie Courregé*. Afterwards, the French newspaper *Le Figaro* described Rodrigue as "America's Rousseau."

Also in the early 1970s George saw his painting, *Aioli Dinner*, accepted for exhibition at the New Orleans Museum of Art (NOMA) during their annual juried show. He grumbles still that his painting was the only canvas in the museum's Great Hall not to win an award. However, I remind him that NOMA and particularly its Director Emeritus John Bullard, more than made up for this oversight with a blockbuster Rodrigue exhibition in 2008, a recent state-wide tour of his paintings from their permanent collection, and NOMA's near-reverence of the *Aioli Dinner*, which divides its time between the museum's American landscape collection and the southern genre paintings at the Ogden Museum of Southern Art.

It was not until the early 1990s and the *Blue Dog* series that museums again noticed George's work. His gallery representation too was minimal at best. He was a figurative artist painting at a time when Abstract Expressionism was the norm in the South and elsewhere. Figurative art was non-existent on the national scene.

"My style," George says, "was outdated and out of touch with contemporary directors that viewed their shows as a reflection of what was going on in New York."

Although he didn't intend it as funny at the time, George and I both laughed recently as we read his quote from a 1974 article in the *Lafayette Daily Advertiser*:

> Today, anything new is accepted as art. Anything that hasn't been done before. But after going through pop art, op art, abstracts—what's left that's new? Not much. That's one reason why things have been slow in the art world for the last eight-or-so years.

Wendy Rodrigue

He continues with a prediction:

At this time, artists should try to produce something from themselves, or from their area—that's where art is headed today. All America really has left in art is what one feels.

Chapter 3

Born on the Beach

I wasn't really born on the beach. I was born on a
military base in Dover, Delaware, a place I don't
recall. At age three we moved to Ramstein Air
Force Base in Germany, and by age six I found
home with my mother and sister on Florida's Emerald Coast.

Dolores Pepper

Dolores Pepper was born on the Miracle Strip, the beaches of Okaloosa Island, behind the condominium where I lived with my mother and sister in Fort Walton Beach, Florida. It was spring break 1982, and my cousin Kelly and I, each of us covered in baby oil and holding a TAB, walked from the umbrellas and families behind our building towards the boys and beer behind the Ramada Inn.

"What's your name?" called a group of guys.

"Flower," replied my curvy cousin.

The boys ogled her as we approached. She flirted and made party plans while I stood behind, an invisible beanpole barely blocking their sun.

As we strolled back to our abandoned babysitting duty (my sister and her friends), I asked Kelly about the name. She explained that we'd have more fun as other girls, namely Flower Anne and Dolores.

"I'm Dolores?"

I couldn't figure it out. My whole life I dreamed of

another name, and she knew it: Emily, the name I gave to every Barbie, Madame Alexander doll, and pet parakeet. (I named my goldfish, every one of them, George, but that's another story).

"It sounds better when I call to you," she explained: "Dolores, Doilin'! Come see!"

(. . . as in, "Dolores, Dahlin'! Over here!". . . as in, "Dolores, Darling! Come with me!")

She was correct, of course.

I considered an appropriate last name and scouted the beach for ideas. My bathing suit cover-up featured a bell pepper, and a full name was born.

That night as the boys, a group from Lafayette, Louisiana, crowded Flower Anne, I tried out my new name. An Hebert (pronounced "a-bear") with a big smile left his buddies and my beautiful cousin and took my hand as we walked. He was probably five inches shorter than me, but he didn't seem to care as we chatted on while he called me Dolores. Later that week he bid me good-bye with a surprise on the beach—a six-inch deep hole in the sand just large enough for my size ten feet. Hidden among the dunes, we stood eye-level for my first kiss.

Although born on the beach, it was in south Louisiana that Dolores Pepper bloomed. I moved to New Orleans full time in the summer of 1989 to be closer to my grandmothers, Granny Wolfe in Metairie and Grandma Mc-Clanahan in Gretna, and to study Art History in graduate school at Tulane University, residing in a newly restored carriage house on the corner of Magazine and Terpsichore in the Irish Channel. My landlord and neighbor, interior designer Judy Girod, kindly cut the rent to fit my limited budget, and I remained two years, spending my days in class and my evenings at Ann Taylor, where I sold women's clothing. It was that weird period of life when one lives on no sleep, hitting the town until five a.m. and the library by seven.

It was during these years that Kelly and I spent

The Other Side of the Painting

Wednesday nights at the long-gone Que Sera on St. Charles Avenue. I donned an Ann Taylor suit, a new one purchased annually with my employee discount during the after-Christmas sale, and trolled the three-for-one happy hour for trouble. We were kicked out for good when Kelly, standing on our table, showed off her "bump and grind it" "Vogue" moves to a flock of men/birds circling her make-shift stage as I watched her carefully from the floor, arms wide in case she fell.

"Flower! Dolores! You're outta here!" shouted the manager.

We returned only once, a few months later, in disguise, dressed as Cindy Wilson and Kate Pierson for a B-52's concert, our hair piled in bouffants. We didn't get far, however, pulled over by a police officer as Kelly plowed through traffic signals, the red and blue lights on her father's car (an oilman with 1980s good-ol'-boy connections) flashing.

"Do you know who my daddy is?" asked Flower Anne, her hands on her hips as she cocked her head towards the angry officer.

It's embarrassing, even humiliating, as I look back on it, remembering how I leaned my head out of the window and taunted the officer with siren sounds as we sped towards the concert rather than central lock-up. In a bizarre twist of fate, Kelly ended up marrying a Kenner cop. They live in Covington with their four children, and I know that her past taunts her as they enter their teenage years and their own rebellion.

It was as Dolores Pepper that I discovered clever, albeit airy and illegal, places to pee on Mardi Gras Day. The rest of the year I snuck out of the bathroom window of Fat City's Gator's Shuck-n-Jive, avoiding the creepy guys who bought us drinks and, just my luck, the only ones we ever met who carried the hots for *me*.

It was as Dolores Pepper that I attended Flower Anne's "Madonna Party" dressed in nothing but my bra and short shorts, with stockings and gloves, no straight men allowed, and had the courage, or stupidity, to sing on stage at the Cat's Meow, "Like a Virgin." This resulted in a twenty-something's dream supply of free drinks: Absolut and cranberry lined up in a row down the bar, and a real coup for my five dollar a night budget.

By the mid-1990s my mentor Flower Anne disappeared for a while, a conservative bastion of family life, trading in her fishnets and wigs for control-top pantyhose and having her hair "done." Since the party-girl Dolores petered out after only a few summers in favor of things like work, school, and a good night's sleep, I pretty much forgot about Flower, aside from the occasional reminiscence of our wild summers.

And then one Mardi Gras, as the young mother Kelly, away from her children for the first time, jumped on our hotel room bed in the middle of the night and shouted, "The cat's out of the cage!," I thought, *She's back*.

. . . or maybe she never left. And that's what made me realize that Dolores is here too. She's older, hopefully more responsible, and she's asleep by midnight. But she's a part of me, taking chances and combating what's left of my shyness.

Mignon's Flowers

Mignon McClanahan Wolfe, born 1940, grew up in Algiers, a New Orleans neighborhood on the west bank of the Mississippi River. As an adult she lived in South Carolina, Delaware, the Orient, and Europe, raised her children on the beaches of north Florida's Gulf Coast, made a lengthy artistic pilgrimage to Highlands, North Carolina, and returned home, in 2003, to a jewel box Acadian house in Abita Springs, Louisiana.

Her parents named her "Felix" because they wanted a boy, and the day she turned eighteen and received a draft notice, she changed it to "Mignon."

"I'm named after a French actress," she used to say.

She was a Chemistry major at Louisiana State University when her pony tail flipped onto her Bunsen burner, catching her hair on fire. And she gained fame as the first LSU student to use the lab shower, when her experiment exploded, disintegrating her clothes and burning her skin to the bone. This prompted her switch to the "safe" major of Fine Arts, despite the fact that she had never held a paintbrush.

She was the kind of person who named her clothes, "The Mermaid Outfit," "The Marilyn Dress," and the "Renaissance Blouse." Her tooled leather belts read "Mignon" amidst roses and bluebonnets; her turquoise and purple jazz class leotards matched her frilly skirts; and she prided herself on the way her "heart-shaped behind" looked in her Gloria Vanderbilt jeans. She wore flowers in her hair, bows on her sandals, and rhinestones on her fingernails. I wanted to be exactly like her.

She was single from the time I was six years old, and her dating life was a regular part of the drama around our house. There was Captain Napp the pilot (oh how I wanted her to marry him!), Russ the psychiatrist, Tom the sailor, Bob the Lt. Colonel, Mike who drove the monster truck (and carried a step stool in the back just for her), Pete the brown-noser (always buying my sister and me records and dresses), and I guess that's a long enough list, lest I tarnish her reputation.

She listened to Don Williams, Charlie Rich, and Donna Summer as she brushed her long blonde hair and, once dressed, played "Vincent" at the piano, meant to impress her dates as they approached the door.

Once I reached dating age, we met for late night horror movies in her bedroom, sharing the details of our dates on commercials during *The Fly* (as we squirmed together, "Help me, Help me . . ."), *Night of the Living Dead*, or *The Raven*. We laughed despite the plotlines, as she reminisced about the rather repulsive, but beloved, Morgus the Magnificent, while awaiting our current hostess, Elvira, Mistress of the Dark's, imminent wardrobe malfunction.

She wanted to be tall and thin, but instead she stood five feet, four inches and struggled with her weight all of her life. Rarely was she as disappointed in me as when I slouched. At five feet, ten inches in the tenth grade, I fought with my mother about what I saw as an awkward, freakish height. Yet she convinced me to parade around our house in her heels, a book and glass balanced atop my head.

She was immensely clever and generous in all things. She couldn't type or sew, yet she plucked out my school papers on a typewriter from a board over her bathroom sink, lest typing from the dining room wake me or my sister. And, like magic, my Girl Scout patches appeared on my sash within days after I earned them.

When I called her at work crying because a wounded bird lay beneath a bush at my bus stop, she canceled her appointments and raced home. I found the bird after school nestled in a towel in the corner of her bathtub, where it remained for several weeks until it flew through the living room and out of our window.

And when she went into the hospital with pain in her hip, she took me aside before her x-ray and said that if she didn't make it, I should find Chesley Adler (whom she knew from Chesley's father's jewelry store where my mother worked) and tell her that her jewelry designs are beautiful and that my mother believes in her talent and potential.

. . . and so I did.

Today I write about my mother often and with appropriate colorful detail, because I owe it to her; and because I should have written about her when she could read it; and because the therapy and psychics and meditation just made me *hope* for closure; and because I should have taken her to Ireland and Egypt; and because I dismissed her discomfort as routine; and because I didn't question the doctors; and because I mocked her belief in fairies and angels and UFOs; and because I rolled my eyes behind her back over something stupid that last week; and because, as my sweet sister managed to choke out and yet state succinctly on the day of our mother's funeral:

"You know, Wendy, Mom was really neat."

And because you too are invisible, and there's a chance that some of you, maybe all of you, knows exactly how I feel.

There is a painting I found among my mother's things that I'd never seen before. It's only two hands, painted in blue. It hangs in my closet, and sometimes I place my hands on hers and I think she's there.

An American Soldier

According to my mother, he never changed my diaper.
Whether true or not, I like to think that's the case. He
wasn't there for me as a child, and I returned the favor
years later, bitter about things best forgotten.

My dad's excuse was better than mine, as he served
in the United States Air Force, stationed in Vietnam during the mid-1960s, rendezvousing while on leave with
my mother, who waited in the Philippines. I never knew
them to love each other, or even like each other, and yet
I was born during the Summer of Love, an irony I used
to explain the flowers in my hair and patches on my bell-
bottom jeans long after the onslaught of shoulder pads and
Dorothy Hamill haircuts.

My sister Heather's first memory is of our dad leaning
over her crib in his flight suit, no doubt saying good-bye

or hello, as he disappeared for another six months. It's the only thing, real or imagined, that she remembers from our parents' marriage, over by the time she was two.

When I think of my dad in those years, I too picture him in his flight suit, but "bellowing out at the night," dancing with me around my bedroom in Fort Walton Beach, Florida, singing Neil Diamond's "I am the Lion," as I modeled the kimonos and senorita dresses carried back from Bangkok and Seville.

Looking back, it was a strange time, a loveless marriage in an otherwise loving household. It was all I knew, and I was okay with it for a while, my dad, handsome and full of stories from strange lands, an American soldier swooping in for a few days of well-deserved hero-worship from his daughter.

John Wolfe grew up in the New Orleans neighborhood of Algiers, graduating from Behrman High School and then LSU. He now divides his time between a beach house on Okaloosa Island in the Florida Panhandle and a farm at the Alabama-Florida border in north Walton County. He has a John Deere tractor, a few cows, and recently acquired some kind of exotic chickens.

He'll turn seventy-five on the Fourth of July, still handsome, still dancing, still a hero.

Last year my sister and I broke the locks on our mother's diaries and discovered gold. We read the story of our parents' courtship, begun in the 1950s in Algiers at the drive-in, around the jukebox, and at LSU football games. We studied her words, picturing her jumping at the phone or running to the mailbox. We laughed in disbelief, reading how she teased her many suitors in order to make our dad jealous. From the beginning, he was the only one for her.

Shocked by this knowledge, we confronted our father:

"You were crazy about each other! How come you never told us? Do you know what it means to us that you were in love?"

Our dad smirked a bit, as he's wont to do, and then he slowly turned the pages of the old photo album, smiling, and, at last, laughing, as he said,

"But of course we were in love. What did you all think?"

A True Fan

I attended a small college, Trinity University in San Antonio, Texas. In the mid-1980s we had maybe two thousand students. Although we had a football team, I don't recall the games. We had a Greek system, but I evaded that as well, opting instead for extra classes and the AIDS suicide hotline.

In short, I received an excellent education in books and sensitivity but, arguably, missed the college experience.

In my family, I was the exception. My parents graduated in '61 and '62 from Louisiana State University, and my sister attended Ole Miss, followed by graduate school at Florida State. Without question, they were the cool kids, fans of football games, dating and parties, while I brownnosed my professors and stood waiting early-morning at the locked library door. In the end, we all graduated, meaning, I suppose, that I missed out . . . needlessly.

For some time now, George Rodrigue seeks to repair this lapse. It began when he insisted that I attend the 2004 Sugar Bowl in the New Orleans Superdome despite my guilt-motivated speech that my ticket belongs with a real fan.

To my surprise, I cheered and cried, losing my voice, but not my enthusiasm, for hours after LSU's win. If I close my eyes as I write this, I picture the energy of strangers' shoulders as we walked together the length of Poydras Street to the Mississippi River. I knew for the first time this sort of exhilaration and, after losing my mother later that same year, cheered for her going forward, for the Homecoming floats and decorated fraternity houses, for poodle skirts and jukeboxes, for young love and life-long friends and, above all, for tradition.

It was the 1957, '58, and '59 seasons, the years my parents attended LSU, that changed Louisiana football forever. In the late 1950s, Billy Cannon won the Heisman Trophy, the Tigers won the National Championship, and LSU stadium filled to capacity. About this same time, national television broadcasted NFL games, watched for the first time by large audiences. People saw the Baltimore Colts with Johnny Unitas play the Green Bay Packers, coached by Vince Lombardi.

"When I went to art school in L.A.," explains George, "the first thing I wanted to see was a national football game live. I saw Johnny Unitas and the Baltimore Colts play the Los Angeles Rams at the L.A. Coliseum. I was shocked to see only 30,000 people in an 110,000-seat stadium. Pro-football still struggled for attendance."

"Years later," he continues, "I'm standing in line at Ray Hay's Cajun Po-Boys in Houston, Texas, and Billy Cannon taps me on the shoulder. Turns out that he's a fan of my Cajun paintings. I could barely speak. It's probably the only time in my life that I felt star struck."

The Other Side of the Painting

Before Art Center in Los Angeles, George attended the University of Southwestern Louisiana (now the University of Louisiana at Lafayette). Considering his football fever today, it's ironic that he remembers little of USL football from school, focusing on his drawing exercises more than the Bulldogs (now the Ragin' Cajuns), a team he follows today with enthusiasm. Rodrigue sought a formal education in the arts, and before graduating at USL, he hopped a train to California, where he watched Louisiana football from afar and painted full-time. For George in those years, tradition was not football. Tradition was the Cajun culture, and desperate to preserve it, he painted it. Gradually, his college football fever returned, an addiction (a wife's word) consuming much of his life, even in the face of painting.

His son André attended UL (George's alma mater), and his son Jacques attended LSU. As a result, George's sense of tradition pulls him both directions, yet still firmly rooted in Louisiana football. In the 1980s he spent ten years supporting UL with paintings of award-winning authors and scholars for the Flora Levy Lecture Series, and in 2003 he painted LSU's mascot, Mike the Tiger. The more than one million dollars in proceeds from Mike's print helped replace the tiger's cage with a habitat, Mike's home on the LSU grounds today.

In my case, I attend games when summoned or stay home when permitted, serving gumbo or red beans, not only because it pleases my husband, but also because it honors my parents. My mother was the first person in her family to attend college. A tradition was born, assumed my grandparents, and as an eighteen-year-old know-it-all, I disappointed them out of the gate, choosing a small south Texas school that I loved over the Baton Rouge campus.

Admittedly, when LSU takes on Alabama, I think about tradition as though I high-fived Billy Cannon himself. I cheer at the top of my lungs for players I've never met, from a school I never attended, against a team no doubt full of nice people—all for a game I hardly understand and a collection of photographs that provide a glimpse of my young parents.

In the museum world, I often hear frustration surrounding the money and attention given sports over art. Yet George is rarely more content than while watching LSU or Saints football from his easel, and my mother, a Fine Arts major, cheered for fifty years with gusto, donned in purple and gold for her Tigers. Obviously a cultural harmony exists within the nostalgia and passion of athletics and aesthetics, making many of us, whatever our reasons, true fans of both.

Guilty

I wandered through college with a guilt complex. Like many naïve students, inspired by a voting voice and new knowledge, I embraced the world's problems as my own, determined to improve things somehow, even as I failed in family relationships and winced at dateless Saturday nights.

Looking back, it was a crazed mental time, when a skipped meal, prayed over, transported magically to a starving child; when vegetarianism meant one less chicken in the over-crowded coop; and when five spare dollars in my checking account meant more money that Sunday in the offering plate. I saw need everywhere, a vision I gradually narrowed, or at least focused, lest I went crazy. Although some of us remain protesters and activists as we age, most concentrate at some point on peace within our own home as opposed to peace on earth. Despite this age-accompanying cynicism, I still believe that one person's actions make a difference, and that even a small difference counts.

Children see the world with broad vision. They love and give without worrying about perception. "We're *all* artists, Mrs. Wendy," explained a young girl recently, as I complimented her on her painting during a visit to her class.

Children also see beauty where adults might miss it. "If you stand here," said a child, taking my hand in the Besthoff Sculpture Garden at the New Orleans Museum of Art, "the light shines from underneath the trees, just like in Mr. George's paintings."

I was a sophomore at Trinity University in San Antonio, Texas, when I met Gladys at the H.E.B. She struggled with her cane and over-sized handbag as she loaded her groceries into the trunk of a cab, while the driver sat helpless and impatient.

"Where do you live?" I asked.

"Alamo Heights," she replied, referring to the old and, were this New Orleans, "Uptown" nearby neighborhood.

She trusted me, and I gave her a ride to a Tudor-style house, classic and cracking on the outside, decaying and 1950s within.

I recognized the old-lady smell, the one that comes from piles of junk mail and dusty lace tablecloths, from floral hand cream and moldy wallpaper, from warmed leftovers and stale coffee. Except for a clock's repetitive "tic-toc," the house was deadly quiet, as though no one disturbed its air with laughter or speech in years. Gladys looked like Miss Havisham, and her home, although not quite Satis House, sat neglected and lonely. We made a date.

That Friday, I fetched Gladys for lunch. She wore her vintage Sunday best to the Mexican cantina (paid for with an advance from my job at the school auditorium) and afterwards served me tea from her floral Windsor china, as we made small talk on a plastic-covered, faded blue sofa. As I recall those days, it's the silence that screams loudest in my memories, broken only by the metered sound of the old clock and Gladys's hesitant answers to my predictable questions:

"Tell me about your husband . . . What is the name of this china pattern? . . . Shall I refill your tea?"

We repeated this visit every Friday for more than a year, eventually expanding our afternoons to include museums, the Alamo, and Olmos Pharmacy (for chocolate malts). Along with my peer tutor class, we decorated a Christmas tree, her first in many years. Holiday music filled the house from a student's boom box.

In January of my junior year, I joined a study-abroad program in Vienna, Austria. Gladys protested, but I left her anyway, and two months later she died.

The following year I returned from Europe, changed but still—perhaps more—guilty. The modern world seemed incongruous with my intense journey through Art History. Without Gladys, I sought diversions. I volunteered at the local AIDS clinic. One by one, scared young men (because honestly—they were *all* scared young men) stopped in for testing. Within weeks I answered the AIDS suicide hotline, forwarded to my college apartment's phone on Monday nights.

I was an unqualified, healthy, heterosexual twenty-one-year-old girl. But it was the 1980s, and gay men died faster than counselors were trained. People feared the infection, and volunteers were scarce. My mother worried, correctly and on several levels, that I didn't know what I was doing. But this was my protest, my creed, and in my mind, I had no choice.

We all remember when we were young and set out to change the world. Maybe you held a picket sign, chained yourself to a tree, or delivered Meals on Wheels. Maybe you still look at the world in this way.

My sister and I learned this vision from our mother. Despite barely covering the weekend's hot checks with Monday's paycheck, she sent money every month, along with our letters, to Ernik Tukiman in Indonesia, a child matched to our family by World Vision. Thirty-five years later, Ernik's photograph still hangs on our Christmas tree.

I asked George about those years in his life, and his answer surprised me:

"All I wanted was to get to art school."

His focus paid off, and he fulfilled that dream and more, supporting his family with his art by his mid-twenties. George's generosity of time and money kicked in later, first in small ways in his Lafayette community, and later with large-scale projects for the University of Louisiana at Lafayette, the Red Cross following 9/11, the International Child Art Foundation, humanitarian and arts-related relief following Hurricane Katrina, and countless small-scale projects involving festivals, school visits, and lectures. Today, through the George Rodrigue Foundation of the Arts (GRFA), these efforts are near full-time, with programs devoted to the arts and education.

At one point, we all realize that the joy of giving cannot match the weight of need. Even through GRFA, it is impossible for George to reach every school, anymore than I could befriend every lonely old lady, or my mother feed every child. But does it mean we shouldn't try?

Blue Wendy

Recently George and I attended an event where the religious leader prayed for and encouraged our suffering. We left watching carefully, unprepared at a gala for this powerful lesson, for the bus that might run us down in the street, safeguarding our empathy with broken bones or worse.

"Suffering and diminishment are not the greatest of evils but are normal ingredients of life," wrote Cardinal Avery Dulles, just prior to his death in 2008. "As I become increasingly paralyzed and unable to speak, I can identify with the many paralytics and mute persons in the Gospels . . . ."

George painted Father Dulles in 1990, one of ten portraits of visiting scholars for the University of Louisiana at Lafayette's Flora Levy Lecture Series.

Wendy Rodrigue

Many doctrines welcome life's hardships, because they tune us in to the suffering of others, making us better people.

"Only the healer, not the healer's subject, must believe," explains George, as he describes his aunt, a Cajun *traiteur*. "It's the same for everyone," he continues. "We each have the ability to make a difference, but it's our belief and compassion that make it so."

To be clear, as a rule George admires doctors and dismisses faith healers; however, he holds a life-long fascination with the power of the mind and the mystery of the universe. Years ago while dating, we split for several months. Upon reconciling, our first conversation involved hours on black holes, the Big Bang Theory, and déjà vu, as though his swirling cosmic thoughts somehow reunited us.

"Give me a few hours to get into the zone, to really believe," explained George recently, "and I could be someone else. I could be so funny that no one would recognize me. I could be Lewis Grizzard."

"I don't have any out-of-body experiences," wrote Grizzard. "I had indeed seen a bright, beautiful light and had followed it, but it turned out to be a Kmart tire sale."

Give *me* a few hours, I thought, and I could slip into

insanity. It seems easy, almost like stepping off of a mountain or, lest my sister worry, from a sidewalk into the grass, into freedom—from cynicism, from suffering, from responsibilities, from guilt (both mine and others in all cases).

"Nothing in life is fair," our mom used to say, followed closely by "I'm sorry girls, but Christmas will be grim this year."

Heather and I, however, rolled our eyes, because Christmas was never grim. Whether new or used roller skates, the pompoms (for the skate-toes) were handmade and hot pink (in my case), and the stuffed animal was the latest or last year's Kermit or Miss Piggy (in my sister's).

I think often on scenes from my childhood. I recall once sharing a joke from school with my mother and baby sister at the dinner table. Ethiopian jokes were popular at Longwood Elementary School in Shalimar, Florida, in the mid-1970s, and I laughed with a mouthful of pot roast, while repeating the latest trendy mockery of a starving people.

My mother, who exudes joy in my memories, wasn't smiling that day.

"There is nothing funny about another person's pain," she said.

"But they can't hear me, Mama; they're in Africa!"

"It doesn't matter whether they hear you or not, Wendy Anne."

. . . and I knew, by the sound of my middle name, that this lesson was very important.

I recall, too, one Christmas with relatives in New Orleans. I was ten or so and opened my skates as though surprised, but became distracted by my cousin's shriek, as she discovered her new stereo, records, and an arcade-size Pac Man video game.

"Come see, Wendy," shouted Kelly, full of love. "I'll share it all!"

But I ran upstairs and buried my face in the guest-room pillow, ashamed of my jealousy and yet helpless to stop it. I remember the feelings like they were yesterday, not wanting to hurt my mother, who gave us the world. I explained through my tears, as she apologized and stroked my hair, how much I loved my skates and how I never liked Pac Man anyway.

I thought of this, for some reason, on a recent Saturday night when George woke me at 3:00 a.m., pleading that I rub his legs and shoulders—"full of tension," he explained, following the LSU vs. Alabama game. Annoyed and half-asleep, I scratched his back for maybe two minutes before dozing off, all the while dumbfounded over the physical and mental trauma following a *winning* football game watched from a sofa.

Within an hour, I awoke again, this time to the sound of a recorded 2009 season Saints play-off game, "the perfect thing," he explained, "to calm my nerves." I almost insisted that he turn off the television, explained how ridiculous this is in the middle of the night, and reminded him that we faced a full day and had to be up in two hours. Instead, however, I marveled quietly at this man and my life.

Oddly enough and unknown to me, he pondered along the same lines, yet in his unpredictable, unique way. Realizing I watched him, he noted, *out of the blue*, as the Saints kicked the winning field goal against the Minnesota Vikings,

"What people don't realize, Wendy, is that all of that funny stuff you write is really me!"

Well, now you know.

Nature Girl: The Art of Modeling

Griping about the challenges of modeling is humiliating. I mean, a model lies on a chaise lounge or perches on a stool or strolls towards the camera wearing costumes, beautiful clothes, or occasionally nothing at all. It's ridiculously easy, right? Just last weekend, however, as I headed towards a previously scouted site for photographer Tabitha Soren, this talented artist, draped in heavy camera equipment, humbled me with her concern:

"Can I bring you some water?" she asked,

. . . as if I couldn't handle *modeling* without dehydrating.

I've modeled for George for years, sometimes posing as Jolie Blonde and occasionally as myself, but most often as no one in particular. He uses my shape and stance within designs for figurative works, even if he's using another person's face or a ficticious subject.

He's quite serious during these sessions, setting up drop cloths and draped backgrounds, or directing me towards a rather uncomfortable perch on a tree branch or windowsill, or sending me, partially submerged, into (sometimes freezing) water. He's photographed me in this way thousands of times, spending many hours on lighting and directing, followed by Photoshop, for images that may or may not result in paintings.

I do admit, with embarrassment, that it took me some time to get the hang of this. The first year's, maybe two, worth of photographs ended up in the garbage. Like most kids, I grew up smiling and posing for pictures, and George nearly gave up on me as he tried to break this habit. I struggled not to look awkward, and we spent months making me not only comfortable in front of the camera, but also attune to George's needs, including his preferences for certain poses, hand placements, head angles, and expressions.

We abandoned make-up from the beginning, preferring the all-natural look, aside from a drop of lip gloss. My hair, he claims, looks better dirty and uncombed for the camera, so that's easy. And clothing, when there is any, is rarely anything other than a prairie-style dress or a t-shirt, jeans, and a broad-brimmed hat.

We learned fast that I work better blind. Without my glasses, I'm undistracted. Directions such as "look straight at me with confidence" or "focus on a loss" or "you've just risen from the dead" become willing suspensions of disbelief. With the world a blur, my imagination takes over. This working-blind, for example, may not have helped me this weekend when it came to avoiding sticks and poison oak as I climbed barefoot in the Big Sur wilderness, yet it did make for a more convincing shot when Tabitha directed "you're being chased by hundreds of wood rats," or later in Palo Colorado Canyon, "by the scary man we passed in the cabin down the road."

George and Tabitha have completely different needs when it comes to photographs. George uses his images in sections, removing the figure from the photograph and pasting it into a painting's design. For example, he might pose me in a chair in our living room for the photo shoot, yet place me outside among the oaks on his painted canvas. For his nude series, *Bodies*, I stand on the stairs outside his Carmel studio as opposed to the above-ground tombstones in the final paintings. The actual cemetery photographs, shot (fully clothed) at Lake Lawn in Metairie, Louisiana, help George with concept and placement only.

Tabitha's photographs, however, are the finished artwork. She's far more concerned with the overall composition and details as she shoots the picture, because she doesn't have the opportunity later to change it with paints on a canvas. In one case, working at 2:00 a.m. in a New Orleans courtyard, she directed that I hold completely still during the ten-minute exposures so that all movement comes from the light and breeze, whether from the swimming pool's surface, the night's moonlit sky, or my hair.

George lights the model so that he sees the details when it comes to painting, whereas Tabitha's lighting is an element of her craft, even as she takes the shot. This doesn't mean that lighting isn't important to George. In fact, it is a key element, especially in his Cajun paintings. However, the light is unimportant until he sits at his easel.

Tabitha's figures oftentimes are less important as subjects than other elements, as in the courtyard example described above. If George paints a figure, however, that figure is the focus of the painting, with all other elements subjugated to it in a highly ordered and contrived manner. Unlike photography, there is no guesswork, no accidents, and no second take on George's canvas. To be clear, neither artist, at least when it comes to my participation, is going for a portrait.

Sunday night, exhausted and yet high on my afternoon brush-with-the-arts, I carefully removed the burrs from my tangled hair, soaked my feet for an hour (after which my friend Barbara fast-tracked her way towards sainthood by removing a dozen or more splinters from my shredded skin), bathed in Tecnu, rubbed Icy Hot on my aching muscles, popped an antibiotic (despite George's thorough inspection for deer ticks), and dropped Tabitha an email of thanks for the beautiful day.

I truly am honored to pose for these artists, creative individuals who I admire and, to a degree, envy, as I think back on my weak and uninspired studio projects from college, along with the pocket-size camera buried somewhere in my closet. Unlike photographers in the fashion world, perhaps George and Tabitha will find use for me even as my wrinkles and "muffin tops" set in.

Risky Business

*It's a dangerous business . . . going out your door.**

This morning I watched from my desk in Carmel Valley, California, as a great-horned owl took a bath. It glanced at me, assessed the danger, and continued, even as I eased open the glass door and stepped into the rain, camera ready.

We all know that the greatest chance for joy and inspiration comes with the greatest risk of pain. It's the reason we stay in a "dangerous" city, New Orleans; it's the reason we argue against our reputation for corruption and a high murder-rate and dismiss dramatic press; it's the reason we stare dumbfounded at anyone suggesting, following 2005, that we leave or, worse, let it go.

On the plane recently from New Orleans to the Monterey Peninsula, I thought, as I do on every flight, about artist Georgia O'Keeffe looking down on the clouds, inspired to paint the experience. I thought of my grandmother Helen McClanahan and her hours of 1950s filmed sky, taken through the airplane window as she puddle-jumped from New Orleans to Lafayette to Houston to Fort Worth. And I checked my superstitions and fear, replacing any form of the word "death" in the book on my lap with any form of the word "life," as I replayed in my head a line I heard years ago on a TV show I can't recall:

"The only thing holding this machine in the sky is the combined will of the passengers."

O'Keeffe was a brave woman, making art in a man's world, resettling alone in the New Mexico desert.

My grandmother (pictured above as Worthy Matron of the Order of the Eastern Star) was also a brave woman, traveling alone in the 1950s and 1960s far beyond New Orleans and Fort Worth to Singapore, Thailand, Africa, and India.

We choose our dangers and balance risks against rewards. I recall the waiver I signed several years ago, as George and I rafted the Grand Canyon with friends:

"You understand that you might die on this trip."

By day two our terror of the ten-rated rapids morphed into elation, as we hooked our arms through the trampoline's ropes and plunged into the freezing water, pulled off balance by rocks and a raging current. We hiked, climbing straight up in the 110-degree heat, to waterfalls and Anasazi drawings. Four days in and now fearless, I swam (blind, lest I lose my glasses) through a deep pond to a mossy cave, where I scrambled like Gollum* to an opening thirty feet above. Standing at the cave's window, I stared across the water at my fuzzy friends, cheering me on and reminding me to clear the rocks below.

For the first time since my childhood, I held my nose, leaping, falling, sinking, choking, laughing . . . and living.

"What's the biggest risk you ever took?" I asked George, who skipped that Grand Canyon leap.

I assumed his answer involved leaving New Iberia for Los Angeles, calling himself "Cajun" when Cajun wasn't cool, or painting a Blue Dog when everyone, from his per-

sonal world to the art world, questioned his sanity. Instead
he replied, without hesitating,
　　"Marrying you."

* J.R.R. Tolkien, *The Lord of the Rings*, 1954.

Chapter 4

A Woolf Inspires a Wolfe

In my husband's shadow, I turn often to Virginia Woolf, who accepted, without resentment, her place in a man's world while asserting, with confidence, her acumen.

STUDIO de RODRIGUE
213 Duclos St.
Lafayette, La. 70501

REILLY GALLERY
832 St. Peter Street
New Orleans, La. 70116

bayou country

Paintings by

GEORGE RODRIGUE
"artist du pays Acadien"

A Gallery of His Own

Be truthful one would say, and the result is bound to be
*amazingly interesting.**

Immediately after returning to Louisiana from art school in Los Angeles in the late 1960s, George Rodrigue wanted one thing: to make a living as an artist.

However, he never imagined that the business of selling his art would be his reponsibility. He assumed his paintings would attract agents and established galleries. They would sell his work, and he would paint. Yet at that time there were no galleries in Lafayette, Louisiana, and with the exception of the Reilly Gallery in New Orleans, which showed his work for a few months in the early 1970s, there was no gallery anywhere that would display George's dark, repetitive landscapes.

He knocked on doors for months with hopes of representation then finally gave up, placing an ad in the back of *Southern Living Magazine* and *Acadiana Profile*, using his home address and phone number. To his surprise the response to the tiny black-and-white words, "Bayou Country Paintings," was immediate. Yet people were shocked to find a young man in his twenties behind these seemingly antique works.

George tells a story of one afternoon when, as he mowed the lawn, a car pulled up to his house on Duclos Street in Lafayette, and a man called from the window,

"Son, is your daddy home?"

"My daddy's dead, Sir."

"Then who paints the pictures?"

For as long as he can remember, George fought to be taken seriously as an artist. Within a year after his return from art school in 1967 he supported his family with his original ideas on canvas, bringing in one hundred dollars a month at first, with sales of two to three paintings from the front door of his house.

In the mid 1970s, after adding Cajuns to his paintings, he hit the road, selling from the trunk of his car with great success in Houston, Dallas, Jackson, Birmingham, Shreveport, and other cities, finding a more receptive audience for his regional subjects, ironically, the further he strayed from home. He raised his prices, selling canvases for $3,000 to $5,000 from his makeshift gallery, the trunk of a bumped-up Lincoln Mark V, because still, despite hundreds of paintings, successful sales, and five years after his return from a prestigious art school, no agent wanted him, and no gallery carried his paintings.

Facing reality and hoping for less time on the road, George rented a space on Pinhook Road in Lafayette. He sold his pictures and painted his canvases with little interruption, one or two visitors per week, eating a hamburger at Lauck & Key across the street each day while eyeing his unlocked front door. (That same lunch spot is the home of Rodrigue's Jolie's Louisiana Bistro today.)

From there he moved to Jefferson Street, raising his house and building a gallery underneath, abandoning any hope of outside representation for his work. This is where George's sons grew up, where his dog Tiffany lived, where he painted hundreds of paintings of Cajun folk life, and where most of his Cajun painting fans, unless they ran into him on the road, came to know his work.

At last, in 1989, things changed. A local doctor and his brother, a wanna-be agent, opened a gallery at 721 Royal Street in the French Quarter spotlighting the art of George Rodrigue. For nine years this agent managed George's career from a rented space and called it The Rodrigue Gallery of New Orleans. After George and I bought the business in 1998, we continued selling the Blue Dog and Cajun paintings from this rented location, a small square room badly in need of repairs and an updated design. Comfortable as his own agent and now routinely declining outside representation, George still hoped for a gallery of his own.

In charge of his career once again, the change was immediate. George painted to please himself as opposed to an audience or agent. When he did paint for others, it was exciting projects of his choosing, such as Neiman Marcus, the Chicago Cow Parade, and Xerox. This self-representation worked in his favor. He pondered both in his head and on his canvas questions of style and meaning, with relief and without fear of criticism. And yet he still wanted a gallery of his own, something unrented, available for his renovations and, in the end, reflective of his contemporary vision.

So did I: a woman, a wife, an insecure accomplice writing about her man, her husband, the breadwinner, the confident and great artist, her supportive and occasionally convincing "I-wouldn't-be-where-I-am-without-you" partner in life.

In 2009 we bought a building, a two hundred year-old brick structure across the street from our old rental space and adjacent to St. Louis Cathedral on Royal Street in the New Orleans French Quarter. George and his son Jacques spent nine months on renovations, and in April 2010 George opened a gallery of his own.

In an irony probably marked by no one but me, it is his first gallery, rented or otherwise, in twenty years that, to a great deal, excludes me. He of course denies this,

"But you're my partner! This was construction, Wendy, and you know that's not your thing."

And then, (and I'm still assessing the motive behind this adulation),

"You are doing something far more important with your blog. You're setting the story straight. That's where I need you."

I listened to him and thought to myself . . .

> . . . how unpleasant it is to be locked out; and I thought how it is worse perhaps to be locked in; and, thinking of the safety and prosperity of the one sex and of the poverty and insecurity of the other and of the effect of tradition and of the lack of tradition upon the mind of a writer, I thought at last that it was time to roll up the crumpled skin of the day, with its arguments and its impressions and its anger and its laughter, and cast it into the hedge.*

I found some confidence, a direction, all within these coincidental events—a gallery for George, a blog for me. I have an audience, and yet I have no illusions. As I write these stories and field the questions of concerned friends, I wonder,

Does it lessen my accomplishment because I write about my husband?

Or do I owe it to womankind and to my mother (the older generation, who did not have thirteen children, but who raised me well) and to the children I forfeited for George (although he didn't ask), nay, for me, and to my husband, who supports me, praises me, encourages me, who gives me credit in public and in private, who takes me seriously as a business partner, as a friend, an equal worthy of my opinions on creation, on the meaning of life, on where to spend the holidays, on what to have for dinner, on how to hang the gallery, *on his art*? Or is it because

> Women have served all these centuries as looking-glasses possessing the magic and delicious power of reflecting the figure of man at twice its natural size. Without that power probably the earth would still be swamp and jungle.*

It is because of George that I keep writing, not because I must tell his story, nor because his ego requires it, but rather because he believes in me, because he encourages this blog of my own.

So do you get it? Have you figured out my deception in this story? My thievery? My homage? The echo, albeit weakly interpreted, of a brilliant essay?

> The best course, unless the whole talk was to be distorted, was to expose what was in my mind to the air, when with good luck it would fade and crumble like the head of the dead king when they opened the coffin at Windsor.*

George has a gallery of his own, just one block from the Reilly Gallery, the location of his first show and the only gallery that ever took a chance on him, now forty years ago.

He has the money and owns the space, to wield as he will, to display his creations. We will see things from him in the coming years the likes of which most viewers never knew him capable:

> Hesitate or fumble and you are done for. Think only of the jump . . .*

And as for me (as much for George as for myself), like

Wendy Rodrigue

Virginia Woolf, I choose to defy the great Alexander Pope ("Most women have no character at all"), and yet I happily define my accomplishments by my husband's. You see, I believe that both Woolf and Rodrigue are correct:

> So long as [I] write (paint) what [I] wish to write (paint), that is all that matters.*

* Unless otherwise noted, all quotes in this post are from Virginia Woolf, *A Room of One's Own,* 1929.

Jealousy in the Art World

*I was the "charlatan" of the art world. Then, when I had enough
work amassed, I became a "satirist"—a tricky word—of the art
world, then "fine artist," but who could live with it? And now,
"We like your old things better."*–Robert Rauschenberg, 1972

Jealousy dismisses itself too easily as an explanation
for bad behavior. Because I don't feel it myself and I don't
see it in my artist-husband, I don't understand it in others,
and the concept seems a convenient excuse, the stock answer for why a successful artist endures ridicule.

And yet the history of art, or at least its written record, proves me wrong. One of the most famous accounts
is the 1964 Venice Biennale, in which Robert Rauschenberg (1925-2008) became the first American artist to win
the Grand Prize at the prestigious international art exhibition.

Wendy Rodrigue

A New York visionary bridging Abstract Expressionism and Pop, Rauschenberg has southern roots. He was born and raised in Port Arthur, Texas, and his family moved in 1948 to Lafayette. Twenty-three-year-old Rauschenberg, however, went on to art school at the Kansas City Art Institute and Black Mountain College in North Carolina, never actually living in our state. His sister Janet married into the Lafayette Begneaud family, a group that rejected his sort of anti-aesthetic despite their interest in art. Rauschenberg's brother-in-law Byron Begneaud, in fact, called artist George Rodrigue in dismay after Rauschenberg designed (literally) a wall of artwork in the family's living room:

"Call the Museum of Modern Art in New York," said a young George, astonished that Begneaud would part with something so important. "You'll have to cut out this wall."

When they next spoke, George learned that Begneaud instead dismantled the installation himself, piling the broken pieces in his attic and eventually selling them to an eager dealer for a pittance.

During the 1964 Venice Biennale, New York art dealer Leo Castelli took the heat for championing Rauschenberg. Vilified by both the international and, ironically, American press, the implication was that Castelli and Alan Solomon (curator of the American Biennale exhibit and director of the Jewish Museum in New York) rigged the outcome in some way, upsetting centuries of European, especially French and Italian, artistic dominance.

This is the complete and utter downfall of culture!" wrote the Vatican paper, *L'Osservatore Romano*. "The objects they are showing bear no relation whatsoever to art.*

This ugliness began with a boycott by American judges who refused to participate in the Biennale because, according to Solomon, they were jealous and didn't want him to win the prize. Solomon (and Castelli) remained undeterred:

> As an art historian, I am a specialist in modern French art, in the grand tradition from David to the School of Paris, and I believe that my observations about contemporary American art are not colored by national prejudice.
> —Alan Solomon Papers, Jewish Museum Archives*

Finally, Brandeis University Professor of Art History Sam Hunter relented, becoming the only American juror. Yet according to Solomon:

> he was impossible about proving his purity, to the point where the Italian Jurors wondered if he wanted the prize to go elsewhere.
> -Alan Solomon Papers, Jewish Museum Archives*

In the end, jealousy persisted even as Rauschenberg received the Biennale's top award, The Golden Lion, showing for the first time America's artistic muscle.

Yet this exasperation was nothing new. Among Americans, professional artistic jealousy reigned supreme throughout the previous decade when "for many ambitious artists, success depended on the degree to which they had managed to dethrone de Kooning." Rauschenberg also played this game, convincing Willem de Kooning (1904-1997) to gift him a drawing, which he promptly erased![†]

Here in New Orleans we are fortunate to know camaraderie among artists. Admittedly I hear rumblings, and I understand that this mutual respect is far from comprehensive, yet it is true in my world, as I admire in our home paintings by local artists David Harouni, James Michalopoulos, Mallory Page, Miranda Lake, and Hunt Slonem, along with sculpture by Sidonie Villere and Thomas Bruno, New Orleans photography by Tabitha Soren and

Dennis Couvillion, and pottery from Newcomb College, a treasured gift from local art dealer Jean Bragg.

One of my favorite memories involves sitting on the stoop of David Harouni's Royal Street gallery one summer, eavesdropping as he and George discussed bronzes. In appreciation of my patience, Harouni gave me a gift, a bronze head, which fits perfectly in my hand and sits today on our mantle.

Although a division exists in New Orleans between the agent and artist-owned galleries, by and large the artists themselves collect each other's works, serve on panels together, and support each other's efforts. Just last week I witnessed an artistic dialogue between George and James Michalopoulos, as they discussed the use of found objects, something begun with Marcel Duchamp and the urinal and perfected by Rauschenberg's stuffed goat with a tire around its neck.

"There's a psychological dynamic underneath this," observed Michaloploulos. "It's energizing to use something found. I can go ahead and throw it away if I want. There is a freedom to a lack of monetary attachment."

No doubt rivalry and jealousy exists on some level within this city. Yet they stem mostly from misconception, ignorance, and a perceived inaccessibility. A New Orleans artist on the fence at Jackson Square admitted this to me recently regarding a well-known New Orleans artist, followed by an explanation of the jealousy's dissipation once the two actually talked.

This is nothing compared to the long history of art. Andy Warhol is famous for his rants on jealousy (as detailed in the book *The Philosophy of Andy Warhol* (Mariner Books, 1977), and the recording artist Madonna (b. 1958) weighs in with frustration over the New York music and art world, defending her friend Keith Haring (1958-1990):

> What stays with me is that very early on, when Keith and I were just beginning to soar, our contemporaries

and peers showed all this hostility. Well, the revenge was that, yes, there's this small, elite group of artists who think we're selling out. Meanwhile, the rest of the world is digging us! Of course, it's what they want too! It's so transparent! They're just filled with jealousy and envy. And it certainly didn't stop us, because Keith didn't want to do his work just for the people of New York City—he wanted to do it for everybody, everywhere. I mean, an artist wants world recognition! He wants to make an impression on the world. He doesn't just want a small, sophisticated, elitist group of people appreciating his work. The point of it all is that everybody is out there reaching for the stars, but only some of us get there!

But the history of artistic jealousy goes back further. Baroque artist Caravaggio (1571-1610) became famous as much for his dramatic painting style as for his jealous tantrums and uncontrolled anger, resulting in his exile for murder. His contemporary Domenichino (1581-1641) endured harsh jealousy from his peers. As he worked on an important commission in Naples, Italy, "rivals that be lieved that originality depended on inspiration were annoyed by the smoothness of [his] altarpiece." Artists attacked his works at night, destroying areas of fresco and canvas. In fact, "the enmity aroused by Domenichino's triumph with [his painting of St. Cecilia] may have led to his eventual murder by poisoning." (*Paintings in the Louvre*, Stewart, Tabori & Chang, 1987)

In the end, perhaps jealousy is an otherwise unpleasant emotion that spurs us onward. Artists do not stumble into success by accident. There has to be both meat and ambition behind the effort. What can be said of choosing one's inherent talent and unique vision over conformity? Well, that's the legacy.

"Every artist after 1960 who challenged the restrictions of painting and sculpture and believed that all of life was open to art is indebted to Rauschenberg—forever."[†]

Wendy Rodrigue

* Annie Cohen-Solal, *Leo & His Circle: The Life of Leo Castelli* (Alfred A. Knopf, 2010).

† Robert Rosenblum, "Notes on de Kooning" in *On Modern American Art by Robert Rosenblum* (Harry N. Abrams, 1999).

A Night at the Opera

As I listened to Sir James Galway (b. 1939) and the Louisiana Philharmonic Orchestra (LPO) during their performance at the Mahalia Jackson Theater, I reflected on how I almost lost this accessible escape. Today, our computerized society tugs at us, leaving little time without interruption. A concert, at least for me, is one of the few experiences commanding an effortless mindfulness, existing without the threat of a waiting message or pressing conversation.

As the perfected tone of Galway's breath on his golden flute darted like a dragonfly (think Monet's *Water Lilies*) throughout the concert hall, I scanned the rows and noticed young and old, all of us abandoning cell phones and computers. A petite Irish knight, a veritable leprechaun, brought us together and stunned us with his technical prowess in a contemporary work by William Bolcom (b.

1938) and enchanted us with "Danny Boy," a piece by Galway's favorite composer, "Traditional."

"Pray for Japan, for your country, for your family," he told us, in the wake of Japan's tsunami. "And pray with your eyes open. The Bible says nothing about closing one's eyes. It says 'watch and pray.'"

I recall specifically the first time a song moved me to such a degree that I retained the echo in my mind for years. Puccini's "Chi il bel sogno di doretto" as sung by Dame Kiri Te Kanawa, launched my still-novice interest in classical music and an on-going passion for opera. At age nineteen, although groom-less, I chose Puccini's *La Rondine* aria as the music for my wedding, as I watched, dreamy-eyed, when George Emerson embraced Lucy Honeychurch in a barley field in the screen version of E.M. Forster's *A Room With a View*.

Two years later as a student in Vienna, Austria, I studied Art History while waiting for hours in line outside of the Vienna Opera to pay one dollar thrice weekly. This allowed me the privilege of standing near the stage within the famous opera house. Dressed each evening in the same long black gown, I stood throughout the performances as the music transformed my homesickness into ecstasy.

While my classmates enjoyed the nightclubs and late-night trains to Amsterdam, I expanded my small-town Florida Panhandle upbringing with opera at the Wiener Staatsoper. I saw Domingo in Puccini's *La bohéme*, Carreras in Wagner's *Tristan and Isolde*, Pavarotti in Donizetti's *L'elisir d'amore*, and many more classic performances and operatic greats, all multiple times. The following year, although happy to be home, I admitted to my mother,

"I will always miss the opera."

Years later George and I attended a concert by The Three Tenors. We sat in prime seats, the tenth row center, thanks to a friend who grew up with Pavarotti and knew of my passion. What struck me most was not the emotional power behind "Nessun Dorma" nor the bravado of "O Sole Mio." As with Galway and our LPO, it was those moments that only occur in a live performance, the musicians' exchanges with each other and their reactions to their audience, which made this the single greatest concert ever.

Between songs, I glanced from the tenors to George, unsure if I was more taken with the dynamics and interaction between the great talents on stage or the uncontrollable, exuberant laughter of the man standing beside me. He laughed without finding humor and without mocking; rather, he laughed out of perfect and undistracted joy.

In the coming weeks, the LPO performs Gustav Mahler's "Symphony No. 7." I recall as a student in Vienna learning of his muse-wife Alma's love affairs with several artists from the Vienna Secessionist movement, including Gustav Klimt (we all know *The Kiss*), architect Walter Gropius, and a passionate relationship with artist Oskar Kokoshka, resulting in his 1914 masterpiece, *The Bride of the Wind*.

Mahler (1860-1911) struggled through personal trauma in his later years, particularly his daughter's death at age five and his wife's public indiscretions, made worse by Alma's desire that he take her seriously as a composer. After abandoning "Symphony No. 7" for months, Mahler searched for inspiration in June of 1905, when he . . .

> . . . set out on a lonely hike through the mountains. On his way back as he was rowed across a lake, the rhythm of the oars suggested the slow introduction to the opening movement. He set to work in white heat, finishing the score, except for some fleshing out of the orchestration, by mid-August.
> —LPO Program Notes by Joseph and Elizabeth Kahn

Once again, as with the knighted Irish flutist, the three Italian tenors, and a troubled Viennese composer, the drama of life mingles with the drama of talent and imagination, providing an escape for the rest of us.

A Writer

"All I see is that you're writing with a pen. Yay!!!"

Author Patty Friedmann cheered the hand-written word after seeing the photo above. It was December 2010, and I scribbled on the pages of a purse-size artsy notebook, purchased annually in multiples from the Morgan Library museum shop.

George photographed me as I sat on the steps of a former military base, one of eight bunkers now housing Dan Flavin neon installations at the Chinati Foundation in the remote town of Marfa, Texas.

The resulting essays became two of my most popular: "New York Art in West Texas" for my blog, *Musings of an Artist's Wife*, and a related story, "Rejecting the Metaphor: Discovering Modern Art in West Texas" for the New Orleans newspaper, *Gambit Weekly*. The paper spotlighted their essay for a week with a photo on their website's opening page, and numerous art sites shared the funny *Musings* account of George's Marfa comments long before he talked me into risking a public facebook page of my own. Thousands of readers, whether or not they accepted concrete boxes and crushed cars as art, related to these stories for their honest and non art-speak account of a Minimalist installation designed, let's face it, for the art elite.

Yet in my mind I still was not a writer. The posts are a compilation of George's photographs and comments and, as he himself stated and I often quote,

"What people don't realize, Wendy, is that all of that funny stuff you write is really me!"

Indeed.

Recently while waiting in line at a pharmacy window, a woman asked me in one breath, as New Orleanians will do, my opinion on this newly renovated Elysian Fields Walgreens and if I thought she overdid it that morning on her royal blue eye shadow, a gift from her daughter. Predictably, we moved on to the Saints and the price of shrimp-per-pound followed by the question that, although somehow inoffensive in her thick yat accent, I hoped to avoid,

"Dahlin', what do you do for a livin'?"

She leaned hard against the railing, obviously in pain from her recent knee replacement surgery, and I knew that my standard reply, "I have an art gallery with my husband," moves quickly to "What kind of art?," followed by "What does he paint?," followed by "What's the story of the Blue Dog?," all more than I felt like answering on this Sunday morning and certainly more than she needed in her uncomfortable condition.

"I'm a writer," I stated verbally for the first time in my life.

"You write books?!," she exclaimed, obviously impressed. "Which ones?"

I back-pedaled, explaining that I work on art books,

and that unless she was into modern art, she probably wouldn't have seen them.

"Which artists?" she asked, and before I knew it I was exactly where I didn't want to be . . . expounding the history of the Blue Dog to a growing crowd at Walgreens while the artist himself waited in the car, where he called our brunch guests, explaining that we'd be late and wondering what on earth detained me.

George, however, introduces me often with the words,

"This is my wife, Wendy. She's a writer."

My heroes are writers, just as my heroes are artists, and I stammer in reply to what I see as an undeserving title. I've contributed to, compiled, and/or edited eight Rodrigue books since 1994. Yet it's not the same as writing my own. It was New Orleans author David Lummis who first labeled me a writer and gave me the courage to use the word within bios and online. With this publication, thanks to a persistent and courageous UL Press, I publish my first solo book.

"Will you join me on tour?" I asked George, laughing, as I imagined him in my established role, swapping out sharpies and spelling dedications in my ear.

"Yes!" he replied, to my surprise. "It'll be fun!"

Moonstruck, Madame Butterfly, and the Mudlark

Bring me the big knife; I'm gonna cut my throat!

Several nights ago, as we walked in a chilly, blowing drizzle across the street from the Metropolitan Opera, I stopped, even as the crosswalk sign suggested we proceed.

"What are you doing?" asked George, as I explained that I saw Cher in my head, breathtaking, emerging from a New York City taxi to meet Nicholas Cage after sighing that morning, "Where's the Met?"

"I love two things," he said (the "he" in my head is George or Cage; take your pick). "I love you, and I love the Opera. If I can have the two things that I love together for one night, I will be satisfied to give up, oh God, the rest of my life."*

The surrealism intensified as we entered the theatre. As the chandeliers ascended into the ceiling, I imagined that I sat in her seat and experienced the Opera for the first time.

"I know!" exclaimed Cher, still in my head at intermission. "I mean, she was coughing her brains out, and still she had to keep singing!"

As *Madame Butterfly* sings goodbye to her son, portrayed by a Bunraku puppet and three masterful puppeteers, she lifts the knife to her own throat, stabbing herself with both the blade and the pain of love betrayed. The tears covered my face, and I was Cher again, as Mimi and Rodolfo (Puccini's *La bohéme*) sing of their passionate love, despite Mimi's wretched illness as she dies of consumption.

"Men!" I choked out after the performance, as though I was Cher. "If anyone deserved to die it was that horrible Pinkerton!"

"That's the way it was . . ." started George/Cage, wisely stopping mid-sentence.

Two days later we found ourselves at the Mudlark Confectionary, a performance theatre in the Katrina-ravaged St. Roch neighborhood, just a few blocks from our Faubourg Marigny home. Far from the Met, we hurried, sans jewelry, from the dark, abandoned street into the front room of a tiny New Orleans cottage. Looking up, George and I gasped at the sophisticated puppets hanging from the ceiling, recalling our Lincoln Center experience in the most unlikely of places.

"It's like *Madame Butterfly* in the dream sequence," I whispered to George, who nodded, snapping pictures as we waited between performances.

To begin, Sir Lady Indee removed her clothes, layer by layer, on stage, until I thought surely she would stand naked before us. George grabbed my leg, and I grew flush, as

I imagined, prudishly, sitting in a room with a conservative friend, also on our adventure, as we stared at the au natural Indee some six feet in front of us. Fortunately, however, she stopped at her step-ins, redressing herself from a roll of cellophane anchored to the wall. As she rolled the clear plastic tightly around her skin, she enchanted us all. She spoke of desire, passion, and indulgence, and I thought of Butterfly, confident in her wedding kimono, even as Pinkerton planned (deep down) to abandon her.

"I ain't no freakin' monument to justice!" shouted Cage, in the movie and in my head. "I lost my hand! I lost my bride! Johnny has his hand! Johnny has his bride! You want me to take my heartache, put it away and forget?"*

Elliot, a woman, seemingly a man, seemingly a woman (not in the least to be confused with Victor Victoria) took the stage.

"Is that a man or a woman?" whispered George.

"A woman," I said, thinking, *Does it matter?*

With a bird's voice, sometimes a lark, sometimes a gull, she sang her anguished creed, alternating between the banjo, bass drum, classical guitar, and small electric piano.

"I'm from Philadelphia," she explained.

The audience cheered in support, as did New Orleans artist James Michalopoulos, our co-host with his wife Reese Johanson, founder of Artist Inc., both great advocates of New Orleans theatre. "Rocky!" shouted James, caught up in the moment.

Elliot, consumed by her expression, began her hometown lament *a capella*.

"This is the most tormented man I have ever known," said Chrissy in the movie and in my head.*

After five songs, we left, passing on the CDs but leaving twenty dollars on the table. Although we appreciated the performances and will revisit the Mudlark on another day, at that moment we never wanted to hear such agony again.

"I'm in love with this man," continued Chrissy about Ronnie Cammareri (Cage), "but he doesn't know that, 'cause I never told him, 'cause he could never love anybody since he lost his hand and his girl."*

Once home, George shook his head and organized his photos. "I'm a little afraid to ask," he said . . .

". . . but what are we doing tomorrow?"

* *Moonstruck*, 1987.

Success

In *Just Kids*, poet/rocker Patti Smith reveals a personal account of life with her closest friend, artist/photographer Robert Mapplethorpe. Earlier this week, I started an essay on Louisiana's Legends, sixteen portraits completed by George for Public Broadcasting between 1990 and 1993, but after finishing Smith's memoir late Thursday night, I suffered a crying-headache Friday, unable to focus on anything other than hydration (mine, but moreso George's, now acute from chemotherapy) and Smith's poem, "Wild Leaves."

"The Legends," along with "Tee Coon," the "Breaux Bridge Band," and any number of other unfinished stories, fall victim to my lingering, as though bruised, emotional state.

If you're a woman, you know this headache well.

If you're a man with this firsthand knowledge, then

you're an anomaly, at least in my world, as I've never met anyone like you.

"Wild Leaves"

Every word that's spoken
Every word decreed
Every spell that's broken
Every golden deed
All the parts we're playing
Binding as the reed
And wild leaves are falling
Wild wild leaves*

Interesting enough, it was George who said,

"Why do you want to write about the Legends paintings? That's boring!"

Yet I knew his comment related to fretful recollections of deadlines and tedious work, as opposed to the subjects themselves, successful, larger-than-life talents like Ernest Gaines, Ron Guidry, and Pete Fountain. Thus, the story remains important, delayed until the day I awake focused once again on Louisiana's best, yet vested enough personally to make it interesting.

I explained this short essay, an effort to get the 1970s New York art scene out of my head, returning me to Blue Dogs in the new millennium, to George.

"Nobody knows who she is, Wendy!" insisted my husband, a fifty-year member of the Johnny Cash Fan Club, about Patti Smith. "Make sure you link to her website," he continued, shaking his head as I gave him *the* look.

"He was worried that I wouldn't be successful if my work was too provocative," wrote Smith about Mapplethorpe in her version of our conversation. "He always wanted me to write a song I could dance to."

Any artist's success lies in a mixture of self-confidence and vulnerability. Whether or not this translates to commercial success is in the stars. However, altering one's creative vision based on outside commentary spells the worst kind of failure, personal defeat. Of this I'm sure.

I circled a passage, as Smith recalls seeing Bob Dylan at her concert:

"Instead of humbled, I felt a power, perhaps his; but I also felt my own worth and the worth of my band. It seemed for me a night of initiation, where I had to become fully myself in the presence of the one I had modeled myself after."

Throughout this book, Smith inspires me, not only through the courage of her personal expression in art and music, but also through the simplicity and sincerity of her words. I believe it was this, as much as the circumstances of Mapplethorpe's death and, in particular, the suffering of my own life's partner, that brought on my sobbing and, afterwards, crying-headache, resonating still.

I asked George, who, despite his weakness, passed me the aspirin without my asking, for a few words on success. He thought only for a moment before he near-whispered,

"Never believe what others write about you—no matter how great or how bad."

* Patti Smith, *Just Kids* (Harper Collins, 2010).

Swamp Women

Oh, this stinkin' swamp water stinks!
—*Swamp Women*, the movie, 1955

Early on Halloween morning I met George in our New Orleans garage for the two-hour drive to Lafayette, where we were to meet friends from California at the Blue Dog Café. I was late.

"What are you wearing?!" he exclaimed. "We're going on a swamp tour!"

Dressed for the day in a skull-covered pirate dress, over-sized spider rings, and spiky heels, I hollered at him as I ran to the house for my flip-flops and bug spray:

"Swamp tour? I thought we were going to brunch!"

In Lafayette we joined our Carmel friends, the Pistos and Ricciardis, in search of southwest Louisiana's best boudin and pecan pie, as Chef John Pisto scouted locations for his television cooking show. We enjoyed an excellent brunch at the Blue Dog Café, with the added bonus of Cajun Swamp fiddler Hadley Castille (1933-2012), who sat in with the Wildflowers Band. From Lafayette we drove through Breaux Bridge to the town of Henderson, where we crossed the levee to McGee's Landing and the edge of the Atchafalaya Swamp.

"Great news!" announced George, after negotiating our afternoon with Captain David in the corner of Mc-Gee's Bar, "We're taking an airboat!"

In the past, I enjoyed dozens of swamp tours, all on pontoon-type, roomy tour boats. The closest I came to an airboat was reruns of *Gentle Ben* (1967-1969).

"What's an airboat?" asked our California guests in chorus.

"Has Captain David been drinking?" I asked George, under my breath.

Within minutes, the roaring airplane-type engine approached the floating dock. I saw mouths moving in the shape of "Oh, no!" but heard no one. Our captain motioned to our seats. . . .

"Put the ladies in the front," screamed George . . . as we donned our headphones and entered a silent movie.

With one life preserver and no seat belts, it was just us, a bench, and the swamp. Captain David accelerated into the makeshift waterway for less than a minute before turning hard right into the lilies, cypress knees, and shallow black water. Inaccessible to boats with underwater engines, this was a new part of the swamp for me. I spoke aloud to myself in amazement at the beauty, and as I write this I feel compelled, before recounting the chaos that followed, to get serious for a moment:

> When I would recreate myself, I seek the darkest wood, the thickest and most interminable, and to the citizen, most dismal swamp. I enter a swamp as a sacred place—a sanctum sanctorum. There is the strength, the marrow of Nature.
> –Henry David Thoreau (1817-1862)

The Other Side of the Painting

In my life, I've seen majesty, both manmade and natural—a weeklong rafting trip on the Colorado River; the birth of our nephews; the Basilica of Santa Croce in Florence—and I recognized immediately such a wonder. The azure blue dragonflies alighted on my shoulders, the alligators peered from among the lilies, and the herons and ducks and egrets reminded us of the shallow water as they walked near the boat. I thought about the Cajuns, harvesting these cypress trees in the mid-eighteenth and nineteenth centuries, trees that grow slowly, struggling after all of these years to once again fill the swamp.

"In another century the trees will be back," predicts George.

As we sat in silence, lost in our thoughts, Captain David moved on, deeper into the swamp. With nothing but each other to hold onto, we raced (quietly praying that the animals get out of the way and the lilies are tougher than they look) through large areas of plant life. We flew over dry land and grew confident in our captain's abilities.

Yet as we headed full speed towards an eight-foot bank, I thought surely he was turning; and as we hit the mound of earth and flew straight up, I thought surely this wasn't happening; and as we nose dived towards the deeper black water on the other side, I thought surely (as I screamed at the top of my lungs for no one to hear) that this was not the way I would die; and as the five-foot swamp tsunami barreled over the bow and into our laps and down (and up) my festive dress, I went into shock.

The motor died, the women sat dripping in slime and disbelief, and the men sat bone-dry, doubled over with cramps of laughter. Collecting himself, Captain David approached the women cautiously with his apologies and a single useless towel.

"Aw, my Gawd," said the Cajun, shaking his head. "Ladies, I am so sawry. In twenty years dat ain't ne'er hap'nd."

Without looking at the men, we women suffered their howling and dismissed our heroes as worthless. As I plucked the snails off of his wife's backside, Tony choked out,

"I thought we were stuck like a dart!"

Dripping in green *gradeaux*,* we ladies wrung out our clothes and wiped our tears (of laughter or disbelief or some swamp disease or whatever) with the towel, while the men focused on the dead engine.

"Look, there's the interstate," pointed George. "This water can't be more than five or six feet, and you gals are already wet . . ."

I conjured a furious look and then laughed some more, imagining us standing in the black swamp water fifty feet below the highway, waving down a passing motorist.

Barbara was the first of the women to speak:

"My mouth was open as we went in. Do you think I'll get cholera?"

At last the engine caught and we sped towards Mc-Gee's Landing, where whiskey seemed the only suitable libation to recount our adventure and toast the dry land. Barbara, Cheryl, and I stood on the deck, unable to handle the a/c in our soaked condition, and stared through the window at our husbands:

"If you look at the guys," observed Barbara, "you'd never know that we almost died."

". . . on Halloween, covered in the monster mash," continued Cheryl.

We refocused, however, as we watched the sunset over the Atchafalaya Swamp. Yet we heard the men, still laughing, as George told the story of him and Dickie in 1950s New Iberia, chased into the swamp by the sheriff after Dickie shot one of the Trajan brothers in the stomach with a pebble-loaded BB gun.

"We knew how to stay dry," said George, "but that sheriff was up to his waist in swamp water before he found our tree house. Boy was he mad."

Following the two hour drive home, I took the second longest and hottest shower of my life, spending a good half hour afterwards cleaning the gradeaux* off of the tiles.

In my dry soft cotton pajamas, I crawled into bed where next to me I found, in place of my husband, a painting of the Blue Dog suspended in an orange color field.

"What's this?" I called downstairs, where George watched the tail end of the Saints game.

"It's a present. You were a great sport today. Happy Halloween!"

---

* Gradeaux: basically, any icky unidentifiable substance.

The Collectible Book

George and I discuss bookstores probably more often than most, usually focused on book tour nostalgia. We spent much of the late 1990s and early 2000s on the road throughout the United States and Canada, sometimes twenty cities in one month, and we developed a personal connection to certain stores and their staffs, as we shared, through lectures and book signings, a growing collection of Rodrigue publications.

In this day of Kindles, iPads, and ebooks, however, the publishing world is changed. Book signings rarely draw mobs; fewer newspapers review books; and that special place called a bookstore is a destination for "collectors." Books, it seems, are headed the same direction as the typewriter.

Recently in Las Vegas's City Center, we stumbled open-mouthed into a new bookstore, Assouline, a New

York City publisher of gift and fine art books. If not the store, George and I both are familiar with the product. Their publications include boxed sets spotlighting fashion and other lofty interests, offered for a serious price through the catalogues of high-end department stores. In addition to these collections, they specialize in large-scale tomes on artists such as Magritte or the history of Penthouse Magazine or their latest project, a tribute to Barbie.

These heavy, beautiful paper objects run anywhere from $300 to $1,500. They are limited in number and, when possible, include the appropriate signatures. The store, its presentation, and its titles are stunning and, for now anyway, impossible to reproduce on a laptop.

"This is where it's going," noted George. "Books are pieces of art."

Making his point, sixteenth-century large-scale original paintings, portraits of royalty and nobility, take up any space not devoted to books, so that the Assouline bookstore ends up a cross between the slick of the contemporary and the idolized of the old world. We couldn't help but compare our bookstore adventure to George's gallery, where we offer the opposite: paintings for sale and books for show.

In New Orleans, my office is a jewel box of special books. They include gifts from authors and friends, first editions of my favorite reads, especially books rooted in Louisiana, as well as assorted award-winning titles. These blend with hundreds of art books, some from my mom, some from George's art school years, and most purchased on our travels, recalling museum exhibitions and friendly debates. I store the titles in plastic and periodically turn out their covers, *Steamboat Gothic*, *The Collectors*, *Ghosts Along the Mississippi*, so that the bookshelves become a changing installation of art.

During our Assouline afternoon, although tempted by

The Other Side of the Painting

Barbie, I spent a chunk of George's slot machine winnings on a reproduction of a 1902 book of French text and paintings illustrating the life of Louis XIV.

George, however, spent the remainder of his winnings on *The History of Penthouse Magazine*.

Lofty, indeed.

The Other Side of the Painting

Oftentimes it takes others to point out our achievements. What begins as small and for oneself can become something else. George paints today with confidence, sure of both his brushstrokes and direction. His paintings are steps towards expounding his vision, whether within a specific series or his career's *oeuvre*.

But this was not always the case. In 1965 George was a student at the Art Center College of Design in Los Angeles. He learned from professional artists and, for the first time in his life, thought of art in abstract concepts, beyond illustration. Although he also studied advertising design, his painting classes focused on fundamentals and technique, as well as the visual transmission of his soul, the impartation of mystery. From his early twenties, art shifted from illustrating a specific idea to eliciting an emotional response.

Wendy Rodrigue

To create the untitled painting above (1965, 24 x 18), George, strapped for cash, rather than purchase a new canvas, glued together two pieces of thin, shiny illustration board. Normally, in presenting a design to clients, he taped his illustration to a press board, covering it with a two-inch matte to hide the tape. Here, however, in a painting class, without concern for clients and their products, he created a makeshift canvas, backing the two pieces with a single heavier sheet of pressboard, all discarded materials from his class in advertising design.

Years later, he stapled the assembled pieces into an expensive, museum-quality frame.

"As I started painting from the model on my glued-down illustration board," recalls George, "the teacher asked me what I was doing and noted that, without a canvas, I should at least use a single piece of board.

"But I shrugged my shoulders and continued to paint. After an hour or so, the same professor walked by and said, 'Stop, it's finished.' So I did."

The scenario was a lesson for Rodrigue. Until this point, he looked at a finished painting, whether a portrait, landscape, or still-life, as best representing its subject, literally. The assignment was simple: paint the model. And yet, in stopping when he did, George's interpretation becomes a visual enigma.

For years, visitors to his studio, especially other artists, asked him when he would finish the painting.

"It's finished, I told them.

"Something else happened. My experience with this one painting helped me see the abstract, beyond the subject. For that reason, it's hung on the wall of my studio for the past forty-eight years."

Similarly, I started blogging mainly to answer the questions of students, collectors, and journalists. *Musings of an Artist's Wife* began as a source for basic information about the art of George Rodrigue, such as the story behind Jolie

Blonde, the origin of the Blue Dog, and the pronunciation of the artist's name.

Yet from the beginning, George was my professor, seeing something else. He encouraged me to drift away from rote answers and instead explore tangents, including not only my observations of his work, but also the nostalgia and perception unique to me and my life. In a way, my audience also guided me, because, as I dared to share the personal and obtuse, those same stories, the ones with obscure references and unanswered questions, drew thousands of readers, oftentimes more than the literal Rodrigue specifics that spawned the blog in the first place.

Like George sitting down to an assignment to paint a model and nothing more, the blog became something else. It's as though we turned over the pieced-together, painted board and, like the other side of the hit record, found something unexpected, something important and true, and, just like the unfinished "finished" painting, something that was there all the time.

Chapter 5

It's like I'm gonna get a stick stuck in my eye, and I can't wait to get it 'cause it's good for me

When it comes to the arts, George Rodrigue and I both have strong opinions, resulting in oftentimes subtle and occasionally lively arguments.

New York Art in West Texas

I could spend the rest of my life traveling and writing about the West, I thought to myself as I sat with George Rodrigue in a café in Marfa, Texas, and watched the barbershop across the street. The barber, partially obscured by a single strand of colored lights and his barber's pole, shaved his own face in the small window, framed by the deserted retail spaces on either side of his shop, before locking up and heading for his pick-up parked out front.

"It's the biggest contradiction in the world," said George about Marfa. "This isn't Texas; this is New York. This is like I'm gonna get a stick stuck in my eye, and I can't wait to get it, 'cause it's good for me."

George's comment does not refer to the barber, or to the flat roofs and Western architecture, or to the golden light and long shadows. It doesn't refer to the lone dog walking down the middle of the street or to the fact that "all of the guys walking by look like the same guy."

He's talking about the deluge of contemporary art that fell, with increasing intensity, on Marfa over the past thirty years. He means that anyone who's anybody in the art world visits Marfa, a remote Texas town near the Mexico border, in order to claim they're in the know. They have no choice.

He has a point. A certain element of Marfa feels like the West Texas annex of Berkeley. If you ask the museums or galleries about restaurants, they name two, both organic, with homegrown veggies, free-range everything, and beautiful young people, sporting long hair or no hair and wearing eyeglasses with dark plastic frames.

"The locals must find this nuts," continued George. "These poor people just had it done to them."

(As he philosophizes, I overhear a Yogi Berra-ism from the bar: "Once you get to know a stranger, then they're no longer a stranger.")

Experiencing art in Marfa is like experiencing art on the set of *High Noon*. At the Chinati Foundation, Donald Judd's (1928-1994) tribute to himself and other Minimalists, we walked between the buildings of a former army base, confronting a heightened sensory perception, an acute awareness of the wind and the light, the squeak of our shoes, and the whir of the grass. This will be here forever, an abandoned fort, windows walled up with impressions of where they used to let in light.

Inside a former military storage bunker, we encounter an installation à la *The Shining* in a, well, shining example of contemporary art, the poems of Carl Andre (b. 1935). We study five hundred pages of patterns typed on a typewriter, or occasionally block-printed by hand, sometimes using nothing but one word or one letter. George tells me that as a young man he did the same thing but, regrettably, did not save the pages.

Donald Judd moved from New York City to Marfa,

The Other Side of the Painting

Texas, in 1979 and created a permanent installation of Minimalism.

"When you become famous," says George, "you tend to go hide somewhere. People (such as Georgia O'Keeffe) have done it before."

"Yes, but why Marfa, where he'll never be understood?" I ask.

"He was making a statement by coming here. It's out of the way, so it didn't create controversy. Only people who thought it was cool and necessary came here. It's like me having an art gallery on Pecan Island."

In other words, Judd didn't really hide; rather, he transformed a community and made it his legacy. A man who rejected painting with brushstrokes because "it's already done and I want to do something new" has his name on half of the buildings of a remote western high desert town.

George and I realized immediately that Judd's idea in Marfa is to exhibit . . . and that is all. The gallery and museum staffs have little or no interaction with visitors, no explanations, no nothing. Our guide at Chinati, for example, presented a brief history of the place and how each artist came to be there. She showed no emotion as she spoke, as though her enthusiasm might betray the artwork. She did not explain the art, because Minimalism is without meaning and requires no explanation.

Accordingly, once inside, she refrained from speaking. We entered the first building at Chinati (unfortunately I do not remember the artist's name; it was not Flavin) and our tour group stood still in silence, first staring at ten fluorescent bulbs along a wall ("I was waiting for it to do something," said one visitor later), and then at each other, at the ceiling, and out of the window, until George finally broke the agony, stating aloud, "I've got it," prompting a relieved eruption of laughter and our guide's sheepish move towards the door.

The overall place is a work of art, combining the installations with old and seemingly, at first, incongruent architecture, purposefully changed to suit each installation, along with the land and sky of West Texas.

Judd related his concrete boxes to the boxes of the buildings. This doesn't make much sense until you realize that the military fort, like Louisiana's oak trees, was already here. Judd took it a step further and created the boxes on purpose, just as George adapted the oaks to his canvas.

According to George, the closest he came to Minimalism was a set of three twelve-inch square boxes he created in the late 1960s. However, he would not pass muster with the folks at Marfa, because he injects too much meaning into his sculpture, creating a warning sign with a STOP, along with a barricade and construction cone.

From Marfa, we visited Marney—not the town, but the person. Marney Robinson is Director of Education for the George Rodrigue Foundation of the Arts. She grew up in Hobbs, New Mexico, a small city with an impressive sign, located about two hundred miles north of Marfa, Texas.

We met her parents, brother, and uncle, visited their family-run pharmacy, and enjoyed their hospitality. We also explored Marney's contemporary art, namely a sculpture influenced by her family's business, the "Tylenol Torso," covered with hundreds of pills and created by Marney for a studio art class at Trinity University.

Like Marfa, the Robinson family home is one that cannot be replicated. It can only happen in Hobbs, under these circumstances and with these people. A painting or sculpture can happen in any number of museums, but not the Marfa experience—it can only happen in West Texas, on an abandoned military base, now enchanted by one man's vision.

Rodrigue vs. O'Keeffe

At the Georgia O'Keeffe Museum in Santa Fe, New Mexico, I unwittingly, as with Degas at the Morgan Library, connect George to Modern Art, this time, however, relating him to an artist whose work he dislikes. Barely through the door, he grumbles,

"The only reason we look at some of this art is because it's hanging here, in the Georgia O'Keeffe Museum. Otherwise a person might walk on by. This museum is the worst collection of her paintings. She needed a good editor.

". . . except for this one," he continued, gesturing to *Black Hollyhock Blue Larkspur*, 1930. "This was a good accident."

Fascinated by O'Keeffe and her biography,* I hoped to convince George of her accomplishments by way of her conviction, an artistic drive evident from an early age and similar to his. I related her struggle with typhoid fever and the temporary loss of her hair to his bout with polio and the interim loss of the use of his legs. Whereas O'Keeffe shared the family's slight good fortune with her siblings, so that each attended school even though alternating academic years, George understood loneliness and misunderstanding as an only child.

O'Keeffe embraced on her own the Prang Art Instruction Manuals, from which she gained "her first impressions of how nature could be reproduced in two dimensions,"* just as Rodrigue embraced the Art Instruction Correspondence Course, based in Minneapolis. In 1957, at age thirteen, George was the youngest person accepted into the program, and yet his parents had little grasp of the significance. O'Keeffe's parents and academic community steered her towards teaching, while George's parents pushed him towards the railroad and telephone company. However, the young people stayed their course, an unpopular path, becoming fine artists.

"And you're a man!" I reminded him. "You had it made."

In addition, just as O'Keeffe understood shape but admittedly "was not a prodigy . . . and had to work to improve her technical abilities,"* Rodrigue struggled with drawing from the beginning, knowing that his inherent skill lies in his ideas. These struggles in life and art empowered both artists. Their suffering, at whatever level, gave them the courage to look inward, to abandon the establishment, and to follow their childhood dreams.

I copied O'Keeffe's words below from the wall of the museum, the same statement George repeats in various forms over the years, whether talking about his Oak Trees, Cajuns, Hurricanes, or Blue Dogs:

"I have a single track mind. I work on one idea for a long time. It is like getting acquainted with a person, and I don't get acquainted easily." –O'Keeffe, 1962

The Other Side of the Painting

Rosalea Murphy, another artist who, like O'Keeffe*
and Rodrigue loved the Land of Enchantment, also could
have written that sentence. Although best known for her
Pink Adobe Restaurant and Dragon Room Bar, she spent
her life (1912-2000) creating an impressive portfolio of
original works, paintings of roosters, dragons, and poblano
peppers. George met Rosalea in the mid-1980s at an exhibition of his Cajun paintings, and their friendship, rooted in their mutual respect for each other as artists, grew
stronger with his increasingly frequent Santa Fe sojourns.
Through Rosalea, George met other creative individuals, including artist/jeweler Douglas Magnus and painter/
sculptor Armand Lara, establishing an artistic camaraderie
that exists still today.

Finally, I leave you with George's thoughts as we ex-
ited the O'Keeffe Museum. Hoping he swayed a bit in her
favor, I asked him once more about the famous artist. He
shrugged his shoulders and replied,

"She loved this land and this place; I'll give her that."

*Hunter Drohojowska-Philp, *Full Bloom: The Art and Life of Georgia
O'Keeffe* (Norton Press, 2004).

The Painting in the Closet

It's a common misconception that George intends all of his art for sale, or at least for public display. If he manufactured tennis shoes, this might make sense, and indeed because George makes a living with his art, it is true that most works end up with a price tag. However, this commercialism is by no means all-inclusive. George loves painting, the process of applying paint to canvas, and he pursues his creative impulses regardless of public opinion. Had he listened to outsiders or even friends and family, there would be no dark landscapes, no Cajuns, and certainly no Blue Dog. Although his paintings for the most part are accessible, there are countless other projects in the closet, so to speak. For example, periodically he calls from the shower,

"Quick, Wendy, write this down. I just wrote a movie."

Or he spends a sleepless night with pencil and tracing paper, designing every detail of some imaginary car.

Yet he's not in touch with TriStar Pictures or Ford Motor Company. Instead these projects, the most important thing in the world to him for a few hours or even a few days, end up buried at the bottom of the pile on his desk or tacked to the wall in his studio or rolled up with rubber bands in my keepsake box, all destined for the archives at some organized point down the road.

Paintings end up in the closet for various reasons. His rejects from a recent figurative series, *Bodies*, for example, filled half a storage room. Yet just because a painting never hangs on the gallery's wall does not mean that it's a failure. On the contrary, some of George's most poignant works are those that he never intended for sale or public viewing.

For example, he painted *No More Dukes* in 1996 following former Ku Klux Klan Grand Wizard David Duke's announcement of his campaign for the U.S. Senate. After it sat twelve years in the closet, George loaned the painting for public display for the first time in 2008 during the exhibition "Rodrigue's Louisiana" at the New Orleans Museum of Art.

After a frustrating look at contemporary art during Art Basel and the Venice Biennale in 2005, he drew *Where is the Art World?*, a sketch he kept for himself and a design he reluctantly offered for sale in a print form, after relentless pleading on my part.

Following the BP disaster of 2010, he created a series of images related to the oil spill in the Gulf of Mexico. He stayed up nights adjusting these designs for no one but himself, knowing that this was a cause beyond his reach, as he fielded calls from offshore oil workers, Louisiana fishermen, environmentalists, and politicians, all on different sides of the issue, and yet each pleading an earnest case. George's oil spill statements remain, still today, in the closet.

Most pieces, without question, stay off of the market

because they're personal. These include gifts for me, paintings designed for our home, and countless photographs, pieces that to George's mind are some of his best works but which he doesn't display, I suspect, because he hasn't the energy for the questions and skepticism that might accompany such an exhibition . . . yet.

Chickens In and Out of Rodrigue Paintings

George's sense of play overflows from his life into his art. Even in his Cajun paintings, which many consider his "serious work," he plays jokes on the public, entertaining himself and his audience with absurd subject matter, scale, and titles. The truth, however, is that when it comes to the process of applying paint to canvas, George is, always, serious. From the ridiculous to the sobering, each stroke, each concept, each finished painting is purposeful, deliberate, and painted in the best way he knows how, painted as if it were a jewel.

Consider *Chicken on the Bayou*, painted in 1986. According to George,

"So fond was the Landry Family of their chicken Clotile, that they commissioned this portrait of her."

He barely says the words before the real fun begins:

"I call it . . . *The Two Hundred Pound Chicken on the Bayou!*"

He then explains in earnest that he painted the chicken like a person, no different than Huey Long at the Evangeline Oak. Its hard edge and strong shape appear cut out and pasted onto the Louisiana landscape and, like the Cajuns, it glows with its culture.

For forty years, certain aspects of George's paintings remain consistent. No matter what the subject, whether Jolie Blonde, the Blue Dog, the President of the United States, or a giant chicken, if the painting is an outdoor scene, then the subject stands framed by a tree, illuminated from within, and part of a carefully planned puzzle, so that shifting any element destroys the design.

This is the reason it all works! If George painted chickens (or dogs) in a realistic scale, if they ran around trees or sat low at our feet, then the mystery vanishes; the subjects become characters or, worse, non-subjects; and the paintings lose their sincerity and power.

Scale is a key element for George in both his paintings and in life. The bigger the story, the bigger the experience. During Mardi Gras 1979, for example, he hosted his annual unofficial "krewe" party in Lafayette, Louisiana, proclaiming himself King on a bandstand in the yard of his Jefferson Street house. This particular year, his friend Louis Mann reigned as the official King of the Lafayette City Krewe, Bonaparte. He arranged an unauthorized stop at George's platform for a photo and gift exchange.

The crowd watched as George presented King Louis with a beautiful box. As he lifted the lid, a chicken sprung out in a frantic fluster, terrifying the eighteen-year-old princesses making their debut. Out of control, the animal tore at and pooped on His Royal Highness's beaded robes.

Louis and George count this story among their favorites. However, Lafayette's city officials did not see the humor. They moved the parade route so that it never again passed by George's house.

My favorite of George's chicken tributes also involves

an actual bird. The silkscreen *Chicken in a Basket* (1993) portrays the Blue Dog front and center with purple and pink chickens on either side, all backed by a yellow moonscape.

I recall the day when George brought home the stuffed real chicken he purchased from a roadside taxidermist in south Louisiana.

"That's disgusting!" I groaned.

"Isn't it cool?" he laughed. "I have an idea for a silk-screen!"

He worked, intently, for a week, and twenty years later the preserved chicken still sits, a mangy and beloved trophy, in our den.

Breakfast at Lea's Pies

Following a recent pilgrimage to the Alexandria Museum of Art, George, son Jacques, friend Wayne Fernandez, and I visited an old favorite, Lea's Lunch Room (est. 1928), located in the tiny town of Lecompte, Louisiana. It was ten years or more since my last visit.

We lived in Lafayette in those early days, traveling by car each fall on book tour. Lea's was our last stop before reaching home after weeks on the road, and I spent that final hour balancing eight pies on my lap, lest they slide or turn over in the backseat.

Although still a destination for many, the place really hopped in the 1950s before and after LSU games, when Highway 71 was the major road between Baton Rouge and Shreveport. Famous for their pies and ham sandwiches, Lea's attracted not only football fans, but also preachers, politicians, and generally anyone looking to hold court.

"There are no calories; it's all air," explains George, as

to why he can eat as much meringue and whipped cream as he wants.

"You got enough pictures so I can start eating this pie?" asked Wayne, as I arranged the slices for aesthetics. (Wayne eventually ate so much sugar that he talked most of the way home about how he was going to stop talking).

"My dad grew up with Lea," shares Lecompte native Teri Welch. "He drove a Stutz Bearcat down the gravel road that ran along Bayou Boeuf and was quite a figure. In later life, with his white hair, he resembled a slimmer Colonel Sanders. He also grew roses and orchids for a hobby. I remember them on the tables at the diner."

After our sweet morning taste of Central Louisiana, our foursome took a slow ride south to Opelousas for lunch. On the way we passed the magnificent Seven Brothers Oak, just west of Washington on Hwy 103.

"You ever painted that?" asked Wayne.

"Nah, it's too confusing," replied George, as he coaxed my sandaled feet towards the tree, hoping for a photograph. I kept my distance, however, recalling our previous week's drive and my near-death encounter with a water moccasin in a Georgiana, Alabama, graveyard.

"Speaking of graveyards, you can bury me here," I announced, as we wandered through a seductive cemetery in Washington, a southern statement made all the more beguiling with its massive oaks, plastic flowers, and blue-washed, crumbling tombs.

"These are the same tombs we sold," explained George, recalling his family's New Iberia business, "Rodrigue's Portable Concrete Burial Vaults."

"We advertised them as air-tight; but it was a problem, because they floated during the floods. In high school, my daddy sent me after hard rains to the cemetery where, using a sledgehammer, I knocked the corners off of the tombs, sinking them for good."

Ready for the next meal, we drove to Opelousas and the Palace Café, "Serving Fine Cajun Cuisine Since

The Other Side of the Painting

1927." The men dined on chicken fried steak and crawfish bisque, while I enjoyed my once-a-year po-boy (fried catfish, dressed).

As I paid the twenty-six dollars bill, the guys flirted with our waitress, a pretty gal sporting Mel's Diner attire and royal blue eye shadow.

"Have a Blue Dog pin," offered Jacques.

"I don't get it," she replied.

"It's an artist from New Orleans."

"Never been there. I don't have a car," she explained, as I added twenty dollars to the tip.

From the Palace Café we drove to Joe's Dreyfus Store and Restaurant, an old favorite in Livonia. Regrettably, we couldn't eat another bite, so we settled instead for photographs of the Christmas decorations, wreaths, and icicles, lights blinking at the steady crowd of customers on a hot summer's day.

"Not too many of these places left," noted George, although after our morning, none of us believed him.

As we turned towards New Orleans, he paused one last time at a crumbling roadside seafood market patched with metal signs and hand-painted banners.

"You'd never know it," he said, "but this started off as a nothin' place."

I lowered the window for a picture.

"Sure wish I had one of those pies," sighed Wayne.

The Price of Beauty

Vanity is the quicksand of reason.
–George Sand (1804-1876)

"I want a face that my husband doesn't feel the need to Photoshop," I told my dermatologist, a licensed aesthetician recommended by a girlfriend.

It was the summer of 2005 and my first visit ever to such a doctor. She explained that my thin skin, the product of my natural, dull blonde coloring, made a chemical peel dangerous, especially the strong type needed to attack large areas of sun damage, the result of my youth at the beach. She asked about my vanity, suggesting cautiously that we freeze the darkest, largest spots.

"You'll have scabs on your face for up to six weeks," she explained. "Once they're fully healed, we'll treat your skin as a whole."

I closed my eyes as she blow-torched my cheeks and forehead in eight or ten places, leaving as many sores, some as large as a dime. Fortunately, George and I traveled much of that summer. Make-up was pointless, and so I ducked George's camera, wearing nothing on my head but sunscreen and a hat.

By summer's end, the sores were gone; I abandoned ideas of further treatment; and George minimized, or at least hid well, his use of Photoshop on my visage.

Then Katrina hit, and I really forgot.

As storm victims go, we were the lucky ones. Not only did we not lose our home, but we also had another place to live, a house in the country in central California, far from reality. In the summer of 2006, we made our escape, spending six months in Carmel Valley, where George painted long hours, creating something other than prints for Gulf Coast relief for the first time since the storm. Meanwhile, I hid from the world while assembling an ambitious art book, *George Rodrigue Prints* (Harry N. Abrams, 2008), a catalogue raisonné of more than six hundred Cajun posters and Blue Dog silkscreens.

Like many, we faced post-Katrina feelings that we hadn't suffered enough. It was the perfect time to attack my face. With a doctor's supervision, I began an Obagi program, seven steps both morning and night.

"Whatever you do," she warned, "don't quit."

It was awful—and humbling. I bled, peeled, whimpered-in-pain, and generally endured vanity torture for six months. Make-up and powder were impossible. One morning George jumped in alarm as I woke him for breakfast, claiming he mistook me, my chin and jaw peeling profusely, for Obi-Wan Kenobi.

According to my doctor, I shed seven layers of skin in all. It was expensive, about fifteen hundred dollars plus products, but in my mind I offset that cost against the money I saved on make-up and dinners out. Most important, I invested in a life's lesson, perhaps better than any therapy.

"You look good in the dark," noted George one evening. I applied a bit of lip-gloss and a cool rag to my face before heading to a friend's house for dinner.

Eventually the holidays arrived, we returned to New Orleans, and I took a break. It was then, as my skin healed, that I saw the changes. I switched to a maintenance program, the same one I use today, visiting the doctor twice a year. I never, ever leave our house without sunscreen.

Astonished by my new face, my family and friends asked me about the program.

"Six months of bleeding and peeling?! No way!" was the general response. I can't say that I blame them. My face was my post-Katrina torture—the outward reflection of my inner shame.

Despite a new face, I can't say that running the gauntlet cured anything long-term beneath the surface. I returned quickly to the makeup, highlights, and dinner parties. For a while, however, the treatments were a strange form of purification, a way of facing the guilt.

And George? He's back to taking pictures . . .

. . . and he hasn't Photoshopped me since.

The Anniversary

George and I married beneath a Louisiana live oak, the same Evangeline-style tree he's painted for years, in Rip Van Winkle Gardens on Jefferson Island, Louisiana. It was a stormy day, and yet the sun emerged just long enough, as we exchanged our vows.

"It seems like yesterday," said George's publishing agent, Roz Cole, last night as we celebrated our anniversary over chocolate cake and Perrier-Jouet in New York City.

"It seems like thirty years ago," mumbled George, half-laughing. And yet I knew what he meant, even as we played gin rummy in our hotel room well past midnight, arguing modern art between hands.

We spent the day at the Museum of Modern Art, where I covet the predictable exchanges:

"It makes you sick," said George, to himself more than me, as we wandered MoMA's contemporary galleries.

"To see what the art world's become?" I asked.

"Yeah, it really does. I mean, am I at a trade show in

Salt Lake City or in one of the most magnificent museums in the world? Video, chop box, trash, candy in piles. I'll come back next year, like I do every year, and hope for the better."

I coaxed him from the giant atrium and the small red tuft, and we shuffled through crumpled pieces of red notebook paper (part of an installation) to "Cindy Sherman."

"Who?" came the question I expected.

I caught him watching me, as my eyes and brain expanded around the magnificent show, forty years of photographs of a single subject: herself.

"What a gimmick!" observed the Blue Dog Man.

People glanced disapprovingly, and I pulled him out, planning my return alone and knowing that he admires Sherman, her gimmick, and especially her fortitude, but that the fun exists in grumbling.

We ran through Diego Rivera's murals ("Genius!" exclaimed George, disappointed that I asked), paused, as we always do, at Rodin's *Balzac*, where George leaned slightly backward on his heels, mimicking the giant bronze figure's diagonal stance, and headed for The Modern (Café), where we spent three hours discussing our new purchase: Sherman's catalogue.

"It was graceful and beautifully surreal," texted my childhood friend, Lisa, about our wedding, as George and I begin our third decade of an art-infused relationship.

The chaotic reality show (long before reality shows) that seemed overnight to become my life, may actually have been a real life fairytale, as I rounded an age-old tree, from ten years alone to twenty years together, cherished, occasionally misunderstood, yet more often redefined. In a word, awesome.

Chapter 6

We Emerged Into the Sunlight Dizzy and Disoriented

First inspired by the *Treasures of Tutankhamun* some thirty-five years ago, today I wander through art with George and my museum pal Emer, transported beyond time, and emerging, always, changed.

Rejecting the Metaphor

The history of modern art is also the history of the progressive loss of art's audience. Art has increasingly become the concern of the artist and the bafflement of the public. –Paul Gaugin

I transcribed my travel notes of the past several days from a downtown hotel in Roswell, New Mexico, home of alien encounters, on the night of the winter solstice and the lunar eclipse. To my surprise, there was no parade, no convention of abductees, and no massive influx of UFO enthusiasts. We stayed anyway, enjoying the irony just two hundred miles from our final destination, Santa Fe.

As we have countless times in the past, George and I crossed Texas in our truck, this time lingering for a few days far west in a town called Marfa, named in 1882 for a Russian heroine in Dostoyevsky's classic novel, *The Brothers Karamazov*. The tiny town is also a movie buff's destination, since hosting the stars and set of *Giant* in 1955.

Texas appropriates the biggest and best for itself, whether grocery stores, barbecue, or two-inch thick toast, and so we shouldn't be surprised to find an expansive beacon of modern art, an almost cult-like destination for New York Modernist enthusiasts, in a town of only two thousand residents, a place so remote that the nearest airport (El Paso) is a three-hour drive.

Yet perhaps it makes sense if one considers the dichotomy that was the New York art scene versus the rest of the country during the 1970s and 1980s. In the age of disco, *Dynasty*, and *Dallas* a small group of New York artists focused on the pure form, the simpler the better, including a complete lack of meaning or metaphor. In contradiction to the excess prevalent throughout American culture during this period, Minimalism did not relate to the general public.

In Marfa, examples include two identical copper cones (1986) by Roni Horn, the only items located in a former military supplies storage building at the Chinati Foundation, as well as numerous examples of John Chamberlain's (1927-2011) crushed cars. (I read somewhere that people followed Chamberlain around his hometown of Shelter Island, New York, retrieving his discarded coffee cups, because "no one crumples like Chamberlain.")

Founded in the 1880s as a railroad stop, Marfa did not choose modern art. Rather, modern art chose Marfa. In the 1970s, Donald Judd, a Minimalist artist in New York City, longed for an escape from "careless exhibitions that often ignored the art's requirements."* He desired large-scale spaces, architecture open to his revisions, and the freedom to create without the demands of museums, galleries, and critics. Finally, he wanted permanence, so that his installations, such as one hundred aluminum boxes spaced evenly in a former artillery shed, would remain intact forever.

The Other Side of the Painting

> It takes a great deal of time and thought to install work carefully. This should not always be thrown away. Most art is fragile and some should be placed and never moved again. Somewhere a portion of contemporary art has to exist as an example of what the art and its context were meant to be. Somewhere, just as the platinum iridium meter guarantees the tape measure, a strict measure must exist for the art of this time and place.
> —Donald Judd

He found this venue in 1979, far from New York, in Marfa, first in the form of two airplane hangars that he converted into his residence. He then added three ranches and more than 40,000 acres of land, including a decommissioned military base where he houses his greatest ambition, the Chinati Foundation, a permanent tribute to Judd, his friends John Chamberlain and Dan Flavin, and eight other artists. In addition, Chinati hosts internships, artists-in-residence, numerous workshops and other programs, attracting both contemporary artists and art enthusiasts to the remote Texas high desert.

Flavin utilized eight of the buildings, installing neon installations at the end of long, cold, almost prison-like U-shaped rooms, filled with nothing but loud and unsettling echoes.

(It's interesting to note that neon artist Keith Sonnier, also linked to the Minimalist movement, talks of establishing a similar artistic venue and foundation in his hometown of Mamou, Louisiana.)

We found Marfa's role in the fading American West just as interesting as its late addition of contemporary art. The long-established reality of this small town of mostly working people of modest means who probably never saw a big city, much less New York City and MoMA, is in humorous contrast to the near beatnik invasion that accompanied not only Judd's project, but also the sprinkling

of contemporary galleries popping up around town in tandem. In one such building known as Ballroom Marfa, George noted, "The idea is to have an exhibition space—nothing more, nothing less."

The restaurants fall into line, particularly Cochineal. Catering to the New York artsy crowd, it too embraces Minimalism in both its décor and its signage. As with similar establishments in Manhattan, we walked past the restaurant four times without seeing the entrance. Surveying the concrete dining room, George observed,

"Nobody looks like they have a job. We fit in real good."

Predictably, we enjoyed a fabulous organic meal and, in my case, a pomegranate mimosa. We strained to understand our server's disinterested mumbling, and labored throughout lunch to ignore a loud and well-enunciated father as he quizzed his young son on Post-Modernism and arugula salad. The lunch experience was Conceptualism at its best.

The critics and museums embraced Minimalism from the start, as though the art that affects the least number of people must be the best. They make contemporary art more important by making it inaccessible, both intellectually and, in the case of Marfa, physically.

Indeed, Minimalism is important and unique as a movement, a philosophy, and—certainly for Donald Judd—a legacy. Before the contemporary art invasion, this small Texas town was already on the map, along with hundreds of others, as a beacon of the fading American West. Yet Judd's contribution makes it a place like no other. The historical significance of his Marfa projects may not attract the *Mona Lisa* crowd, but perhaps it's only a matter of time.

* Marianne Stockebrand, *Chinati: The Vision of Donald Judd* (Yale University Press, 2010).

Green Light

"He must be Irish," noted Emer Ferguson about artist Dan Flavin, "because it says here he spent three hours
drawing in the rain."

Emer and I, on the other hand, spent three hours in a
dry New York museum studying the drawings, notes, and
ideas of the "Minimalist monk"* during our biannual visit
to the Morgan Library, Pierpont Morgan's monument to
books, papers, and great works of art.

Familiar with his fluorescent light bulb installations,
I approached the exhibition, "Dan Flavin: Drawing," the
first of its kind, with curiosity. Flavin's fame centers on
rooms transformed by his decisions: the size, color, and
placement of one or more of the most ordinary, industrial,
and—within our homes or workplaces—irritating utilitar-
ian objects.

I expected large plans and proposals. Instead I found

Wendy Rodrigue

tiny renderings, many written on notepaper no larger than three inches. In addition, most of Flavin's drawings include notes, such as "alternate green and yellow five times on west wall," near impossible to study without a magnifying glass. In essence, when it came to drawing, the great Minimalist, when he wasn't transforming former military bunkers in Marfa, Texas, into expansive, curiously lit rooms-without-meaning, rejected Minimalism in favor of "mini."

Flavin scribbled messages with sketches, plans for museum installations, and public spaces such as train stations and office buildings, and scrawled demands, such as this note to Richard Koshalek, then director of the Walker Museum and today director of the Hirshhorn:

"Raise the damn ceiling, Richard, or else you are cramping my style. Love, Flav."

Flavin (1933-1996) admired from the beginning artists such as Barnett Newman and Piet Mondrian. He collected their drawings, also on view, quick sketches on cocktail napkins and cigarette packages.

"Mondrian," wrote Flavin, "knew that his essential discoveries should extend far beyond the limited space of his canvas but he had no way to move out (neither have I yet). . . . I am trying in my way to understand the great research of this man."

Imagine what he could have created had he had a computer, I thought to myself, as I studied the repeating perfect lines and patterns within his plans. Reading further, I learned that many of his larger drawings were not rendered by Flavin at all. Obviously it was not important that he execute them, only that he conceive the idea.

There were exceptions, of course, notably Flavin's pocketsize notebooks and his free-form (sans ruler) sailboats and landscapes, as though recalling Ireland, a clear interest for this lifelong New Yorker, who collected nineteenth-century drawings of the Irish coast.

The Other Side of the Painting

Yet it was the light bulb that seduced Flavin repeatedly, making him famous as a Minimalist, despite that school's taboo: suggestion of meaning. Perhaps this referenced his confounded past, specifically the death of his twin brother in 1962, and an Irish Catholic father who pushed him, without success, towards the priesthood.

For it was the Irish-American artist himself who described his first sculpture, a single fluorescent bulb leaning in a corner, as . . .

". . . the diagonal of personal ecstasy."*

- All quotes from The Morgan Library, except those marked with (*) referencing Robert Rosenblum, "Dan Flavin: Name in Lights," in *On Modern American Art: Selected Essays by Robert Rosenblum* (Harry N. Abrams, 1999).

Modern Art in a Day

Modern Art, a predecessor to Contemporary Art, breaks ranks with traditional representational painting. It includes everything from Monet's reflections to Pollock's drips, and its paintings are among the most popular in today's museums.

Such was the case with the New York Guggenheim Museum's *The Great Upheaval*, a selection of Modern Art from 1910-1918, specifically European artists and their output just prior to and during World War I.

Surprisingly, this early twentieth-century collection includes an almost hopeful view of the oncoming war, as philosophizing artists focus on possibilities of renewal, liberation (particularly for women), and a rejection of elitism. The artists transfer their open-mindedness to their paintings, rendering natural subjects in unnatural colors. They reveal emotions and essences, looking beneath the subject, even inside of it, to expose more than its physical makeup. Franz Marc's famous *Yellow Cow* (1911), for example, spawned endless debate regarding its meaning, most often interpreted as a portrait of the artist's new bride.

Art walks an interesting line, both dated and timeless. Even though bound by a date or an -ism, if effective, it endures as universal and eternal in its mystery. I thought about this while strolling the Guggenheim's snail-shell shape. Frank Lloyd Wright's architectural anomaly, opened in 1959, twirls like a corkscrew into Fifth Avenue, built to house a collection of a family's foundation formed between the world wars.

The early 1900s were an exciting time for the arts, with thriving groups such as Die Brücke and Der Blaue Reiter, and a plethora of -isms, including Cubism, Futurism, Rayism, and Expressionism.

"What happened to the -isms?" I asked my artist-husband.

"The agents killed them with their selections," he said. "Art is now predicated on what the agent can sell, and not on what the artist can do. Early on the agents followed the movements; now they dictate them. Castelli (agent to the art stars) was a pro at this. He picked only one artist of each type and rejected the others. That way he could say he had the best."

Artist Franz Marc (1880-1916) and his contemporaries supported the war effort, hoping it would bring positive change. Marc enlisted for service and soon realized the horrible and seemingly endless reality of battle. Concurrently, the German government realized that it was losing its cultural minds and issued deferments for the country's artists. Marc, however, was mortally wounded at the front only days before his scheduled return.

The Other Side of the Painting

These artists painted about war without painting the war itself. Like poetry, the German Expressionists sought deeper meaning on their canvases. As a result, the wartime paintings resonate with the human condition, whether in times of war or peace.

This is also true of the Austrian Expressionists, on view at the Neue Galerie for the exhibition *Vienna 1900: Style and Identity*, without question the best show I've seen in years. Following our Guggenheim experience, I recognized immediately these transparent paintings of the human psyche and the near-literal loosening of the corset strings. George, however, saw much more. He opened my eyes to line and shape, to the way the artists relate their drawings to the edge of the canvas. Through his eyes I considered the exaggerated long and angular limbs, enormous heads and hands, and large negative spaces.

> Schiele is free to exaggerate, dissecting the page with lines instead of following the body's accurate form. It's the same thing with the paintings, and it's the same thing with Gustav Klimt. He filled in the negative spaces with whatever design was going on at the time. It's real easy to figure out once you see the drawings.
> —George Rodrigue

Finally, we contrasted the Expressionists with the founding king of -isms, Picasso, with a tour of *Picasso and Marie-Therese* at Gagosian Gallery. Painted between the world wars, Picasso's paintings inspired by his young mistress break new and personal ground, revealing again his superiority, independence, and vicissitude as a Modern artist.

Whereas Klimt and Schiele focused on line, Picasso focused on shape and form. Yet in all cases the artists hint at or shout something other than the obvious. Picasso abstracts his forms, revealing hidden meaning not only in what he observes, but also in what he interjects, ultimately abandoning the literal and surface subject.

Picasso rules twentieth-century art because he boldly follows his own direction. Others follow his -isms but not his lead, unable to break this kind of ground repeatedly. And yet, when the great bronze sculptor Rodin (1840-1917) invited Brancusi (1876-1957) to apprentice in his studio upon his move to Paris in 1904, Brancusi declined, noting,

"Nothing grows in the shade of a tall tree."

The Human in the Painting

*She was like a woman of Leonardo da Vinci's, whom we love not
so much for herself as for the things that she will not tell us.*
–Cecil Vyse, *A Room with a View* by E.M. Forster, 1908

Certain paintings, particularly a certain era of paintings, transport us, if we let them, to another age of humankind. I say "humankind" instead of the more colloquial "mankind" because too often we women face oppression on some scale or, more accurately, the fight for women's rights, as though this is the United States 1913 and the question of women's suffrage hangs in the balance. If we still fight for a voice today in the United States of America, how must it have been for the Italian girl in the portrait above, immortalized (by men) like a few elite others, within frowning, idealized wedding impressions sixteen years before da Vinci's smiling subject suggested that just maybe a woman carries a secret or, Heaven forbid, an opinion.

The Metropolitan Museum of Art recently hosted a magnificent exhibition of Renaissance portraits, men and women, prior to 1510. I considered each painting in relation to the *Mona Lisa* (1504)—whether Florentine with endless vistas behind the subject, or Venetian, captured on shiny black backgrounds, more like figures painted on polished obsidian rather than an empty, infinite space—and how this famous painting of a woman, painted by a man and copied by many, altered perceptions, so that mankind became humankind, and humankind became the individual.

"What do you think of the *Mona Lisa*?" I asked George.

"In that vein of 'humankind,' the *Mona Lisa* became the most famous painting in the world portraying an unknown subject. It represents a common person rather than a noble one.

"Da Vinci's contemporaries saw the painting in his studio and were shocked that he painted it not as a commission, not to make someone famous, but rather for the pure joy of capturing a persona on canvas. With the *Mona Lisa*, the artist was no longer exclusively a craftsman interpreting other's ideas."

From "The Renaissance Portrait," I spent hours within the Met's "The Steins Collect," falling in love again with Matisse, and laughing at the all-too-familiar deals wielded by a young Picasso, strapped for money in 1907 Paris.

As a teacher, Matisse reminds me of George who, although he enjoys students' renderings of the Blue Dog, prefers that they use their imagination and spirit to create things in their own way.

"The idea is more important than the execution," I've heard him say many times. It's the reason Salvador Dali, despite no visual connection between their works, remains his favorite artist and the only artist he claims inspires him.

"Matisse," wrote Annette Rosenshine, a friend of the Steins, "was disappointed if the students merely followed in his footsteps. He had struggled desperately for his own artistic freedom and was not interested in creating little Matisses, but wished to help the students find their own individual expression."

The most famous of the Stein collectors, Gertrude Stein (1874-1946), immortalized in paint by Pablo Picasso in 1906 (also at the Met), encouraged creativity across the board. She embraced painting, opera, and writing, and enjoyed great friendships with Picasso and Matisse, artists struggling at the time for public and particularly critical recognition. Even her portrait, which she adored, is a testament to this mindset. When others commented that the young Stein looked little like her painting, Picasso responded, to her amusement, "She will."

From the Met, I encountered "Renoir, Impressionism, and Full-Length Painting" at the Frick Collection. There I reassessed humankind/womankind again. I thought of Lucy Honeychurch in the screen adaptation (1986) of F.M. Forster's *A Room With a View*: "I don't want to be a Leonardo, I want to be myself."

Enchanted by Renoir's women, I noted that they are not portraits, but rather subjects filling his vision of French society, from their stylish clothing to the light reflecting from their shapes. And yet, unlike the harsh criticism of the day, I see nothing offensive in these dancing figures, in a woman who dares to remove her gloves in public. In fact, in thinking about contemporary art, I wonder whatever happened to the notion of a beautiful painting.

I asked George about Renoir, and his answer, in part, surprised me.

"I never particularly liked him, but I understand what he was doing and I admire the concept of Impressionism. I mean, photography was a shock, seeing how the light bounces off of the figure into the film. Before photography, the artist drew a form first, emphasizing the shape in an almost technical way . . . think of Michelangelo's Renaissance drawings. The artist was as aware of the backside of the head as he was of the front. The Impressionists could care less about the backside of the form; they only wanted an impression of what they saw."

From Renoir's impressions at the Frick, we encounter Cindy Sherman's illusions at MoMA, an interesting contrast. Again, George and I disagree—not a squabble, but a way of seeing, linked I believe, directly to notions of "womankind." He says "no," however, insisting that our differences derive from his artistic understanding, which may partly be true. It's the kind of discussion we live for, an exchange of ideas in which he gives my female brain as much credit as his own.

Miniatures

Jean de France, duc de Berry commissioned the *Belles Heures*, an elaborate calendar and religious volume, in 1405. Created by the German Limbourg brothers, Herman, Paul, and Jean, over five years in Paris, the illuminated manuscript is a mere 9 x 6 inches, with many paintings no larger than a postage stamp.

My friend Emer and I spent half a day with this illustrated text in a dark room at the Metropolitan Museum of Art in New York City with our glasses first on (best for reading the extended labels) and then off (best for squinting at the tiny images), finding a little relief after discovering the stockpile of magnifying glasses at the guard station. Three hours later and carrying our heavy copies of *The Art of Illumination* (Yale University Press, 2009), we emerged into the sunlight dizzy and disoriented, and in my case in need of a chiropractor, since each of the four hundred pages hung suspended in display cases nearly a foot below my height.

It was Easter Sunday, and although we couldn't read the Latin and French text, our intense study of the Limbourg's paintings of the Psalms, Jesus' death and resurrection, and the martyrdom of fifty saints surely gained us points upstairs. As we headed to meet George and Emer's friend Jack for fancy egg dishes and mimosas, we agreed that we'd as good as gone to Mass.

The Limbourg brothers painted these pages six hundred years ago, and yet I easily imagine the boys, apprenticed first to a goldsmith as young adolescents and then employed in their late teens by the duc de Berry, engrossed in creating one of the greatest works in the history of western art. To complete one page must have taken weeks, and had they not all three died of plague before reaching their thirtieth birthdays, surely they would have gone blind from their detailed work.

Just a guess, but I am probably the first visitor to think about George while viewing these medieval images. I've written stories about his paintings of giant chickens, along with his interest in creating large-scale works. There is perhaps no more bold a comparison than that between a two-inch square "jewel" from the *Belles Heures* and a six-foot Blue Dog canvas!

And yet for a time George painted dozens of miniatures. We have several of these 2 x 3 inch paintings in our home, all landscapes painted in the early 1970s. Although I easily imagine the Limbourg brothers, I struggle to imagine George straining over something so small, especially when I know that he painted landscapes as large as eight feet across during this same period. I asked him about the tiny canvases. Did he paint them out of curiosity? Were they easier to sell?

His answer surprised me. It had nothing to do with the paintings or their salability. Rather it had everything to do with the frames.

In a way, the limitations of a frame are like the limitations of a book. The Limbourg brothers painted on parchment created from animal skins, a process nearly as time-consuming as painting the pages. Today we're spoiled when it comes to these materials, but in the year 1400, stretching the skins, choosing and shaping just the right bird's feather for a quill, and acquiring, grinding, and blending each color, required intense labor and skill.

In the case of his miniatures, George spent more time finding a molding, cutting its shape, and restoring its finish than he did on the painting itself.

Our framer today uses an electric saw hinged to a vice that cuts the molding at a perfect forty-five-degree angle. George, however, used a vice with a fixed handsaw. The awkward saw took loads of muscle and made a clean cut difficult. He glued the pieces together in another vice, and if they didn't fit at the joints, then he shaved the wood further with a small knife or began again. Establishing a close fit, he filled the remaining cracks with putty and liquid wood. He then sanded the joints and painted the putty, carefully matching the wood's finish to the larger pieces. Recalling this labor, George laughs,

"All of this resulted in the frames not being square at all."

Once he completed his frame, only then, in a process contrary to the normal order of things, did he paint a canvas. In other words, instead of painting a picture and finding or making a frame, George painted *to the frame*.

George admits that part of his motivation was financial. He cut most of his frames from old moldings. But even this, at four dollars a foot, was expensive. Cutting a frame resulted in extra, odd pieces at the corners, usually about eight inches altogether, the sort of pieces normally discarded by a professional framer. He combined these as described above, and as he explained in details with a diagram on the back of our lunch receipt, as I grilled him on the process.

To create the painting, he stretched a tiny canvas to fill the frame, usually 2 x 3 inches, holding it in his left hand while painting with his right. The images were too small to use his mahlstick (a sword that steadied his hand). Therefore, he often taped the canvas to a board and propped it on his easel or table, resting the heel of his hand against the back surface for the detailed work. After selling several of these finished paintings and frames at fifty dollars each, he purchased new molding for a larger painting.

As I mentioned, I have a hard time picturing George, a man who uses large brushes and thick build-ups of paint, working in this way. Today he groans at the thought of anything detailed, and one look at my new book of the Limbourg brothers' manuscript prompts a strong reaction:

"That would kill me."

Indeed even with his larger paintings, I'm reminded of my Met adventure with Emer, glasses on, glasses off, struggling to see the *Belles Heures*. George wears his reading glasses as he paints and then rolls his chair back six feet, removing his glasses from a distance before returning to his easel for changes. It's a constant back and forth, a move he makes subconsciously, not realizing that within every minute he probably rolls his chair and removes his glasses two or three times.

Today, although referring to large canvases, George admits, "Something else truly happens when scale becomes a part of your concept."

The Other Side of the Painting

Most of George's recent detailed work appears in some of his silkscreen designs and even on a necktie, which he created for himself and friends.

It turns out that the Limbourg brothers also created *lagniappe* in the form of fake books, gold medallions, and other special items as gifts for the duke, items supposedly prized among his greatest possessions, but which they refused to be paid for or create in multiples.

When I looked at the Limbourg brothers' manuscript, I thought about their devotion to a project that consumed their lives. Although it resulted in income, it was much more than a job. I imagine that, like George, they felt fortunate to be paid for their passion.

I enjoy connecting six-hundred-year-old religious manuscripts to forty-year-old Rodrigue landscapes, and I propose that just because something is popular or commissioned (or tiny) does not mean that it is less inspired or less personal. Rather, the artist's importance and the quality of their work make them worthy of appreciation and compensation and, fortunately for the Limbourg brothers and George, others agree.

A Passionless Style

We traveled to New York this week, meeting with publishers and celebrating the launch of Deb Shriver's elegant tribute to New Orleans, *Stealing Magnolias*. With only a few hours to explore the city, I again joined my museum pal Emer, this time at the Morgan Library. Far from the abstract art I hoped to see at the Museum of Modern Art (which was closed), we encountered Edgar Degas's drawings, a classical and familiar art history nook for us both.

Everyone knows Degas's ballerinas and horses, and those of us in New Orleans especially know his painting of a cotton exchange, painted during his lengthy visit here in 1873. Coveted for years, we watch it from afar, now hanging at the Museum of Fine Arts, Pau, France.

Expecting the familiar, I was surprised to see in his sketches studies of the old masters, especially Michelangelo, the same drawings that inspired and indeed educated George as an art student. To understand the human figure, both artists copied the old masters, Degas from Casa Buonarroti in Florence and Rodrigue from art books printed from that collection.

In addition, like George, Degas (1834-1917) rarely accepted commissions, preferring his own passionate direction over the dictated instructions of others. This independence led him to experiment with various mediums, including print-making. After our recent studio visit with artist Woody Gwyn in Galisteo, New Mexico, I did not expect our impromptu discussion of monotypes to pay off so quickly. However, as Gwyn explained, it was Degas who embraced this medium with enthusiasm, adding paint to his prints and creating a form of mixed media. In at least one case, he embellished in 1885 with pastel a lithograph he originally printed in 1877.

This reminded me in turn of George's mixed medias. He paints on silkscreens, occasionally revisiting and reworking prints from years back, exchanging his easel and palette for the fun of garage walls and paint-from-the-can.

Furthermore, I couldn't help but draw a connection between Degas's ballerinas and Rodrigue's Blue Dogs and their effects on each artist's career. After years of painting without significant notice, both artists achieved fame when the public embraced their new subjects.

I do not presume to connect the styles of Rodrigue and Degas. However, there are certain similarities regarding their interests and artistic development that crossed my mind as I viewed the Morgan's collection.

Following the Degas drawings, Emer nudged me towards the Roy Lichtenstein exhibition across the hall, specifically his black-and-white drawings from 1961-1968, the same years George attended art school in Lafayette and Los Angeles.

"Come on, Wendy. They're just plain fun," she said in her expressive Irish accent.

My passion for George's paintings, ironically, does not spill over to Pop Art in general. Over the years, I've seen numerous exhibitions and studied the relevant artists. However, I'm far more excited about the ballerinas. Maybe Lichtenstein himself unwittingly described the reason when he said of his own work,

"The passionless style is my passion."

Despite there being five times the number of pieces, Emer and I blew through the Lichtenstein exhibition much faster than the Degas. There's not much to study or to say beyond the overall clever and, certainly at the time of its rendering, innovative concept.

Lichtenstein used stencils and common household window screens to create his dot patterns. I found his "cheating" intriguing, even refreshing, especially since he also copied his images from advertisements and cartoons found in newspapers, images he appreciated for their "startling quality of visual shorthand and their sense of cliché." (Lichtenstein, quoted on the Morgan Library wall.)

Hey, I like cliché too! And this candor, the willingness of Lichtenstein to admit his insensitivity and "sort of mindless drawing," renewed, ironically, my interest . . . and, although not quite the swoon from a Degas ballerina, my passion.

After Tut

Despite the debate in the museum world about the value of block-buster exhibitions, . . . the show became a watershed in the cultural history of New Orleans, with people speaking of "before Tut" and "after Tut." –Prescott N. Dunbar*

Recently, coinciding with the death of *Encyclopedia Britannica*'s print edition, I toured the exhibition *Hard Truths: The Art of Thornton Dial* at the New Orleans Museum of Art and thought about information. I researched the show beforehand on NOMA's new and improved website, impressed with the museum's education efforts, particularly in sharing the exhibition with middle school children.

In my youth, the show was *Treasures of Tutankhamun*, and the research came not from websites and social media, but from small images and dense text in a fat set of alphabetized books stored along the school library wall. There were no links, no games, and no videos. Outside of *Encyclopedia Britannica*, Tut existed only in Egypt until one magical year it visited six U.S. museums, including the New Orleans Museum of Art, its only southern stop. I sat on a bench within *Hard Truths*, a poignant compilation of found objects, assemblage, and statements, and googled "Selket" on my iPhone, triggering a flashback:

Wendy Rodrigue

At 4:00 a.m. on December 26, 1977, my mother, giddy, woke me.

"Hurry up. Wear your new coat. It's cold."

I was ten.

Along with my younger cousin Kelly, we left my uncle's house in Gretna, Louisiana, on a moonless, stormy night. We ate Pop-Tarts in my mother's canary yellow Oldsmobile as we crossed the Mississippi River and a then single structure Greater New Orleans Bridge to a parking lot located somewhere in Mid-City. With hundreds of families we waited one hour in the dark for a bus that carried us past a Nile-blue painted Lelong Avenue and the New Orleans Museum of Art to a distant City Park path, where we joined thousands already in line.

I recall clearly the ten dollars in my mother's purse, an amount that translated to either the double album (with fold-out pictures) of the *Saturday Night Fever* soundtrack, which I did not receive for Christmas, or to admission for two children (50 cents each), one adult ($1), and the full-color exhibition catalogue ($6.95 plus tax), amounts I've confirmed according to the brochure still tucked within the now treasured book on my shelf. (*Treasures of Tutankhamun*, The Metropolitan Museum of Art, 1976)

By lunchtime, it sleeted, and we were six hours in line.

"You girls decide," said my mom, who huddled near a fire-filled steel drum without us, lest we blacken our white rabbit fur coats, Christmas gifts from our grandmother.

"We're staying!" I exclaimed, even as we resisted the Valley of the King hot dogs, knowing their purchase meant foregoing the catalogue.

"The Fairmont Hotel chefs have created a special Pharaonic menu for the Pavilion," states the exhibition brochure, "featuring such specialties as Egyptian dolmathes, Lotus of the Nile Salad, and Sphinx Burgers."

On my mother's budget, considerably less than that

of the rest of her family, NOMA's King Tut Fast Food Pavilion might as well have served lobster and filet mignon. The couple beside us overheard our discussion and, in a gesture I'll remember for the rest of my life, shared their sandwiches. Kelly and I ate quickly while my mother went without. As the dull day darkened further, we reached the holding tent and, at 4:00 p.m., sat for the first time.

According to museum historian Prescott N. Dunbar, NOMA and City Park leaders

> oversaw the installation of a temporary transformer for electricity for the tents and for lighting in the bleachers that were built to seat the crowds awaiting entry to the Museum. [They] supervised the installation of sewage and water lines to the tents as well as the installation of air conditioning and heating for the tent.*

I first learned of the heat, however, in Dunbar's account. On that below-freezing day, I recall huddling, tired and hungry, with my mother and cousin on the icy metal bleachers. It was there, in the tent, that we despaired.

After nearly twelve hours in line, we walked in the early evening through one last burst of sleet into the New Orleans Museum of Art. The heat hit us hard, and my nine-year-old cousin blocked others from the door as she fainted.

"Get up!" I screamed, shaking her, as my mother, shocked, pulled at me. People stared, and a guard radioed for medical assistance.

From a bench, a nurse revived Kelly with juice and smelling salts, suggesting we abandon our plans. My mother watched my face: I was too young, crushed, and self-centered to forego Tut, even for the cousin I loved. We entered *Treasures of Tutankhamun*, the greatest wonder of my short ten years, surpassing even the Three Tenors and the Roman Coliseum in the following thirty-five.

It was the golden goddess Selket, who stood my height

and wore a scorpion on her head, that most captured me. From the catalogue:

> [Selket] is one of four goddesses who stood outside the gilded wooden shrine that housed the chest containing Tutankhamun's mummified internal organs, the goddesses' outstretched arms spreading protection over their charges. Selket's divine role was not limited to funerary duties: also associated with childbirth and nursing, she was chiefly noted for her control of magic.

Concerned for Kelly, we spent less than an hour within NOMA's exhibition, and yet it changed my life, setting me on a course for Art History. My mother and I returned home the next day to Fort Walton Beach, Florida, where I held court with our Tut catalogue each Friday afternoon, the star of my fifth grade class show-and-tell.

With my mother's help, I created a life-size papier mache sculpture of Selket, painting her in gold. I remember my hand shaking as I applied her black eyebrows and eyeliner. That March, on my eleventh birthday, I carried Selket onto the school bus and shared her with my class. Like the exhibition itself, that day stands out as one of the happiest of my childhood, made all the more so by my mother's gift, a birthday surprise, the *Saturday Night Fever* double album.

Today, in a life I never imagined, I sit on the Board of Trustees of the New Orleans Museum of Art. I meet artists, museum directors, and collectors. I'm spoiled with V.I.P. access, world-class lectures, and gala events. I enjoy fine dinners within the very room where I stood as a child staring at King Tutankhamun's solid gold funeral mask. I visit the museum weekly, absorbing not only today's exhibitions and programming, but also the classic paintings and decorative arts that enticed me on every New Orleans visit as a child.

I have not forgotten where my love of art began, nor what it means to part with lunch money in exchange for a museum visit.

I also walk, as I did often with my mother, in the Besthoff Sculpture Garden, a perfect amalgamation of the finest Modern and Contemporary artwork and the finest Louisiana terrain. I recall a cold day thirty-five years ago, before the sculptures, when a long line snaked through those same trees.

Within this garden I reflect not only on a winter's day, but also on the sculpture positioned among the oaks, an eight-foot, three-sided Blue Dog created by George and installed by Mr. and Mrs. Besthoff, a gift for me in memory of my mother, who, along with a Boy King, planted a seed in me, sprouting a lifelong love of the arts.

* Prescott N. Dunbar, *The New Orleans Museum of Art: The First Seventy-Five Years* (Louisiana State University Press, 1990).

Chapter 7

Treat Your Painting Like a Jewel

Fifty years later, George Rodrigue still applies the lessons he learned in art school. He experiments and practices, growing even now within his art.

The Art Contest

George Rodrigue entered two local art contests in his life and failed at both. By "failed," I'm not talking about losses, but more significant, he was disqualified or learned a hard lesson about cheating.

"Nothing in life is fair," my mother used to say, and maybe she was right. But in the end perhaps that's not a bad thing. In George's case his contest experiences taught him life lessons; they helped him understand people and, most important, that no one reaches their star by proxy. Either you work hard and make it on your own, or it doesn't happen.

The first contest George entered was in 1954 at the Sears Roebuck Catalogue Store in New Iberia, Louisiana. For some time, in an effort to widen its reputation beyond automobile tires, Sears hired actor Vincent Price as their cultural ambassador. He traveled across the country with art exhibitions for the store. It was one of these shows, in Baton Rouge, that first exposed George a few years later to paintings by professional artists.

In keeping with this direction, the New Iberia store, too small for an exhibition, held an art contest for local grade school students. They produced a coloring sheet so that each child worked on the same image.

"I knew that no one colored better than me in my class," says George. "I remember going to Sears with my mother to turn in my picture, and I remember staring at that tool set, knowing it would be mine."

At age nine, recently recovered from polio, young George wanted nothing more than to win the child's tool set offered as a prize. His mother, frugal since the Great Depression, was not fond of gifts, and if he didn't win it, he knew he would never have one.

From an early age, if George wanted something beyond necessities such as food and clothing, it was up to him to buy it. By the time he was a teenager he earned money by working in his father's tomb business and by selling his paintings of swamp monsters. He also took the occasional portrait commission, until 1959, when the director of the local funeral home, George Burgess, refused to pay the agreed-upon price of fifty dollars. For George, at age fifteen this was a hard lesson learned, and the Burgess portrait hangs in his studio today, lest he forget.

He didn't win the tool set. Rather, the boy who sat behind him in the third grade and who "couldn't color at all" took it home. His aunt, the manager at the Sears Roebuck Catalogue Store, presented him with the prize.

Ten years later, in his early twenties, George entered his second and final art contest. It was in Morgan City, Louisiana, where he was disqualified from the start because the contest's organizers thought he passed off antique landscape paintings as his own. In other words, they assumed he cheated.

It's ironic, given this track record, that in 2009 George launched, through the George Rodrigue Foundation of the Arts, his own art contest for Louisiana high school students. With sixteen winners and $35,000 in scholarship awards, the first contest was an enormous success, as rewarding for George, I believe, as for the winners. As a result, the now annual contest includes higher scholarships and cash awards, attracting hundreds of entries from across the state.

Remembering the rigged Sears contest, he avoids judging himself, ensuring fairness as much as possible with guest judges and nameless entries. Remembering his own academic struggles, he eschews GPA requirements, test scores, and declared majors, hoping all juniors and seniors in Louisiana, regardless of their grades, will find confidence in their creative abilities and give this competition a try. George visits with the winners at a luncheon in their honor and follows their progress during the year, hosting an art show of their works within our foundation's Education Center. The exhibition travels to several venues throughout the state, including the Louisiana Governor's Mansion in Baton Rouge, the Ogden Museum of Southern Art in New Orleans, and the Masur Museum in Monroe.

"It gives me a lot of joy," says George, "to sponsor in Louisiana a statewide art contest, because it provides excitement and goals for young artists. It's a friendly competition that, should they win, not only helps pay for their college, but also boosts their confidence."

Remembering Lafayette's
Advocates for the Arts

When George speaks of supporters during his early
years, as a determined yet struggling Louisiana artist, he
mentions three names: Rita Davis, A. Hayes Town, and
Frances Love. Between them they spent only a few hundred dollars on his canvases, however their influence in
the community contributed greatly to George's direction,
reputation, and fame.

It was Rita Davis (pronounced "Ree-tah") who introduced George to A. Hays Town. The famous Louisiana architect assessed George's paintings in the late 1960s and
transformed his approach with this advice:

"Treat each painting like a jewel, because if it is precious to you, it will be precious to others."

Young George returned to his easel with this abstract
concept shaping his method, and he never painted the
same way again. Both Davis and Town purchased the resulting Rodrigue landscapes, now dark, seemingly antique,
painted with care and sparkling like jewels. The small Da-

vis landscapes, painted in 1969, later returned to George when her son requested he "lighten them up." George instead exchanged the paintings for a later work and retained the early canvases, his first paintings in this "jewel-like style," now treasures within his personal collection.

It was A. Hays Town who recommended George to the Reilly Gallery in New Orleans, the only gallery other than his own to display his work in Louisiana. The London-based operation specialized in seventeenth, eighteenth, and nineteenth century paintings and broke their own rule in 1969 with a solo show for the twenty-five-year-old Rodrigue, their first exhibition for a living artist.

In 1969 George also met Frances Love, director of the permanent collection of the art museum for the University of Louisiana at Lafayette Foundation (then called the University of Southwestern Louisiana) from 1965 to 1983. In 1968 A. Hays Town designed and built the art museum that would house the university's collection of works, compiled from gifts to the USL Foundation for the Art Center for Southwestern Louisiana.

Modeled after Hermitage Plantation (1812) near Darrow, Louisiana, the impressive building stands today on St. Mary Boulevard in Lafayette, adjacent to the campus, and shares property with the Paul and Lulu Hilliard University Art Museum (est. 2004). Although the new climate-controlled contemporary museum houses the permanent art collection and temporary exhibits today, for years Town's plantation-style "Pink Building," now painted white, serviced the community as the Lafayette Museum.

It was Frances Love who dedicated her efforts to this institution for nearly twenty years and who, after a long line of outside shows, chose twenty-five-year-old George Rodrigue as the first local (and living) artist to exhibit at the museum. The 1969 exhibition was hugely successful, and it was a milestone for George who could have no way of knowing that it was the only time the university's mu-

The Other Side of the Painting

seum would devote their major galleries to his work.

The museum and the university's foundation together own more than twenty original Rodrigue canvases, largely donated due to the persuasive efforts of Mrs. Love and the generosity of local collectors such as Mr. and Mrs. Robert Shelton and Dr. and Mrs. John Straub. However, with the exception of a small exhibition in 2009, not since Mrs. Love's retirement in 1983 has the art of George Rodrigue hung on the museum's walls.

This irony was not lost on Frances Love, who supported George's career throughout her life and encouraged local support of the arts. I asked George for a few words in her honor:

"Mrs. Love brought new talent to the museum and got local people involved in the arts—neither of which had been done before. She put on many shows, not necessarily dedicated to traditional painting and sculpture, but also unique exhibitions that attracted a wide audience.

"She was heavily involved in the Louisiana Gulf Coast Oil Exposition (LAGCOE) and geared museum exhibitions towards attracting its participants. She created a yearly design fair for exhibitions, bringing in artists, interior decorators, and fashion. She also produced periodicals and books about the museum and its collections and was instrumental in getting local participation for industries to support the university's art programs.

"Mrs. Love worked tirelessly for the arts, the university, and the community. She acted not only as the museum's director, but also as the lead public relations person in exposing the arts to Lafayette.

"After my show in 1969, she became one of my closest, best supporters, and there's no doubt that her devotion to my art established my strong early beginnings in and around Lafayette.

"Mrs. Frances Love was a true promoter and supporter of local artists in the Lafayette community for forty-five years."

The Nude Figure

As a student, it was important to George to learn the fundamentals of art. He grew frustrated early on with his college education, a 1960s academic art world rooted in the abstract, as opposed to classical notions of compositional design, chiaroscuro (play of light and dark), and an accurate study of the human figure.

He longed to understand the effectiveness of a da Vinci, specifically those elements of its design, color, and shadow that make his paintings such obvious masterpieces, not just to the sixteenth-century eye, but to every eye since.

At the University of Southwestern Louisiana (now the University of Louisiana at Lafayette), George's education was wholly abstract, and the closest he came to traditional art studies was through his own efforts. It wasn't until he reached a graduate school, the Art Center College of Design in Pasadena, California, that he received a classic art training. Although Art Center was cutting edge and far from a conservative school, the curriculum blended hard-edge and abstract painting with the fundamentals. George relished this formal approach.

It was not easy for him. George has always said that his forté is the idea. He was never the best painter in class, and he struggled in particular with drawing. During a two-semester life drawing class, he entered the Christmas break with his lowest grades, not for lack of trying, but because he could not transfer the three-dimensional nude model to his two-dimensional sketchbook.

George excels, however, in a crisis, and this struggle with life drawing was no exception. He spent that holiday break with an art book of Michelangelo's drawings, and over a three-week period he learned from the best. Rather than return to Louisiana that December, he spent his days copying these Renaissance drawings until he understood the proportions, movement, and shape as rendered by Michelangelo.

At his first class that January, he glanced at the model, noted the pose, and drew a magnificent sketch, à la Michelangelo. George's professor stopped at his drawing table,

"What happened to you? You're like a different artist!"

The professor used George's drawings that semester as the example for the class. He emerged not only with an "A," but more importantly he left school no longer intimidated by working with the human figure. This does not mean that George set out to be Michelangelo. However, a better understanding of the Renaissance master contributed to his confidence in his own ability to experiment and find a style of his own, a "Rodrigue figure."

George painted nudes intermittently throughout the 1970s and 1980s within his Cajun series. Usually these reference Evangeline or Jolie Blonde, and they were rather unpopular with his conservative audience, particularly the local crowd in southwest Louisiana. In several cases collectors returned paintings with the request that George "cover her up," after repeated complaints at home. Twice he gave into this because he needed the money, but when possible he accepted the painting's return.

George remained (and remains) undeterred, however, and pursued his figure studies well into the *Blue Dog* series and the early 1990s, when his battle with chemical hepatitis forced him to abandon turpentine and oil paints in favor of the fast-drying acrylic paint, a medium unconducive to the blending necessary for painting female flesh.

Considering the trouble George experienced with the public regarding his early nudes, it's ironic that among his most popular Blue Dog paintings are his recreations of famous classical figurative works, such as *Right Place, Wrong Time* (1991), based on Ingres's *The Turkish Bath* (1862), and *Wrong Century* (1991), based on Manet's *Olympia* (1863).

With a handful of exceptions, these were the last of George's nudes for many years. He painted a few figures in acrylic paint but in most cases was unhappy with the results. He did experiment once with an original silkscreen of a nude, *Love Among the Ruins* (1994), referencing a Roman statue among the Louisiana oaks.

Frustrated with the fast-drying acrylic paints, George abandoned the nude figure for nearly a decade until discovering a water-based oil paint in 2002. With minimal fumes, the paint is safer, especially when he works from his studio in Carmel, California, where the windows remain open and the paintings dry on the outside deck. Excited by this new medium, he sketched once again as he re-examined his interest in the classical nude and prepared to paint in oil.

Over a three-year period beginning in 2002, George developed a series called *Bodies*. To my astonishment, this included more than a dozen paintings relegated to the closet. For the first time since I'd known him, I watched George pursue his vision of excellence by both rejecting and learning from his own work.

This was different from the overlapping series, a collection of abstract and expressionistic works called *Hurricanes*, painted on round canvases and without mistakes during 2002 and 2003.

These nudes remind me that George is still a student when he approaches his canvas. Each painting is a puzzle to be solved and with *Bodies*, at least in the beginning, there were more failures than successes. Rather than paint over the rejected works, George studied them. This process traces back thirty years to his early landscape paintings, when he realized that underneath each painting existed a dozen rejects. At one point he forced himself to leave a painting as is, even if he was unhappy with it, so that he could study his steps, learning from his mistakes and moving forward in his art.

After more than a year devoted to this project, George completed his first, to his mind, successful *Bodies* painting. Once he found this direction, the others followed over many months. He then scanned the images into his computer and played with their color and design, creating

remastered digital prints. He describes these works on paper, as opposed to the original paintings, as the completed *Bodies* artwork.

In addition, George refers occasionally to *Bodies* as an extension of his ongoing series, *Jolie Blonde*, which began with his loose rendition of an imaginary female figure in 1974.

It's interesting to note that it was *Bodies* that consumed George just prior to Hurricane Katrina in 2005. In fact, we were in Houston for a premiere exhibition of these works when the storm hit the Gulf Coast. Immediately, George abandoned not only *Bodies*, but also painting of any kind, devoting his time and energy to relief prints benefiting humanitarian and arts organizations affected by the storm.

In recent months, as he plans a year or more (2013-14) in his Carmel studio, he mentions returning to *Bodies*, yet in a new direction affected by life-changing events, including his battle with cancer. He enjoys the water-based oils and uses them regularly within his landscapes, so it seems likely that the paints will once again factor into his figurative interests.

However, even as I make these predictions, I am ever mindful of George's favorite expression,

"I refuse to predict what I'm going to paint next."

Oil Paint or Acrylic

After experimenting in art school with several mediums, including designer colors, pastel, water color, and chalk, George settled in 1969 on oil paint to create his dark Louisiana oak trees. Money was tight in those days, and each stroke of his brush equated to less paint in the tube. To make the paints last, he thinned them with turpentine. As a result, forty years later, many of those early landscapes are cracking.

By the time he incorporated Cajun figures into his work, money was better, and George was careful not to overly thin his paints. He used oil for more than twenty years, eventually creating thick canvases layered with texture and blending. These glistening, jewel-like works required months to dry, and their dark tones showed off best following several treatments of spray varnish.

For years George painted in small, enclosed rooms, first in the rear of an advertising agency owned by his

Wendy Rodrigue

friend Kenny Bowen in Lafayette, then in the attic of his Jefferson Street home, and finally in a side shed off of Landry's Restaurant in Henderson. The unventilated spaces and the humid Louisiana air required air conditioning, window units straining and humming throughout the hot summer months.

I think of him painting in this environment, with Roy Orbison or Hank Williams on the radio, his friends Dickie Hebert, Romain Frugé, or Bud Petro stopping by with the latest gossip (in Dickie's case), female conquests (in Romain's), and duck calls (in Bud's). They enticed him out for oyster po' boys and gumbo, and he laughed and relaxed before returning to his studio where he remained most of the night.

As he describes those years, I picture George alone, inside a closed, quiet room, surrounded by, engulfed in, drowning in . . . fumes.

He used heavy oil paints and turpentine, and before turning in, sprayed his canvas, the air, and his lungs with varnish. It coated his insides and poisoned him, and in 1984 he was hospitalized for several months, weak, dizzy, and without the energy to paint, to play with his kids, or even to think.

The doctors ran tests and sent him home, having no idea what caused the problem. He stopped painting for six months and felt better, and still no one, not even him, connected his illness to the toxins present in his everyday life. George returned to his easel and, two years later collapsed again. This time the doctors asked the right question,

"Do you work around chemicals?"

Diagnosed with hepatitis brought on by spray varnish and paint fumes, George skirted death yet faced losing the thing he loved most—painting.

You can imagine this devastating news! Not only was painting his career path and the means of supporting his family, painting is his life, no different than eating or sleeping. It's true that George goes long stretches without painting, sometimes three or four months, but he knows it's there, waiting, and he does the rest, the selling, the schmoozing, the books, and the interviews, so that he can return to his easel. Without that, the rest is for naught. Without that, I think he would sink into a depression; he would cease to function.

According to his doctors, the only option included wearing a gas mask hooked to a tank, a prospect inhibiting for anyone, but impossible for this creative free spirit. Nevertheless, he painted under these difficult conditions for a number of years before it became unbearable.

George never accepts situations like this. And in this case the answer, on the surface, was surprisingly simple. Acrylic paint, a water-based paint, was invented in the 1950s and became available in artist colors in the 1960s. It's a fast-drying paint, completely different from oils, and the change for George would not be an easy one. As I mentioned, oil paints take months to dry, and he could re-work areas and smooth things out and scrape and shift and blend, creating new colors on his canvas.

With acrylics, however, the paint dried within minutes, and by the time he rolled back his chair and lowered his glasses to look from a distance, it was too late to manipulate that area of paint he'd applied shortly before. But there were no fumes, no dizziness, and no danger, and, despite the artistic challenges, he was determined.

Coincidentally, it was about this time that George began in earnest the *Blue Dog* series. Although the early loupgarou paintings include bayou settings, the series grew increasingly abstract. George's learning process is evident in these early 1990s paintings. Many works include simple, flat backgrounds, not as a favorite option, but because he struggled with acrylic paint.

It took several years and one hundred or more paintings before George felt somewhat comfortable with this fast-drying paint. He complained repeatedly, and I panicked when on several occasions, in a fit of frustration after painting a solid, one-color background, he hauled his canvas outside, broke out his old colors, and painted the dog in oil. It wasn't until maybe eight or ten years ago that I first heard him tell an interviewer that he likes and sometimes prefers working in acrylics. By that time he'd been using them nearly ten years.

Because the nature of the Blue Dog paintings lends itself to acrylic paint, George says the Blue Dog "saved his life." The colors are brighter and more intense than oils. On occasion he paints straight from the tube without blending. He produces clean lines without risk of smudging the paint he applied an hour previous. In some ways, his paintings of this period look more like his silkscreens—an odd observation, since one would think it would be the opposite.

By the late 1990s George was comfortable with acrylics. His only regular complaint concerned the human female figure:

"A woman has to be soft. I have to be able to blend without producing thick layers. Otherwise she looks rough, like a man."

As recently as 2004 when he painted Louisiana Governor Kathleen Blanco, he struggled with this. After weeks of work, he abandoned the canvas and began again, painting her face in oil and the rest of the painting in acrylic.

These challenges increased as George considered returning to figurative painting, specifically the classical nude. About this time he learned of a new paint, a water-based oil. There is no turpentine. There are no fumes. It still needs the spray varnish, but George's long-time assistant Douglas Shiell takes on this task, wearing a mask and working outdoors.

Beginning in 2002 George explored the nude figure on canvas in a series of paintings and prints he called *Bodies*. To my surprise, he rejected the first eight or ten paintings, a year's worth of work, and began again. It was a shocking reminder for me that George is still learning. One would think that by this time every stroke is perfect and every painting deserving of public display. But that's not the case at all, at least not in George's eyes.

What also surprised me was his patience. He wasn't frustrated by inferior works but rather lined them up in the studio, studied them, shut them in the closet, and began again. He seemed obsessed, and he enjoyed it like a scientist discovering a new planet.

By 2005, after more than three years of work, he completed five *Bodies* paintings worthy, in his mind, of exhibition. He used these to create a series of remastered digital prints, altering colors and overlaying the Blue Dog.

Today George paints in both acrylic and water-based oil. He chooses the paint according to the painting, sometimes using both on one canvas. In the past several years, in addition to figurative work, he revisited landscape painting in a style similar to his early dark oaks.

Forty years after those first turpentine-thinned, cracking oils, he squirts his paint onto his palette in large

Wendy Rodrigue

dollops. He paints with verve and without restrictions. His studio still bustles with visitors—his sons André and Jacques, his football buddies Tony and Rich, and even Dickie, his oldest friend, who drops by with the latest Cajun jokes. He still paints through the night, and Elvis and Johnny Cash still play on the radio.

All the while, George couldn't know that, despite his switch to acrylic paint, the old fumes continued poisoning his body, emerging in the form of tumors, resulting in another life's change with the shocking diagnosis of advanced lung cancer in the summer of 2012.

Painting to the Frame

Years ago George coined the phrase "painting to the frame," a process linked to his original art from his earliest landscapes to his recent Blue Dog paintings. Although his paintings and frames are often unrelated, at times he encounters a frame that dictates the design, color, and imagery on his canvas.

Following his return to Louisiana from California and art school in the late 1960s, George faced the challenge of earning a living, while determined to paint full time and avoid a "real job." He not only saved money by thinning his paints, but also purchased old frames at junk shops and flea markets throughout the South. Custom-made frames are expensive and for years were beyond his reach. Yet from the beginning he utilized gilded and wooden frames, adding importance, weight, and interest to his landscapes. At age twenty-five, he wanted his paintings to look like they came from the Louvre.

In some cases the frame was so interesting that George spent more time restoring it, stripping paint, oiling the wood, and cleaning the details, then he did on his painting. This is true of two small landscapes from 1969, both in his possession today, the carved cypress frames stripped of their gilding by his own hand, as precious to him as his dark oaks.

Oftentimes he worked for days to restore a frame before beginning his painting. Rarely have I seen George as disappointed as when he purchased his 1969 painting *Bayou Country House* at auction several years ago and discovered that the painting's original buyer, at $150, painted over the stripped cypress using a grey house paint. George hired a conservator to restore the painting who, to my surprise, left the frame alone. It hangs today in our living room, a reminder of struggles with clients and their preferences, and a reminder that art takes on a life of its own beyond the artist's intent, depending on where it hangs and who takes notice.

George's most famous image painted to the frame is his *Aioli Dinner* (1971). He found its 32 x 46 inch frame at Bob's Junk Shop in Lafayette, and it inspired the painting's size and greenish color. Even now, forty-five years later, one side of the frame is considerably darker than the other. When George found it, the frame held a vertical photographed portrait of President William McKinley, and the dirt gathered on one edge for decades before he turned the canvas horizontal for his dinner scene.

Today we have a framer on staff, and George prefers many of his works custom framed with a contemporary and simple molding that, as much as possible, remains invisible. However, that's not always the case, and although he doesn't set out to find the frames anymore, he still comes across them occasionally and creates a painting to the frame.

The Other Side of the Painting

The concept of "painting to the frame" is a reminder of George's inventiveness, as well as his devotion to his own rules of painting, such as hard edges, graphic interpretations of his culture, strong design, and repetitive imagery, all rules he set for himself more than forty years ago.

Landlocked Pirogues
and Blue Dog's Eyes

People are moving in time and in history, in a pirogue, on land.
–George Rodrigue, 1975

John Courregé's Pirogue is one of seventy-eight images featured in the book *The Cajuns of George Rodrigue*, the first book published nationally on Cajun culture (Oxmoor House, 1976). As with all of his paintings within and since, Rodrigue imbues his artwork with symbolism, from his hard-edged, topless oaks to his glowing white figures. His rivers and roads blend as one.

"When the Cajuns arrived in southwest Louisiana," he explains, "the bayous, creeks and other waterways were the only roads. The people used them in the same way the Native Americans did for centuries before. All early settlements were on the bayous—Bayou Teche, Bayou La-fourche, the Vermilion River, and the Mississippi. People needed this transportation for trade.

"I named the painting after my cousin, John Edward Courregé, who, the minute he got his driver's license, drove me to Catholic High every day for four years. Later on, he worked in the junkyard with his father and sisters."

Oddly enough, it was an unrelated photograph that reminded me recently of George's surreal concept of a boat floating on the land. *What is a Photograph?* is a new exhibition at the New Orleans Museum of Art (NOMA). Through a series of images and processes spanning more than 150 years, curator Russell Lord shows us why "photography, it seems, is not one medium, but many."

Amidst this wondrous variety, a small dark image caught my attention, a portrait of a family in a studio's prop boat, a hand-colored tintype from 1885. Lord writes, "In this humorous example, a family poses for their portrait indoors with studio props and a contrived backdrop intended to make them appear to be enjoying a leisurely outing in a boat."

It turns out that George modeled his painting after a similar family photograph (circa 1910, unfortunately lost). The figures, probably members of the Courregé family, sat in a pirogue on the bank of the river and posed for a picture.

What's more, the 1885 NOMA photograph includes subtle hand-coloring, pale reddened cheeks suggesting the healthy effect of the outdoor air. This charming application sent me on another tangent, as I recalled George hand-coloring the Blue Dog's eyes in his earliest silkscreens. As with photography, his method hinged on technological limitations.

In the early 1990s, silkscreen ink and colors dictated, to George's frustration, both quality and variety. Therefore, he preferred paint, pulling his prints by hand and applying each color individually. The expensive materials and time-consuming process, further complicated by the frequent scratches, dings, and splattered paint, necessitated improvisation. Rather than pull the prints again, he used a simple paint pen, adding yellow pigment to the dog's eyes, thereby reducing both expense and damage.

Traditionally, artists conceive new methods of fulfilling their creative goals and conveying their message. Whether the symbolism of a land-locked floating boat, the illusion of a contrived studio portrait, or the practical application of hand-applied paint to a printed image, this improvisation spurs both artist and art-lover forward.

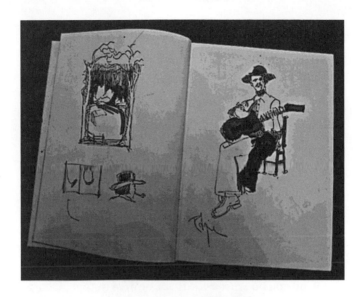

The Sketchbook

It was in 1960 that Coach Raymond Blanco, later Vice President for Student Affairs at the University of Louisiana at Lafayette, famously threw George out of class for drawing. He sat in detention in the hallway of Catholic High in New Iberia, Louisiana, and, rather than repeat the assigned lines, continued sketching, already with the knowledge that he was far more artistically than academically inclined.

Today he piles his old sketchbooks to the ceiling, all shapes and sizes stored in his warehouse, studios, and even his closet, a new one always on his desk. Some are leather-bound and small for his pocket, while others are thirty-six-inches, made of tracing paper, and protected in portfolio cases. Within the pages he designs cars, houses, billboards, and statuary; writes books, movies, and poetry; and draws everything from plans for paintings to mindless doodles.

Without a sketchbook, George grabs any surface

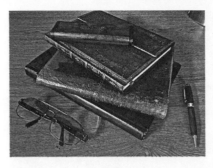

available, obsessed with graphically expressing his ideas. At the time, he speaks of these concepts as though they are the most important projects of his life, whether he's on an airplane, at a restaurant, or in the shower. Once I awoke in the night and found him on the floor of our bedroom with a flashlight, the underside of a roll of wrapping paper spread out before him.

"What are you doing?" I asked. "It's the middle of the night!"

"Designing a car," he replied. "Come see."

While on book tour for *Blue Dog Man* in 1999, George improvised on a long flight when he found himself without his sketchbook. As I recall, he was inspired by Lewis Grizzard (1946-1994), author of such books as *They Tore Out My Heart and Stomped that Sucker Flat* (1982) and *Elvis is Dead and I Don't Feel So Good Myself* (1984).

As we flew home from a Hawaiian vacation, I recounted our trip in letters to friends and family while George drew on the back of the stationary box. Instead of the beach, he drew *his* landscape, the bayous, and oak trees of south Louisiana, with a pirogue waiting. Beneath his sketched world he wrote,

"Wendy—A perty picture for a perty girl." Signed "George Rodrigue 1995 —Day

after a long vacation in the Pacific."

Without a sketchbook, George absconds random surfaces, even if it means the drawings might be damaged, stolen, or discarded. I was as happy as if Robert Browning himself had composed a love poem in my honor when, while installing a Rodrigue exhibition in Frankfurt, Germany, I received a package covered in doodles.

Saved today in my keepsake box, the back of the cardboard reads in my hand,

"12/11/95, On a FedEx box full of Christmas goodies-from Janique Boutique, the shop attached to The Time is Always Now gallery. George was in NY for his show and sent them as a surprise. That's a "Blue Ball" Christmas tree!"

Tablecloths and napkins are George's favorite sketchbook substitutes. It was on a cocktail napkin that he designed the large-scale painted metal Blue Dog sculptures, such as the one in the Besthoff Sculpture Garden at the New Orleans Museum of Art and on Veterans Memorial Boulevard in Metairie, Louisiana. His preliminary design included an oak tree, similar to his bronzes of the mid-1970s, and, because it was never built, exists only within his head and on the stained, crumpled napkin.

In our home, I frame George's restaurant drawings, complete with tomato sauce and coffee stains, and intersperse them with my mother's paintings and hand-made cards, all priceless memories hanging in my office. Recently, it was in my notebook during a visit to Marfa, Texas, that George sketched a diagram of his early and now-lost attempt at Minimalism. And just a few weeks ago he experimented with paint-by-number, using his computer as a sketchbook, as we researched together the 1950s phenomenon.

Yet the impromptu sketches remain my favorites. Once he found inspiration as I left the house for an Aerosmith concert, using a sharpie to cover my back with a bayou scene and Blue Dog. And twice he doodled on French bread at the classic New Orleans restaurant, Galatoire's. He drew the first in 2001 as a gift for David Gooch, the restaurant's long-time manager. He drew the second after a food fight in 2005 resulted in irreparable damage to the original baguette. Mr. Gooch stored the bread on a pillow and carefully shellacked the unusual artwork for years, now on permanent display in the Southern Food and Beverage Museum.

Blue Dogs, Ghost Ranch, and Mrs. Wertheimer

"She created her own world, and I created mine," explained George to a packed audience at the Alexandria Museum of Art, as he nodded from a New Mexico landscape to a wet Blue Dog canvas. I made a mental note to remember the line, the nicest thing he's ever said about artist Georgia O'Keeffe.

"I've been to Ghost Ranch," he continued, "and this painting has no relationship to the actual mountains. But that's okay. That's the prerogative of the artist, to interpret what he or she sees and make it their own."

Normally we present these events within an auditorium. However, this unusual painting demonstration occurred within the museum's largest exhibition space, surrounded by *Copley to Warhol*, a collection of thirty American masterpieces from the New Orleans Museum of Art (NOMA), on tour throughout Louisiana during 2011 as the museum celebrated its centennial.

In a bit of irony, NOMA also toured its significant Rodrigue collection that year, visiting Monroe's Masur Museum, the LSU Museum of Art in Baton Rouge, and

Wendy Rodrigue

Shreveport's Louisiana State Exhibit Museum. Due to logistical problems, however, Alexandria missed the Rodrigue show.

The Anne and Wendell Gauthier family of New Orleans came to the rescue, loaning Alexandria the *Saga of the Acadians*, a series of fifteen paintings created by Rodrigue between 1985 and 1989. Without an auditorium, the museum's lecture plans, we assumed, included the small gallery housing these works. Anticipating a large crowd, the Alexandria Museum of Art had other ideas, however, which is how George ended up nodding to Georgia O'Keeffe, and I ended up speaking in the presence of Sargent's *Mrs. Asher B. Wertheimer* (1898), as the painted London socialite stared from across the room.

It was recently that I dove into the scandalous story of John Singer Sargent and *Madame X* for the essay "American Artists in Paris." Now the elegant Mrs. Wertheimer watched me as though she were the face of art history and patronage, evaluating my delivery and checking my facts.

George painted as I shared his story with the audience. He worked quickly, with large brushes and paint straight from the tube, completing a painting in less than one hour for entertainment's sake, only to repaint it later over several days in his studio. As he turned a blank canvas into something else, I spoke, reacting to the great works in the room.

"As a young man returned from art school," I explained, "George decided almost immediately to paint Louisiana. He visited the New Orleans Museum of Art and studied the great masters, especially the Hudson River School. He reacted to the works of Richard Clague, Joseph Meeker, and Ellsworth Woodward."

I gestured to the dreamland of visual aides hanging on the walls. The heads turned from George's canvas, straining instead to see this European style, both the birds-eye view of the classically trained artists and the painted reflections of the Impressionists.

For George, I continued, this is not Louisiana. He found his own direction, pushing the oak tree to the front of his canvas, cutting it off at the top so that the light shines from beneath its moss and branches, and defining his distinct shape with hard edges. From the beginning, he graphically interpreted Louisiana with hopes of preserving the fading Cajun culture.

"The difference between everyday art and great art," explained George, turning to the audience, "is that everyday art might look good when you first see it, but after two or three days you lose interest.

"These paintings," he continued, as he gestured to the walls, "continue to ask questions; they retain mystery; and they retain a distinct quality so strong that each artist holds his own among the others, even in a room of paintings spanning two hundred years."

A man raised his hand.

"Your painting looks alive to me," he said. "I watched you paint, and yet I can't explain in my mind why your approach differs from illustration. I see it, but I don't understand it. How did you paint something that looks so alive?"

George referenced the walls again, unable to resist the energy in the room, as though America's greatest artists depended on his answer.

"It's in the artist's mind, in his approach," he explained, as he looked towards Warhol, Rivers, and Inness. "All of the paintings here look alive. In great art the viewer has a constant communication with the painting, no matter what the painting's age.

"An illustrator's role in creating art is to hold the viewer's attention for two or three minutes. He doesn't intend his art to have a lasting effect with permanent communication."

Following the painting demonstration, George visited

with the crowd. Some remembered him selling his paintings on the road from the trunk of his car during the 1970s and 80s. Others shared their children's versions of Blue Dog. One couple presented him with a letter describing their feelings for *Tee Coon Gone Fishing*:

"*Tee Coon* looks wonderful in our dining room, and he reminds us daily how happy we are to be 'home' in Louisiana. Your painting is one of our most treasured possessions."

Another pointed out a Rodrigue steamboat painting, circa 1972, donated by their family to the Alexandria Museum of Art.

George ended the evening with a favorite piece of advice recalled from art school:

"Art is like a yardstick (held horizontally) with the *Mona Lisa* at one end and black paint on a black canvas at the other. Most artists move back and forth along the stick, getting nowhere. It's important, however, to find your place on that stick and go up."

He looked again at the masterpieces hanging in the room, pausing with begrudging respect at the O'Keeffe.

"Once you're up here," he continued, pointing to an imaginary spot in the air some two feet above the imaginary stick, "you're by yourself."

"Once you're up *here*," he emphasized, "no one can touch you."

Chapter 8

"A Maiden Who Waited and Wandered"

-Longfellow's "Evangeline: A Tale of Acadie," 1847

After returning to Louisiana from California and Art School, George Rodrigue committed to preserving what he feared lost. For twenty-five years, through his art, he graphically interpreted the Cajun culture.

Early Oak Trees and a Regrettable Self-Portrait

It was on the long drives back to Louisiana from the Art Center College of Design in California that George Rodrigue developed his style. He considered for sometime how south Louisiana differs from other places, as well as the eighteen hundred miles of cities and countryside and Americans he passed along the way. From Los Angeles he drove Route 66, a two-lane highway that hugs the terrain, making every hill and gulley and stretch of flat land a part of the experience. And at Amarillo he turned onto smaller roads, traversing seven hundred miles across Texas before crossing the Sabine River and entering Louisiana.

Today, with our straight, cut-through-the-mountains highways, along with our big engines and high speed limits, it's a three-day drive with time for several good nights' rest in between. In the mid-1960s, however, it was a three-day drive non-stop.

Traveling alone, George had plenty of time to think . . . and to look. Its beautiful hill country aside, Texas is defined by its large stretches of uninterrupted land and even more by its big sky. After many hours crossing that land and observing that sky, George was struck by the change as he entered Louisiana. Almost immediately, it seemed to him, the sky was small. The land is flat, even sinking in spots, and there are no hills or mountains. Rather, massive oaks block the sky. The road is hidden between the trees, and the sky is visible in the distance underneath the dark branches.

The more George thought about this, the more he realized how unique this vantage point is to his state. He began researching Louisiana paintings, particularly landscapes and other outdoor scenes, with trips to the Louisiana State Museum at the Cabildo, as well as the New Orleans Museum of Art. What he found was that artists painted Louisiana in a European tradition. Most paintings are two-thirds sky, with small trees, streams, cabins, and cows at the bottom. Nearly every canvas shows Louisiana from a bird's eye view. The few, such as Drysdale and Heldner, who obviously stood on the ground when they conceived their compositions, captured Louisiana with an Impressionist-type idealism.

However, fresh from art school, George's mind swirled with Pop Art, hard edges, and strong design. He was never a plein air painter. Although he photographed thousands of scenes of the Louisiana countryside, it was the tree and its relationship to its surroundings that captured him. Rarely did he identify with a particular place.

Eventually photography became an indispensible part of his Cajun paintings. With the tree, however, the camera was an abstract tool that emphasized the importance of this symbol and shape. People often ask George the locale of particular landscapes and are surprised to learn that, with few exceptions, his trees are imaginary.

The Other Side of the Painting

His first landscapes include other elements, such as small figures and cabins. However, he quickly dropped those in favor of the tree alone. He broke his canvas into three elements—tree, ground, and sky—and he found endless combinations. For three years, from 1968 to late 1971 (when he completed the *Aioli Dinner*, his first painting with people), George painted hundreds of these landscapes. His well-defined style set the groundwork for the Cajun paintings to come, as well as a later strong image, the Blue Dog.

He pushed the oak tree to the front of his canvas and cut it off at the top so that the light shines from beneath, forming an interesting shape between the bottom branches and the ground. The paintings are problems within a canvas world, and solving those problems consumed him. For George, although the oak tree in his works symbolizes Louisiana, he doesn't see a tree. Rather, he sees shapes.

This direction was very exciting for George. He was a young man in his early twenties, and he discovered a unique path within a traditional painting genre. In the beginning, he hoped to find his own direction just once. But when he dropped his inhibitions and stopped caring about the opinions of critics, neighbors, and friends, he created only new things, uninfluenced not only by the public, but also by the art world—by styles and labels, by what's happening in New York or Art Basel, by what's happening anywhere other than inside his own head.

With one exception . . .

George was unprepared for the negative hometown reaction to his landscapes. Most locals entered his gallery on Duclos Street, and later Pinhook Road and Jefferson Street, in Lafayette, Louisiana, with skepticism. *Why are your paintings so dark? Everything looks the same. Can't you paint anything else?*

And in response to his prices (at that time, one hundred dollars on average) . . . *You'll never get that kind of money for those paintings.*

Worse, after a cousin who worked at the Old State Capitol in Baton Rouge managed to secure him a show, the exhibition of seventy Rodrigue landscapes prompted George's first newspaper review, a full page in the *Sunday Advocate*, with the headline, "Painter Makes Bayou Country Dreary, Monotonous Place."

To combat the criticism, young George painted his self-portrait. He never offered it for sale. Rather, he propped it in the corner of his gallery and motioned to it anytime he thought it might boost his credibility. Sure

enough, as recently as the New Orleans Museum of Art's Rodrigue exhibition in 2008, where it hung in a room filled with landscapes from the same period, he overheard people,

"Man, he really can paint."

I heard them too, and I felt George's frustration and imagined what it must have been like to have broken the mold in landscape painting and to be redeemed by something he saw as ordinary. He resented it, and he's always disliked this early self-portrait (1971), so different from the hundreds of portraits he painted over the years, and yet still prized by many as his best.

The Other Side of the Painting

George's success provides him with the freedom to paint when and what he wants most of the time. There are periods, however, when he feels chained to his easel. The mid to late 1980s come to mind, when he spent countless hours painting family portraits. But the money was good, and there are times when paying the bills overrides, well, almost everything.

Even today, in the slow summer months or during a struggling economy (or following a major real estate purchase, such as the new New Orleans gallery), I see him compromise that freedom, and I hear him grumble as he returns to his studio to finish a donation for a friend's foundation, a cover for a book of fiction, and a ballet dancer (the three projects currently on his easel). These are the times that the end result—whether promoting a worthwhile cause, pleasing a friend or, frankly, because the money will pay for an old building's new air conditioning system—means more than the art. These are the times that painting becomes work.

He still puts his all into it and, unlike that early self-portrait, these current projects produce rewarding results beyond the art, making them worthwhile. He gets through them to resume painting for himself, just like one makes it through a difficult work week, knowing that Friday afternoon waits at the end.

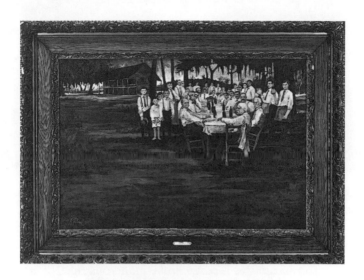

The *Aioli Dinner* and a Cajun Artist

The first time I saw the original *Aioli Dinner*, I was struck by its monochromaticity. It is a green painting through and through. Unnoticeable in a photograph or print, the painting exudes the swamp, and one senses the mugginess, smells the sweat, and feels the mosquitoes biting.

Probably his most famous Cajun painting, the *Aioli Dinner* (1971, 32 x 46 inches) is George's first painting with people. It is based on the Creole Gourmet Societies, in their heyday between 1890 and 1920 when they met each month on the lawn of a different plantation home in and around New Iberia, Louisiana. The six-hour meals included a lavish spread, cooked by the women standing along the back, served by the young men standing around the table, and enjoyed by the seated gentlemen, each with their own bottle of wine. The very French meal was not the Cajun cuisine one expects. In fact, the men denied "Cajun." They were French, and their cuisine was Creole.

(In nineteenth-century Louisiana the term "Creole," as applied to a person, refers to someone of usually French or Spanish parents who was born in the Louisiana Territory before the Louisiana Purchase of 1803. The term Creole, as applied to the food, refers to the cuisine of the French high society living in Louisiana. The term "aioli" refers to a garlic-butter sauce.)

After three years of painting landscapes, George began to wonder, *What does a person look like who walks out from behind one of my trees?* They are primitive, he decided, like the land. They are timeless residents. *Is it 1800 or 1900?* Perhaps they are ghosts, floating and caught—by the trees, by the land, and by their heritage.

To capture this George broke numerous rules of art, especially in his use of light. With his landscapes the light shines in the distance, underneath the trees. This continues in his Cajun paintings, but he begins to view this light with a broader symbolic connotation. He interprets it as the hope of a displaced people, the hope for their future in the swamps and prairies of south Louisiana.

After the 1755 Grand Dérangement, the Cajuns thought they would be welcome in New Orleans. Yet New Orleans society was not a home to these farmers. Instead, they traveled west on the Bayou Teche and made Acadiana their home, supporting the big city of New Orleans with cattle and crops.

George's mother never claimed to be Cajun. She was French. This is true of the members of the Creole Gourmet Societies as well. As late as the 1970s, the word "Cajun" was considered derogatory by some. A Cajun was poor and ignorant. A Cajun worked hard and lived off of the land. When George announced to his mother after completing the *Aioli Dinner* that he is a "Cajun Artist," she begged him to reconsider.

The Other Side of the Painting

Most of the country, in fact, was unaware of Cajun culture in 1971. In 1976 George was introduced at his own gallery exhibition in Boston as a "Ky-yoon" artist. He credits Chef Paul Prudhomme and his blackened redfish, along with the McIlhenny Family and their Tabasco sauce with getting the word out.

George, from the beginning, was proud of his Cajun heritage. His years of art school in California increased that nostalgia. He saw his heritage fading, unable to resist a modern world, and he strove to capture it with a contemporary and radical approach to art. In his words, he would "graphically interpret the Cajun culture on canvas."

The people who walk out from behind a tree in a Rodrigue painting are not hidden in the shadows of heavy branches and drooping moss, as one might expect. Rather they shine with an unnatural light, framed by the trees and bushes, their heads rarely touching the sky. They are cut out and pasted onto their landscape, removed from Nova Scotia and inserted into south Louisiana. Most important, in every Rodrigue painting the Cajun people glow with their culture.

In the six months it took him to paint the *Aioli Dinner*, George developed many of these ideas and honed his abilities as a portrait painter. His grandfather's face alone took him three days. After finishing this painting, he moved forward as a different artist.

Ironically, after three years and hundreds of landscape paintings, George was awkward in painting the *Aioli Dinner*'s foreground. He was, however, confident in the design, dividing the canvas into a strong diagonal. I was surprised when I saw the original painting at how the ground treatment almost seems like an afterthought, as though George said, "Whew, I finally got through all of these portraits; now I can just knock out this grass." The truth is that he had not yet found his comfort zone when it came to painting large areas of ground.

Wendy Rodrigue

He chose the Darby House as the setting for his paint-ing, because in his research of these Gourmet Clubs, it was the only one referenced and still standing in 1971. The house was in bad shape and has since burned down, but it was a grand estate in its day. In addition to George's grand-father, Jean Courregé, seated front left and looking at us, Octave Darby, the house's owner, makes an appearance, as does George's uncle, Emile Courregé, along with several members of the Chastant family, in-laws to George's son Jacques Rodrigue.

In reality, never at one time were all of these men at one meal together. George placed them that way using a combination of photographs from various dinners. I guess it could be described as a dinner of ghosts. The only time they gathered was in George's painted illusion.

After completing the *Aioli Dinner* in late 1971 George asked a big price, $5,000, far higher than the several hun-dred dollars he charged for landscapes. The painting took him six months of work, and he recognized immediately its importance. It hung on the wall for sale in his gallery

in Lafayette for fifteen years. As he raised other prices, he raised this one accordingly. It was always the most expensive painting in his gallery. When the Zigler Museum in Jennings, Louisiana, asked to borrow a Rodrigue for display, George pulled the *Aioli Dinner* from the market and sent it to this historic house in a small Cajun town, where it hung for more than ten years.

By the early 1990s the Blue Dog paintings broadened George's appeal, and museums made regular requests. Still not sure how to handle his Cajun masterpiece long term, he loaned the *Aioli Dinner* numerous times. Finally, in 2000, he gave the work to his sons, André and Jacques, and they placed it on alternating loan with the American Landscape paintings at the New Orleans Museum of Art and the regional paintings at the Ogden Museum of Southern Art.

The *Aioli Dinner* continues to inspire George over the years. He painted several versions of these dinner scenes during the 1970s and 1980s, and in 2001 he reinterpreted the scene with the Blue Dog in a painting, *Family Business*, for the Xerox Collection.

George made several print versions of the *Aioli Dinner*, but this caused problems from the beginning. The painting's overall green tone led to large black areas in early lithographs, and much of the subtleties were lost. Finally, in 1992 he tried a new approach, creating a 30 x 40 inch direct image transfer of the painting (essentially a photograph glued to masonite board). He then repainted the work on top in lighter and more contrasting tones, removing much of the green and approaching the foreground with the confidence and skill developed over the previous twenty years. He photographed the re-worked piece and eventually, in 2003, used the new transparency to make a fine art silkscreen. The resulting print is far superior in color and clarity to earlier versions.

Thanks to the 1992 re-painting, George found himself with an extra *Aioli Dinner*. He couldn't resist including the

Blue Dog in the foreground, calling this new original *Eat, Drink, and Forget the Blues*, a piece he made for his own collection, never translating it into print form.

The *Aioli Dinner* continues to inspire not only George, but others as well. In depicting one tradition, it encapsulates a unique and some would say dying culture, one that remained intact and isolated longer than most within America. In 1971 George set out to record his culture, to "graphically interpret southwest Louisiana and the Cajuns," and for the next twenty years he stayed the course. Yet I argue that, even if he had changed direction after completing only this painting, he still would have met that ambitious goal.

Evangeline

There are enough Rodrigue Evangelines to fill a museum exhibition. George has painted the Acadian heroine one hundred or more times over nearly forty years. Like Jolie Blonde, the Oak Tree, and Blue Dog, she is a staple in his work, a protagonist as much for him as she is in the story of Acadiana.

Famously portrayed in Henry Wadsworth Longfellow's epic poem, "Evangeline: A Tale of Acadie," from 1847, this mythical heroine followed the path of the ancestors of many Cajuns, including George. She lived as a young woman in the town of Grand Pré in Nova Scotia where, according to Longfellow,

> Fair was she to behold, that maiden of seventeen summers.
> Black were her eyes as the berry that grows on the

thorn by the way-side.
Black, yet how softly they gleamed beneath the brown
shade of her tresses!

Her lover, her fiancée Gabriel, "a mighty man in the
village and honored by all men," was the son of Basil the
blacksmith. Among her many suitors, it was only Gabriel
who won her heart.

But their star-crossed fate emerged when the British
invaded Nova Scotia in 1755 and when, along with their
friends and families, they learned,

> that all your lands, and dwellings, and cattle of all
>   kinds
> Forfeited be to the crown; and that you yourselves
>   from this province
> Be transported to other lands. God grant you may
>   dwell there
> Ever as faithful subjects, a happy and peaceable
>   people!
> Prisoners now I declare you; for such is his Majesty's
>   pleasure!

In the persecution that followed, Evangeline and Gabriel were separated, and she spent the rest of her long life
searching for him, mostly through the swamps and prairies of southwest Louisiana, a path she took having heard
he had done the same:

> a maiden who waited and wandered,
> Lowly and meek in spirit, and patiently suffering all
>   things.
> Fair was she and young; but, alas! before her extended,
> Dreary and vast and silent, the desert of life, with its
>   pathway
> Marked by the graves of those who had sorrowed and
>   suffered before her,
> Passions long extinguished, and hopes long dead and
>   abandoned. . . .

The Other Side of the Painting

Reunited in old age, Evangeline, now a nun, tended to Gabriel in the last few minutes of his life, when she happened upon him by chance as she cared for the sick in Pennsylvania.

It's a heartbreaking, romantic story, the vision of Evangeline wandering for years along the banks of the Bayou Teche and beneath the splendid Louisiana oaks. The legend inspires many artists, and its mystique is so great that the towns of New Iberia and St. Martinville disputed the location of the Evangeline Oak, purportedly the place she wept and "stood like one entranced." George's mother remembers the public controversy in the 1920s when both cities claimed this landmark tree. Although St. Martinville eventually won out, for many residents any grand and ancient oak in southwest Louisiana deserves the title.

> As, through the garden gate, beneath the brown shade
> of the oak-trees,
> Passed she along the path to the edge of the measure-
> less prairie.

From the beginning, Evangeline was a natural painting subject for George. He also incorporated her into his first major public sculpture, *Legacy* (1983), a twelve-foot bronze statue of Longfellow, Evangeline, and Gabriel, located in Kaliste Saloom Office Park in Lafayette.

He used several models for Evangeline over the years, including a waitress he barely knew, a silent movie actress (Dolores del Rio) he never knew, and most often the daughter of his good friends Bertha and Curtis Bernard.

He photographed Diane Bernard Keogh hundreds of times during several sessions in the 1970s and used her photographs for Evangeline paintings over the next twenty years. In an ironic twist that Evangeline herself would appreciate, Diane came to work for George in 1996 and remains an important part of Rodrigue Studio today.

Wendy Rodrigue

Stood she, and listened and looked, until, overcome by
   emotion,
"Gabriel!" cried she aloud with tremulous voice; but
   no answer
Came from the graves of the dead, nor the gloomier
   grave of the living.

Once established on his canvas, George never aban-
dons a subject. He adds to and manipulates those symbols
and shapes that he makes his own. As with the Louisiana
oak tree, Evangeline remains important on his canvas well
into the *Blue Dog* series. In the early 1990s when he painted at a side building at Landry's Restaurant in Henderson,
Louisiana, he photographed one of the restaurant's em-
ployees and adopted her image as a modern-day Evangeline, painting her numerous times with the Blue Dog. At
the same time, he continued to use photographs of Diane
Bernard and other models in contemporary designs of
Louisiana oaks, the Blue Dog, and Evangeline.

Admittedly, it's been several years since George last
painted Evangeline. However, I would be surprised if she
never appeared again on his canvas: "Something there was
in her life incomplete, imperfect, unfinished."

The Other Side of the Painting

Jolie Blonde, however, appears regularly in Rodrigue paintings today, as she has since he first painted her in 1974. (I'm afraid I unwittingly swayed the artist in this case.)

But in this essay we pay tribute to Evangeline who swooned,

> O Gabriel! O my beloved! Art thou so near unto me,
>   and yet I cannot behold thee?
> Art thou so near unto me, and yet thy voice does not
>   reach me?
> Ah! how often thy feet have trod this path to the
>   prairie!
> Ah! how often thine eyes have looked on the wood
>   lands around me!
> Ah! how often beneath this oak, returning from labor,
> Thou hast lain down to rest, and to dream of me in
>   thy slumbers.
> When shall these eyes behold, these arms be folded
>   about thee?

. . . perhaps a heroine not just for Louisiana, but for all who search for love.

* All quotes from Henry Wadsworth Longfellow, "Evangeline: a Tale of Acadie," 1847.

Jolie Blonde

According to local legend, in the 1920s a Cajun imprisoned in Port Arthur, Texas, pined for his lost love, his beautiful "Jolie Blonde," and wrote a waltz from those feelings of longing. Over the years the song became for many the Cajun anthem based on a sort of modern-day Evangeline, and Cajun men throughout Louisiana sang in French some version of . . .

> Pretty blonde, look at what you've done
> You left me to go
> To go with another than me
> What hope and what future can I have?

On the internet there are more credible versions of the history of this song, notably its copyright origins with Cleoma Breaux (1906-1941), famous as an early performer

Wendy Rodrigue

with her husband Joe Falcon. Cleoma was from a town of fifteen thousand people near Lafayette called Crowley, Louisiana, Rice Capitol of the World, a place renowned not only for its charm, but also for growing Louisiana characters like brothers Marion Edwards and Governor Edwin Edwards, Senator John Breaux, and Judge Edmond Reggie (father-in-law to Senator Ted Kennedy). This small town with its motto, "Where Life is Rice and Easy," as well as its annual rice festival and its newly renovated opera house, is an ongoing source of Louisiana's colorful history, including the most famous of Cajun songs.

Ironically George, although unfamiliar with her connection to "Jolie Blonde," painted Cleoma Breaux and Joe Falcon in 1977. He recalled her as famous for accompanying her husband on a modern cowboy guitar, an unusual instrument for an early Cajun band. The Breauxs played for years at Oneziphore Guidry's dance hall in Rayne, Louisiana, Frog Capitol of the World, and Joe Falcon (1900–1965) recorded "Allons a Lafayette," the first Cajun music recording, in 1928.

But for Rodrigue's *Jolie Blonde* paintings, what matters is the story George clung to as a young man; what matters is the romantic myth of this convict who wrote a waltz for the woman he loved, a faceless Cajun beauty waiting for an image.

By 1974 George lived in Lafayette and painted Cajuns. It was three years since his first painting with people, the *Aioli Dinner*, and his collectors expected complex works with large groups of people, rooted in old photographs and Cajun history. To paint these intricate designs, he remained tense for hours, steadying his hand with a mahlstick, a Knights of Columbus sword he pulled like Excalibur on a hot summer day from the mud of the Bayou Teche.

It was 3:00 a.m., and George worked on such a painting promised to a client. His right hand ached, and his head swirled with thoughts of tiny faces and deliberate brushstrokes. He returned to his easel and in one hour, as he listened to Joel Sonnier and Doug Kershaw sing his Cajun favorites, without model, photograph, or mahlstick, he painted *Jolie Blonde*. She emerged from his head and onto his canvas, quickly and with loose brushstrokes, painted for himself without a collector standing by.

To George's surprise, the painting sold the following day, with four couples fighting over the purchase.

Rodrigue's *Jolie Blonde* paintings, like his *Evangelines*, could fill a museum exhibition. He photographed dozens of models over the years and painted hundreds of versions. However, it is that first version, the one he invented from his dreams in 1974, that remains not only his most famous, but also the quintessential Cajun portrait of that culture's "beautiful blonde." Jolie Blonde is as much a repetitive subject for George as the Oak Tree and the Blue Dog. In fact, he often paints the three subjects together.

I've modeled as Jolie Blonde for George over the years, beginning in 1994, including for his recent series *Bodies*, when he revisits Jolie Blonde as a classic nude in cemetery settings and contemporary arrangements. This is where it's important to remember that these are not portraits, but rather means to an artistic end. Like George, I can't help but view these paintings with an eye like no one else. I see them not as me, but as George—or rather, as paintings of his feelings, of his soul.

This vulnerability is also true of George's first Jolie Blonde, the one he painted from his imagination in 1974. The rest, no matter whom the models, are just attempts at recapturing that spontaneous and mysterious original.

Or are they? He might argue that he's moved on and that the Jolie Blonde of forty years ago has been replaced, both in his life and on his canvas. As much as I love the early painting, I like to think that this is true. For an artist so associated with repetitive imagery, when it comes to the classics, to the artworks that define his career, he never repeats himself. He moves forward, always looking towards that next great masterpiece.

Broussard's Barber Shop

After painting the *Aioli Dinner* in 1971, George's confidence soared in rendering not only the Cajun figures, but also a style of his own. During the six months it took to complete the painting, he developed specific rules for himself, things separate from and often contradictory to the established rules of art.

He would shape trees and bushes around his figures, he decided, so that their heads never touch the sky. In this way his paintings are puzzles, as he manipulates everyday scenes into highly structured designs. His figures are locked in, unable to move without disturbing this serene snapshot existence of their world, the world of nineteenth-century Acadiana as George envisions it.

Because his motivations involve his concern for a dying culture, he traps slices of time. This also grants him license to brighten his figures, even when reason tells us they should live in shadow, beneath the trees. In Rodrigue's painted world, the Cajuns shine in white as though their bodies are light bulbs, illuminating them in the dark Louisiana landscape and within a culture known for seeking shade, whether beneath the trees or on the front porch of their houses.

Glowing white, the figures in *Broussard's Barber Shop* (1971) sit underneath an overhang as opposed to within a building. In this way the oak trees maintain the structure of their world, holding it together by framing their bodies and, in a sense, the very essence of who they are as displaced Acadians living in Louisiana.

According to George, the Broussard brothers opened the first barber shop in the New Iberia area near the turn of the century. On a limited budget they spent all of their money on their barber chairs, leaving no funds for a building. Undaunted, they cut hair beneath the trees.

I've heard this story from George for twenty years and, since my hope is to be as accurate as possible in these essays, I questioned him further,

"So George, that's true, right? I mean, did your mama know these guys? Did your daddy get his hair cut there?"

"Um, no. I don't remember them talking about this place."

"But you're sure it existed, this portico in the woods?"

"Mmmmm, probably not."

Then you made it up?!

"Oh, I don't know! Does it really matter? After all these years, can't it just be true?"

Similarly, I asked him about the photograph on which the painting is based. Was this place in New Iberia? Was it called Broussard's Barber Shop? Where did he get the picture?

"Just say it came from my mama's album. I have no idea."

I did manage to glean a few believable notes. For example, the chairs remind him of the one he sat in as a boy when he visited the barber. The chair was so important to him that he spent several years searching for one, finally tracking it down at the Ragin' Cajun Junk Shop in Ville Platte, Louisiana, in the 1980s. In an effort to recreate the exact memory, he spent another six months restoring it, covering the seat of the white porcelain chair in red leather and re-chroming the metal.

Weighted with oil to run the hydraulic lift, the heavy barber's chair sat for years in the corner of George's studio in Lafayette and later Henderson and Butte la Rose, Louisiana, until it made its way in 1995 to his restaurant, Café Tee George, where it joined other novelty items and memorabilia. Unfortunately, the restaurant burned just a few years later, and the only thing salvaged was a moose head mount, painted blue, and now hanging over the door of the Blue Dog Café.

Ironically, there is an actual Broussard's Barber Shop located for the past seventy years in Lafayette on Pinhook Road, a mere block away from both the Blue Dog Café and George's first gallery.

"Is that where you got the name?" I asked.

"I don't think so. I think I just made it up. I never got my hair cut there, and I never much thought about it."

He did say that not long after he finished the painting, some men from the barbershop approached him to purchase a print.

"I remember telling them that it was twenty-five dollars, at which point they decided it was too expensive and dropped the idea."

Many years later (thirty-five, according to George) as he walked by the window of Broussard's Barber Shop, he noticed the print hanging on their wall. He peeked in and asked about it, knowing that they hadn't purchased it from him.

"We really love that picture," replied the barber. "We had to pay a lot for it . . . Now who are you again?"

Cajuns, The Book

By the mid-1970s George painted on average forty canvases per year, all scenes of Cajun folk-life stemming from his first painting with people, *Aioli Dinner* (1971), while incorporating the distinctive oak trees from his landscapes. Although he rented a gallery in Lafayette, he sold most of his work on the road in Houston, Dallas, Birmingham and other cities, usually from the trunk of his car to collectors he met on referrals from restaurants, banks, and jewelry stores.

Following the birth of his son André in 1975, George longed for new clients without the road trips. He sought gallery representation, but options were few in those years, especially in the South, and his efforts in New Orleans, with the exception of a short stint at the Reilly Gallery, proved unsuccessful.

Out of nowhere, opportunity knocked. Oxmoor

House, publisher of *Southern Living* magazine, approached George about a book. Based in Birmingham, Alabama, they knew his paintings and envisioned the work in a large coffee table-type format, linking it to their 1974 publication, *Jericho: The South Beheld*, by James Dickey and Hubert Shuptrine, a book hailed as a southern publishing phenomenon.

Despite the obstacles, George jumped at the chance. According to his contract, he would write the text, provide transparencies of his artwork, and commit $75,000 to book purchases. He learned quickly that books, especially art books, rarely generate profit for the author/artist. He also learned, however, that books sell paintings.

He signed the contract late on the Friday afternoon of a holiday weekend. With $400 in the bank, he wrote a hot check to Oxmoor House and spent the weekend knocking on doors, paintings in hand. In three days, using his hometown connections, he made some of the money and borrowed most of it, covering the check.

It was a long shot, typical of George, the type of challenge he relishes, no different than raising his Jefferson Street house to build a gallery underneath, purchasing a building adjacent to St. Louis Cathedral, or for that matter shifting from Cajuns to Blue Dogs.

"Anytime I'm broke or in trouble," laughs George, "I buy a car. Once I figure out how to pay for it, the rest of my problems work themselves out."

George wrote the book the following week, hiring a translator for the French text, printed alongside the English. The large format features seventy-eight paintings with George's detailed descriptions. *The Cajuns of George Rodrigue* (1976) was the first book published nationally on Cajun culture and the first bilingual American book ever printed.

The book caught the eye of the Director of the National Endowment for the Arts who showed it to First

The Other Side of the Painting

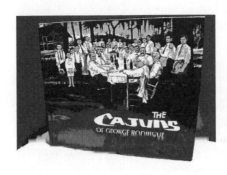

Lady Rosalynn Carter. Mrs. Carter chose the book as an official White House Gift of State during President Carter's administration. *The Cajuns of George Rodrigue* also made the Top 10 Best Southern Book List of 1976.

George was ecstatic. *The Cajuns'* accolades elevated his résumé. But the $75,000 presented a problem. At the time his paintings sold on average for between $500 and $5,000, and the short-term sales couldn't possibly cover his debt. He devised a plan.

In exchange for his investment, Oxmoor House sent George his share of the books. However, selling them was difficult. In pre-internet 1976 only six bookstores existed in the state of Louisiana. And think about this—2,500 large-scale hardcover books weighing four pounds each, delivered to his house on wooden pallets by a semi-truck. It was daunting.

However, George is creative in all things, and he relished this challenge. He secured a mailing list for every French teacher in the United States and offered *The Cajuns* at $15, discounted from the $24.95 list price. He recruited friends to package the books and process the payments. Within days, the orders poured in. Simultaneously, area banks sold the books alongside their teller windows, offering a special price for customers opening new checking accounts.

Within two months George repaid his loans. Within six months he felt the book's long-term effect on his painting sales as it impressed potential buyers. He broke his own sales records and, unable to meet demand, raised prices.

In addition, as a direct result of *The Cajuns*, George painted in 1976 a gift from the State of Louisiana to the President of France, Valéry Giscard d'Estaing, increasing George's reputation internationally, especially on the heels of his Paris Salon award of 1974.

Most important, *The Cajuns of George Rodrigue* taught the artist the power of publishing. It was books that would sell his paintings; it was books that would make him famous.

Iry LeJeune

Since the early 1970s George has painted dozens of music-related scenes, including southern music legends from Elvis Presley to Mahalia Jackson. However, the Cajun music subjects remain his favorites, returning repeatedly to his canvas like painterly records of a once isolated culture.

It was 1972, the year following George's first painting with people, *Aioli Dinner*, that he painted accordion player Iry LeJeune. This early work shows a twenty-seven-year-old Rodrigue already confident in his graphic symbolism, as he seeks to preserve the Cajun culture on his canvas. The figures, spirit-like, all in white, are shapes set against the Louisiana landscape, the land that produced an ardent people devoted to their culture, veritable symbols of themselves, long before the American Cajun craze and stereotype.

Born near Church Point, Louisiana, to a farming family, Iry LeJeune (1928-1955), near blind from birth, turned to music as a young child. It was his cousin, Angeles LeJeune, who first introduced him to the accordion. But it was the records of Amédé Ardoin that most inspired him, influencing both his Cajun-French style and his recording future.

Known for his soulful music, many consider LeJeune to be the greatest Cajun accordion player and recording artist of all time. Produced by Eddie Shuler and Folk-Star, a subsidiary of Goldband Records out of Lake Charles, Louisiana, LeJeune's recordings of "Calcasieu Waltz," "Jolie Catin," and "Evangeline Special" were big hits.

Despite the musician's near blindness and impoverished means, he became a legend in his twenties, much like his Alabama contemporary, country music star Hank Williams (1923-1953).

Shuler first met LeJeune as he walked down a dusty road, carrying his accordion in a flour sack. It was the first accordion the music producer had ever seen.

"He walked up to me and asked me about making records," recalls Shuler, who agreed to take a chance. "In those days the Cajuns didn't write no letters and things; they shook hands, and that was their contract."

In 1949 Shuler produced a 78-rpm record, LeJeune's "The Calcasieu Waltz."

"I bribed the engineer at the radio station to cut the disc for us. It was easy; just a fifth of Old Crow."

The men made seventy dollars on the record, and a Cajun legend was born.

Sadly, Iry LeJeune died at age twenty-six when he and fellow musician, fiddler J. B. Fuselier, were struck by an oncoming vehicle while stopped to change a flat tire late one night on their way home from a performance at the Green Wing club in Eunice, Louisiana. Fuselier, who was driving, survived the accident, but LeJeune, unable to see, had no warning and died instantly. He left behind a young family of five children, dozens of recordings, and a Cajun music legacy.

> Oh, my "little world," I know that last night
> I went everywhere
> To meet you, pretty heart.
> Hey-aie, the promise you made me!
> You turned your back on me to go meet another.
> —Iry LeJeune, "The Evangeline Special," 1948

Sources:

Ann Allen Savoy, *Cajun Music: A Reflection of a People* (Bluebird Press, 1984).

Les Blank, Chris Strachwitz, and Maureen Gosling, *J'ai ete Au Bal (I Went to the Ball): The Cajun and Zydeco Music of Louisiana*, narrated by Barry Jean Ancelet and Michael Doucet, 1993.

The Patchwork Gift

In 1978 George tackled a 5 x 7 foot canvas, piecing together a group of women at a church quilting party, a common Acadian gathering during the 1940s and 1950s. The ambitious project combines twenty figures, including a portrait of the painting's new owner with her child, all gathered beneath Rodrigue's typical Louisiana oaks.

As with his other Cajun paintings, such as the *Aioli Dinner* and *Mamou Riding Academy*, the concept originates with a photograph or series of photographs (now lost), adjusted to suit his needs. In the original image the figures sit indoors, perhaps within a fellowship hall or other meeting space, working on the quilts sold to benefit their church. Rodrigue moves the women outside, contriving a setting so that the scene gains generalities of place and time, becoming anyone's quilting party rather than a specific one.

The figures' heads never the touch the sky, framed instead within oaks, bushes, and quilts. The children sit locked within the outline of adult women. The landscape nurtures the traditions; the oaks stabilize the people; and the mothers protect the future.

Reinforcing this concept is Rodrigue's choice of clothing, dressing most of the women in traditional frocks, while the back row stands in modern-day attire. The painting rejects time, the figures floating like ghosts. Without feet they melt into the landscape and each other as a unit, locked within both an artist's design and a Cajun tradition.

"I first got the idea for a quilting painting," explains Rodrigue, "when I saw quilts on the road between Alexandria and Monroe, Louisiana, as I visited clients in the 1970s. On the small two-lane highway on the east side of the Red River, local quilters hung their quilts for sale on clothes lines strung between the oak trees in front of their homes."

Quilting parties continue today not just in Louisiana but also widely, as we've learned through gifts over the years, including a treasured compilation of Rodrigue images formed into a quilt by a group in South Carolina at the request of George's friend, Linda Kuykendall, who donated her collection of Blue Dog and Jolie Blonde t-shirts for the project (a remarkable gift on more than one level, since George is unable to replace her collection, because the shirts were made only in small quantities and never sold.)

During the summer of 2012, as George battled cancer in Houston, the Community Prayer Quilters of Estes Park, Colorado, quilted a gift to aid his healing through the traditional comfort of a quilt and power of prayer.

"My cousin Kay tells me," explains George's Lafayette friend Bertha Bernard, "that as they work on the quilt, they pray for the person for whom it's intended. When they finish, they hang the quilt in a church where the congregation prays individually for that person. Kay is a member of the group, and they are called to make hundreds of quilts each year."

The Other Side of the Painting

Early in our marriage, George and I collected several quilts during drives through the Texas Panhandle, specifically the stretch between Amarillo and Wichita Falls. In the small towns we purchased heirlooms from area antique marts, seeking tradition in our young marriage through these found handmade treasures. Although we ceased collecting long ago, the quilts remain, whether on beds, within trunks, or framed on the wall, destined within our family as a continuation of a cultural tradition, *The Patchwork Gift*.

The Kingfish and *Uncle Earl*

For years George has claimed that he is not a portrait painter. He explains that others better interpret likenesses, and his models are just that, models. If he paints Jolie Blonde, in other words, it's not about the person posing, but rather about the legend. In the case of his mother's school class, it was not about her and her friends, but rather a depiction of a culture and a slice of time.

The *Aioli Dinner* (1971) is a table of actual New Iberia Frenchmen, yet only in recent years has George referred to their faces as portraits, even after his torturous struggle with their likenesses. In Rodrigue paintings, the milieu and sentiment trump any individual part.

He describes even his paintings of his sons in terms of what the figures represent, as opposed to the real boys we know as André and Jacques. The paintings reveal little about them, his sons, because George designed the works to enlighten his viewers about something else, the Cajuns.

George denied the title "portrait artist" even after painting three United States presidents, five Louisiana governors, musicians Louis Armstrong, Hank Williams, and Clifton Chenier, and Chef Paul Prudhomme. He believed for years that his portraits didn't measure up. Because his goal was to capture the essence of a culture as opposed to a person, perhaps he dismissed the individual's likeness as insignificant.

In addition, I've often thought that this denial stems from resentment, from what he saw as an albatross of family portrait commissions in the 1980s or even that first self-portrait of 1971.

In spring 2008, the New Orleans Museum of Art opened its exhibition *Rodrigue's Louisiana: Forty Years of Cajuns, Blue Dogs and Beyond Katrina*, showcasing over two hundred Rodrigue paintings and sculptures in their main galleries. The museum's director John Bullard chose the categories and insisted on a gallery of portraits. Once installed, "Portraits," with sixty paintings, comprised the largest section of the exhibition. There were more portraits than Oak Trees, Cajuns, Blue Dogs, Hurricanes, or Bodies, the show's other categories, totaling 260 works in all. It never occurred to Bullard to group the Portraits with the Cajuns. And yet it never occurred to George not to do so.

As NOMA installed the exhibition, George stared at the word "Portraits" stenciled on the wall. He walked the large area in silence, pausing in front of a painting in the far corner.

"This was my first real portrait, maybe the best one I've ever done," he said, standing before his painting of Huey Long and referring to himself as a portrait artist for the first time.

Painted in 1980 *The Kingfish* (60 x 36 inches) is

The Other Side of the Painting

George's interpretation of Louisiana Governor and U.S. Senator Huey Long (1893-1935). As with his other Cajun paintings, he painted Long not in shadow as one would expect beneath a tree, but rather glowing with his culture as though cut out and pasted onto the dark trunk. His white clothing and barely discernible feet leave him floating within the composition, as though he is a ghost, timeless and historic.

The setting is Huey's famous campaign speech. He stands beneath the Evangeline Oak in St. Martinville and says,

"Just as Evangeline cried for her Gabriel, Louisiana cries for roads, schools, and bridges."

George uses the tree to frame not only Huey, but also a vision of the capitol building he would construct in 1932 in Baton Rouge. In addition, the apparition refers to Long's assassination, occurring three years later in that structure.

Soon after its completion the painting hung on exhibition in the Senate Rotunda in Washington, D.C., during a show of Louisiana artists.

Again, when George painted *The Kingfish* he did not think of it as a portrait, but rather as an extension of his efforts to preserve his culture and record Louisiana history. It wasn't until that day at NOMA, when he looked around the room and saw what he'd done, that he dared to discuss his works in this way.

After painting Huey Long it was natural that George paint his brother. *Uncle Earl* (1989, 60 x 36 inches) depicts Louisiana Governor Earl K. Long (1895-1960).

As with Huey, George paints Earl on the campaign trail, this time in north Louisiana where he drove door to door in his white Cadillac, purchasing vegetables from farmers in one parish and distributing the food to working people in the next. He too stands within the oak tree, but instead of the capitol building, George includes pea

patches, shown in three rows to Earl's left.

"There he is, Crazy Earl, screaming into the microphone," says George about this painting.

During the NOMA exhibition, I noticed that whereas Huey is George's favorite, Earl belongs to the people. They love this painting, and among the public it is considered one of George's best.

At last, according to the painter himself, George Rodrigue is a portrait artist. In addition to the Longs, he painted Louisiana Governors Edwin Edwards, Kathleen Blanco, and Bobby Jindal. And in 2009 he tackled an ambitious historical painting of President Eisenhower and Andrew Higgins for the National World War II Museum.

The portraits, however, do not change the intent of his earlier paintings of individual Cajuns or his more recent figurative works. He still uses models to express a comprehensive idea separate from the person posing. For example, although he paints from photographs of me, as with his sons, he never, with the possible exception of *Wendy and Me*, approaches the paintings as portraits. With regards to my face and person, my likeness in series such as *Jolie Blonde* and *Bodies* is a means to an artistic end, unrelated to my portrait or personality.

And yet when it comes to the Long brothers, after more than twenty years of denial, George admits, finally, that these larger-than-life Louisiana characters usurped his original intent the moment he applied the last brushstroke to each unmistakable visage.

The *Saga of the Acadians* *

Between 1985 and 1989, George painted the *Saga of the Acadians*, a series of fifteen paintings chronicling the Acadian journey from France to Nova Scotia in the seventeenth century, from Nova Scotia to Louisiana during the Grand Dérangement of 1755, and the first official return visit from southwest Louisiana to Grand Pré in the 1930s. The series, a labor of love for George, tours Louisiana as his interpretation of the story of his ancestors.

In 1984, the year before beginning the *Saga*, George painted his first Blue Dog. Over the next five years, while working on these paintings of the Acadian story, he painted not only the *Loup-garou*, but also a number of important Cajun works and portraits, resulting in a lengthy crossover period of both Blue Dog and Cajun works.

George narrowed the Acadian story to thirty paintings and, after completing them, to a final fifteen. (In other words, fifteen remain together as a collection and fifteen were sold separately, no longer part of the series.) He's said many times that had he committed, the expansive saga could have been two hundred paintings.

Painted in oil and completed just prior to his battle with hepatitis, George blames the marathon pace of painting both this series and the forty canvases for the book *Bayou* as having brought on his illness, planting a seed that resulted in cancerous tumors, discovered in 2012.

The *Saga* paintings typify George's style, established years earlier with works such as *Broussard's Barber Shop* (1971) and *The Class* (1972). The figures appear to be cut out and pasted onto the landscape, just as the Cajuns were cut out of Canada and pasted onto south Louisiana, where they made a home for themselves in the swamps and prairies. The oak trees are cut off at the top so that light shines from underneath, representing the small sky of Louisiana, as opposed to the big sky of neighboring Texas, as well as a distant hope for these transplanted people. Rather than shadowed beneath the trees, the people beam from within.

The *Saga of the Acadians* originally belonged to the Landry and Defez families of Henderson, Louisiana. They donated the works to the Acadian Village Museum in Lafayette, where for ten years a George Rodrigue annex spotlighted these important works, along with supplemental paintings loaned from the artist's private collection.

Eventually the Anne and Wendell Gauthier family of New Orleans, by way of southwest Louisiana, acquired the collection. Through their generosity the fifteen paintings tour museums throughout the state of Louisiana, focusing on small venues in Cajun communities.

The first painting in the series, *The Sailing of the Jonah*, depicts the beginning of a journey in 1604 from Normandy, France, to what is now Nova Scotia. Arriving just north of Plymouth Rock in 1604, the French *Pilgrims* (painting number two) lived a family-oriented lifestyle in the harsh Nova Scotia wilderness. Now Acadians, these imaginative settlers, shown planting seed in painting number three, developed fertile farmland in their marsh-like territory. So successful were their efforts, many historians feel the Acadians were deported to make room for British settlers who coveted these productive grounds.

In *The Fight for an Empire*, French soldiers board a ship just ahead of advancing British troops. Caught between two military giants, the Acadian settlers face losing their tranquil lifestyle forever. British troops use the *Church at Grand Pré* (painting five), the first Catholic Church built in Nova Scotia, as a prison for the soon-to-be-exiled Acadians. Finally, in *Leave Our Homes? Hell No!*, soldiers force evicted residents from their homes and into the wilderness.

These French Pilgrims originally settled in Nova Scotia to satisfy the expansion needs of Motherland France. Following British victory, however, they were required to forsake the Catholic religion and swear allegiance to the British king. Refusing on both issues, as depicted in the painting, *With No Country to Call Home*, they were deported to many lands and often refused entry. Even in France, they were considered "no longer French." The exiled Acadians endured the harsh winter in open vessels in the North Atlantic, and in one controversial painting, *Final Insult*, a soldier of the Crown offers a diseased blanket to a child.

In *A Final Look at Acadie*, the original Acadians bid good-bye to Canada. Forcibly driven from their homes and separated from those they loved, the stage was set in 1755 for the odyssey to begin and for Longfellow to immortalize this epic journey. After many years without a homeland, these steadfast Acadians reached their long sought "Land of the Oaks" and became *The First Cajuns*, portrayed by Rodrigue as they arrive on the Bayou Teche.

In *The Last Novena for Gabriel*, Longfellow's Evangeline, symbol of forced separation of families, friends, and those in love, offers a prayer for her Gabriel, as she waits beneath a Louisiana oak.

Native Americans assisted the Cajuns in understanding the indigenous ingredients available to them for cooking, as illustrated in the painting *Macque Choux*, with an offering of corn.

From here, George jumps forward in time to 1912 when Louisiana Governor Luther Hall issued a special edict that French could no longer be spoken in schools. The resulting painting, *He-bert, Yes - A Bear, No*, is the most popular from the series.

In 1929 Hollywood produced *Evangeline*, a film starring Dolores del Rio, who stands beneath the Evangeline Oak in George's fourteenth painting in the series, *Evangeline—A Silent Classic*.

Finally, in *Return to Acadie*, Dudley LeBlanc is the first Cajun on record to revisit his roots: the historic church of Grand Pré in Nova Scotia. At the time, LeBlanc's Hadacol was second in America for advertising expenses behind Coca-Cola. From Hollywood to the Hadacol Caravan, the Cajuns were now, solidly, American.

George's *Saga of the Acadians* shares through art the history of the Cajun people. It is an excellent teaching tool for young and old, not only as a tribute to the Acadians, but also as a reminder to all cultures that, as computers and travel encourage homogeny, it is important that we honor our roots and treasure our uniqueness.

* With thanks to Museum Curator Dana Holland-Beickert, who helped research the Acadian history for traveling exhibitions of Rodrigue's *Saga of the Acadians*

Chapter 9

More than a French Legend, More than a Dog

The *loup-garou* and Tiffany are mere roots of a series that freed George Rodrigue on canvas, while propelling him towards worldwide fame.

Blue Dog in the Beginning

In 1980 a Baton Rouge investment group approached George Rodrigue for help with creating a lasting Louisiana memento, a book of Louisiana ghost stories for the 1984 World's Fair in New Orleans. Author Chris Segura embellished forty rather gruesome tales, and George researched regional myths and legends for appropriate imagery, resulting in *Bayou* (Inkwell Press, 1984). Not big on fiction, I doubt the Cajun artist read these stories (he doesn't recall), which is probably a good thing, because they are wrought with macabre literary vignettes, better illustrated by Hieronymus Bosch than George.

Instead he painted from titles and themes relating to familiar legends, completing the works long before Segura wrote the stories. Each of the forty tales inspired one painting suggesting a vague reference to the content. In this way George enjoyed artistic freedom without feeling bound by specifics in the text.

He devoted three years to painting the forty canvases, now known as the *Bayou Collection*, all typical of his Cajun style, most with large oak trees and ghostly figures. But it was one story *Slaughter House* that launched an artistic phenomenon. The story tells of an evil dog that guards a house. Although unreferenced in the story, George used this opportunity to paint the *loup-garou*, a word translated from the French as "werewolf," and a myth Rodrigue heard often as a boy. In his mother's version, however, the loup-garou was more of a crazy wolf or ghost dog that lurked in cemeteries and sugarcane fields. She threatened young George that if he misbehaved today, the loup-garou would eat him tonight.

Ironically, there is another story in *Bayou* called *Le Loup-garou*, and for that George painted not a dog, but rather Genevievre, an Evangeline-type figure, standing beneath an oak tree at the edge of a cornfield. In George's interpretation, she shows no hint of the horrible death awaiting her at the story's end, other than the red outlines of a wolf painted into the trim of her dress.

To capture his loup-garou, the artist searched his vast photo files for a suitable image, settling on photographs of his dog Tiffany, deceased four years by this time. It was her strong shape, not her memory, that caught his attention. From the beginning, he divided Tiffany the pet from Blue Dog the design. This cute terrier-spaniel mix lived in his home since she was a puppy—named "Tiffany" to give her importance as the runt of the litter and the last puppy left in the box (although he has mentioned, always while laughing, that she was a mean little dog, snipping at friends and eating the furniture). Tiffany was his studio companion, and as George painted throughout the night, she sat watching. He kept his camera nearby and leaned often from his stool, capturing her expression as she stared up at him at his easel.

The Other Side of the Painting

Although I've softened on this point in recent years, early on I felt a need to convince people that these loup-garou paintings were in no way representative of Tiffany, the family pet—a compendium that reduced the artwork's significance to nothing more than a pet portrait or a memorial. The photo of Tiffany, no question, was important, but it was secondary to the strong shape and George's personal, even vulnerable, translation. In his design, the loup-garou, not Tiffany, was the subject of the painting. It was not a small dog sitting in the background. And never, in all of the years and hundreds of Blue Dog paintings since, has it suggested "Where's Waldo?"

George's dog image is out front and center, painted like a person, locked in. As with all of his paintings, whether Cajun people or trees or other subjects, there exists a strong sense of deliberateness—that if the dog or any element shifted even a bit to the left or right or up or down, then the composition would crumble. In a sense, it would also lose its illusion of simplicity. George's paintings are actually complex, ordered worlds. Every detail of design and color is specific; there's no randomness, and there's no room for change.

Pleased with his loup-garou shape, George sketched a design. It was time to paint. The dog stands on tomb-like steppingstones leading from a red haunted house. The original loup-garou, as explained by his mother, said nothing about the dog being blue. Rather, George imagined a dark night sky casting a blue-grey shade on the dog's fur. As a late decision he painted the eyes red, further suggesting the devil-dog legend.

The resulting painting did not cause an overnight sensation in the art world, or in the gallery, or among his friends. But it did haunt George. He liked this strong image and its odd color, a powerful shape that held its own, similar to his tree and Cajun figures. There's a common misconception that George painted the Blue Dog and immediately stopped painting Cajuns or exploring other ideas. It is true that over the next five or six years he painted dozens of these loup-garous, always in bayous and reminiscent of that childhood tale.

But at the same time, he painted the Cajuns, ambitious historical works such as *Fais do-do* (1986) and *Louisiana Cowboys* (1988), as well as iconic non-Cajuns, such as *Hank Williams* (1987) and *Louis Armstrong* (1989).

In addition, his reputation as a commissioned portrait artist expanded greatly during this period, including large-scale family portraits, paintings for the National Republican Party of President Ronald Reagan (1988, at the Lod Cook Alumni Center, Baton Rouge), President George H. W. Bush with his grandchildren (1989, at the Bush home, Houston, Texas), as well as three portraits of Chef Paul Prudhomme (1984-9, at K-Paul's Louisiana Kitchen, New Orleans).

It was at an exhibition of sixty Rodrigue paintings in Los Angeles in 1988 that George first heard a new phrase. Up until that point, he called his dog-image loup-garou, and he thought of its grey-blue color as the logical choice, given the atmosphere of these works. However, at this exhibition he overheard gallery visitors refer to the ten or twelve loup-garou paintings as "Blue Dogs." George says that his first reaction was, "Blue Dogs? What are they talking about?" He honestly had no idea that people looked at his creation in this way.

The show was a sell-out—the Cajuns, the Landscapes, and the Blue Dogs, which, following this exhibition, took on a category of their own. George left Los Angeles thinking about his years at Art Center and the city that introduced him to Pop Art in the mid-1960s. In retrospect, he says, it should not have surprised him that it took a California audience to recognize this new, strong idea in his work. From the beginning, even as a painter of regional landscapes and Cajun folk life, only 2 percent of his sales were to Louisiana residents, a percentage that holds true today, whether paintings of Blue Dogs or other subjects, even as his home base remains New Orleans.

Upon his return to Louisiana, George experimented at his easel. The first simple but important step towards changing a loup-garou into a blue dog was the eyes, which he changed from red to yellow. The other changes, and there are many, took place over the next twenty years, resulting in an image that no longer resembles or even suggests its dark roots. Each change, each period of development, deserves its own round of images and its own detailed essay. Truth is, I've barely touched on the history here.

Even now, folks rarely understand that the Blue Dog is something George invented. Although Pop in nature, it is unlike Andy Warhol, who took everyday commercial products such as Brillo boxes and dollar bills from the popular culture and inserted them back into that same culture as works of art. In George's case, he invented the image as a unique painted illusion, which he introduced to the public from the beginning not as a cartoon, not as a stuffed animal, not even as a logo, but always, only, as a piece of art.

For children who grew up knowing the Blue Dog, and for many adults who forget life-before-Blue-Dog, this explanation is a challenge. In lectures, I approach it this way:

"Imagine if I asked you to draw the bogeyman. What would you draw?"

Blank faces.

Wendy Rodrigue

"I believe you would each draw something different. That was George's challenge with the loup-garou. There was no picture of what it looks like. He created it from his head. And in turn, he created the Blue Dog."

It's about this time that I see light bulbs, and I imagine that I hear their thoughts:

"If he can do it, maybe I can too . . . ."

For a detailed history of the *Blue Dog* series following this introduction, please see the online essays at *Musings of an Artist's Wife*.

Starry, Starry Eyes

In 1991 George's printed artwork bolted forward with new color and precision as he applied the latest in ink and technology to his silkscreens. This marked a substantial advancement over his earlier Cajun posters and Blue Dog prints. For the first time he created complex original print designs using intense hues.

Prior to the silkscreen *Starry, Starry Eyes*, George's Cajun posters were four-color, offset lithographs. His Blue Dog silkscreens were two or three colors, dull in shade and thick in texture, as he experimented with silkscreen ink. He guessed at colors and struggled with splattered paint, scratches, and dings, sometimes pulling as many as thirty trial prints to obtain a final artwork without damage and in perfect registration.

With *Starry, Starry Eyes*, George swaps paint for ink

and hand for machine. He experiments for the first time with the computer, increasing the complexity of his designs and, because his silkscreen prints transfer from his mind to his paper without an intermittent painting, allowing him to see the final image and make changes before his printer produces the work.

Starry, Starry Eyes became George's bestselling print to date, despite its $350 price, a staggering amount at the time. A victim of backyard familiarity, the New Orleans gallery sold only a handful of prints to locals. We shipped worldwide, and the gallery phones rang non-stop for weeks, long after the prints sold out.

This was remarkable in those pre-email days, because, other than New Orleans and Carmel foot traffic, we relied on photographs and the U.S. Post Office. We produced our first high quality mailer, a tri-fold piece with die-cuts, overlaying the eye-filled sky on the dog. Today these mailers are a casualty of the computer age, as we dismiss the delay and expense in favor of digital photography, websites, and Facebook.

It is the Blue Dog's eyes, according to many enthusiasts, that draw them in and create the mystery. Early on George changed the loup-garou's red eyes to yellow, shifting the dog's meaning away from the Cajun werewolf legend. In time the oval dog-like eyes become unnatural round saucers, uniform in their structure and hue, shifting the artwork's meaning again, this time away from real dog associations.

"Without variation in shape," explains George, "one would think these round saucer eyes would cause a static expression. But this is not the case. The other elements in the dog's face become very important. In changing those elements, even slightly, in relationship to each other, the dog's expression varies.

"In fact, the paintings show a wide variety of interpretations, which is unexpected when one considers the basic premise. And it's certainly unexpected if a person has seen only one image."

It was a gift, an art book from New Orleans artist Mallory Page, that started this discussion of eyes, reminding me of Rodrigue's Van Gogh salute. *The Look of Love* (Graham C. Boettcher, 2012) features magnificent late eighteenth- and early nineteenth-century eye miniatures from the Skier Collection, the subject of a recent exhibition at the Birmingham Museum of Art.

Swept up, I pulled a book of poetry from our shelf and turned to Percy Bysshe Shelley's famous lines (1772-1822):

> How eloquent are eyes!
> Not the rapt poet's frenzied lay
> When the soul's wildest feelings stray
> Can speak so well as they.

"It's pure romance," says Page, known for her emotive paintings, as she reveals her heart not through a painted gaze but through abstraction and color.

I asked George about the importance of eyes in expressing emotion; yet he dwells on character, referencing the timeless stares within his paintings: the ghostly Frenchmen within his *Aioli Dinner* (1971), the crazed gaze of Louisiana Governor Earl K. Long (1989), and the unwavering strength in his portrait of General Eisenhower (2009).

Whether an imaginary dog's questioning, yellow saucers, a beloved's gaze within Victorian miniatures, or the strength of character within historical portraits, it seems that the eyes lead to the soul of the subject and, in the case of George's Blue Dog, perhaps the soul of the artist himself.

Blue Dog, The Book

To find her you must lose her. The Blue Dog knows the way.
—Blue Dog, 1994

In March of 1992 journalist Bridget O'Brian interviewed George for an article, front page, center column, in the *Wall Street Journal*. Although George had no control over the content, O'Brian allowed him one special request. Without hesitating, he replied, "Please say that I'm looking for a publisher."

On the day of "How Many Dogs Can Fetch Money?," my Carmel, California, home phone rang at 5:00 a.m. with the news. Long before the internet, the Rodrigue Gallery phone continued ringing for a month. At daybreak I purchased ten newspapers from the Carmel Drugstore, where two men asked for my autograph. I was flabbergasted.

In addition to clients, reporters, and publishers,

George received the one call he most wanted. The following week he flew to New York and met Roz Cole, Andy Warhol's legendary book agent. Mrs. Cole lined up several meetings, and the challenge began:

"What is a Blue Dog?" asked the publishers. "Is this a children's book? Will people buy a book of Blue Dog paintings?"

I wasn't in on those meetings, but after years of working with publishers I imagine what it was like. George grew frustrated defending his work and convincing the book world of his project's star quality.

Eventually, Viking Penguin committed to a Blue Dog book, and George and I committed, coincidentally, to each other. This landed me, albeit peripherally, in my first publishing project. We began at Viking's offices in New York City in the fall of 1993. The book, *Blue Dog*, would feature Rodrigue's paintings and an imaginary story by George and author Lawrence Freundlich. In a large boardroom, a team of editors, art directors, and marketing strategists explained the book, a paperback retailing for twenty dollars.

George sat dismayed and considered abandoning the project. They still did not understand his work. A cheap book only cheapened his art, and he had no interest.

Suddenly, Peter Mayer, Penguin Books' near-mythic CEO, burst in the room. In five minutes he transformed the paperback into a hard cover book with slipcase, hologram, and other special features, retailing for fifty dollars. He congratulated George on his art, leaving the room as fast as he arrived, having altered permanently a project and attitudes.

The book, with an innovative design by Alexander Isley, tells a touching story of Blue Dog, first as Tiffany living in George's Lafayette studio and, following her death, her ghost's cry for his attention. In the fictitious tale, she haunts his dreams and eventually lives again through his art.

The Other Side of the Painting

When I had finally begun to paint Blue Dog alone in a world of her own kind, I sensed that Blue Dog was giving me my freedom—freedom not so much to love but to accept love from the infinite bounty of a dog's heart. I might be her master, but to my own master I was only a servant.
–*Blue Dog*, 1994

Viking printed a cautious five thousand copies of *Blue Dog*, released fall of 1994. The book's popularity surprised nearly everyone but George, and the publisher reprinted quickly. *Blue Dog*, now topping two hundred thousand copies in five languages, is a legend in the world of art books, something people still talk about when we visit New York.

Since *Blue Dog*, George published books and calendars with Stewart, Tabori & Chang, Harry N. Abrams, Sterling, and Rizzoli. He embraces these books as works of art, reflecting his ongoing confidence in his vision and his enthusiasm for such projects.

With *The Art of George Rodrigue* (Harry N. Abrams, 2003; revised 2012) and *George Rodrigue Prints: A Catalogue Raisonné* (Abrams, 2008), he experienced his proudest publishing achievements since *The Cajuns of George Rodrigue* (Oxmoor House, 1976), career retrospectives with critical texts by Art Historian Ginger Danto and Director Emeritus of the New Orleans Museum of Art, E. John Bullard.

Today, unlike the early Cajuns and Blue Dog years, the pressure's off. George meets annually with Roz Cole and publishers, producing new projects according to his whims, including children's books and wall calendars in recent years, as well as numerous collaborations in the form of loaned artwork for publications such as Ken Wells's *Rascal* (Knopf, 2010), Deb Shriver's *Stealing Magnolias* (Glitterati, 2010) and *In the Spirit of New Orleans* (Assouline, 2012), the recent *A Unique Slant of Light: The Bicentennial History of Art in Louisiana* (Louisiana Endowment for the Humanities,

2012), and *The Other Side of the Painting*, a Fall 2013 project for me with UL Press.

Blue Dog 2000, the Year of Xerox

Although most collectors understand by now that George avoids mass-production, products, and other projects that might be described as "sell-out," there was a period of time when I (and I daresay much of the gallery staff) approached each day on the defensive.

The late 1990s brought a flood of projects his way, and to many on the outside it appeared George grabbed at everything. These included three catalogue covers for Neiman Marcus, posters for the New Orleans Jazz and Heritage Festival, and the Official Presidential Inaugural Poster for Bill Clinton and Al Gore, just to name a few.

However, behind the scenes, although we were very busy, it didn't feel like a sell-out. Every project was unique and chosen for some purpose other than money. In fact, in retrospect, nothing brought in much money—not directly anyway. Rather, they were interesting projects, things to be worked out, that excited George both artistically and, there is no denying, promotionally. Each one of these helped increase his fame in certain arenas on a positive level, while at the same time challenged his creativity.

Yet I was shocked at the number of projects he turned down. People often asked him, "How did you get the Blue Dog paintings on the show *Friends*?" or "How did you come to paint President Clinton for his inauguration?" Folks assumed we sought out these projects (or even paid for them!) when in fact, they poured in. Many nights we sat on the couch going through that week's stack of offers. And 90 percent of the time, before I barely outlined the proposal, George's answer was "no."

He declined (and continues to decline) everything from cartoons to major motion pictures, stuffed animals, needlepoint, clothing lines, and even mascots for major league football teams and women's roller derby, as well as the more obvious—magnets, coffee cups, and baseball caps.

I'm amazed at the number of licensing companies that still contact him, thinking that because they're not out there, surely he never thought of making t-shirts or posters.

To George's mind, however, while he's here on this earth, alive and painting, any of those projects might ruin his art. That's not to say that there won't be posters on every street corner one day, but it will be long after he's gone, after his art reaches that elevated status that comes with a complete *oeuvre* and a lifetime's achievement, so that the gap between the original artworks and products is so wide as to be insignificant.

There was one project, however, that appealed to George not only creatively and promotionally, but also financially: Xerox.

The Other Side of the Painting

When we received their letter early in 1999, although intrigued, George initially declined. He hesitated in favor of the project only because the letter came not from Xerox, but from Young and Rubicam, the legendary New York advertising agency. His years at the Art Center College of Design in the 1960s focused heavily on advertising design, and as a student George considered the profession.

Unsatisfied with his reply, the Y&R team, specifically Barry Hoffman and Bob Wyatt, visited our their home in Lafayette, Louisiana. They presented Blue Dog designs for a worldwide advertising campaign for their client Xerox. George was torn. On the one hand, he was like a child with excitement at the thought of working with these talented designers, and he dreamt of plans for the generous payment they offered for the use of his art in their campaign. On the other hand, he winced at their initial work. In all cases, they had removed the dog from his paintings, so that it stood on its own or appeared as a design-element in their layouts. In at least one example, a speech bubble protruded from the dog's mouth.

If there is one hard and fast rule for George regarding whether or not to allow the use of his artwork in any project, it is this:

The Blue Dog exists only within a complete painting of his design.

He declined again.

Within a week, they flew us to New York and tried again. I'll never forget that meeting, because I knew then that it was going to happen, and admittedly, the thought of that big pile of money, the likes of which we'd never seen, was like winning the lottery. Y&R agreed to George's terms regarding his art. They would give him tag words, and he in turn would design the complete painting and ad, so that the campaign was more about his art as a whole than the Blue Dog (or, frankly, Xerox).

This included not only print ads and billboards for

the United States and Europe, but also television commercials filmed in museums, as well as unexpected locations throughout rural America, with George's paintings as the focal point.

That meeting's icing on the cake was a last minute arrival. Aldo Papone, the legendary ad man who coined the phrase for American Express, "Don't leave home without it," popped in to meet the Blue Dog Man in person. Yet it was George who was as excited as if he'd met Elvis himself.

The Xerox campaign gave George the opportunity to work with America's advertising giants. He became friends with these men and looked forward each day to exchanging ideas and sharing his work. He painted on the Xerox campaign throughout the year 2000, working on little else. Rarely have I seen him so excited about a project.

So was this a sell-out? I don't know. I do know that it was not a mistake. Whatever flak he took over the campaign was mostly in Louisiana. The national press was, well, impressed. And indeed, I'm not sure that the nine-month worldwide promotion didn't do more to promote George's art than it did Xerox.

The naysayers made the obvious analogy that George paints the Blue Dog as though he's running it off on a copy machine. But those of us close to the project never saw it that way, especially given the complexity of these works. Also, remember, this was one man sitting in his studio at 3:00 a.m., Hank Williams turned down low, a glass of milk beside him, lost in his thoughts, his designs, his paints. For a project that came from the Big City and from the Big Time, in the end it was just George sitting in Lafayette at his easel. High art or low art? You decide.

And so what about the money? He got a big hunk of it, and we used it to buy a house in Carmel, California. We found a property on eighteen acres in the country, in Carmel Valley. Even better, there was enough space for George to build his dream studio. It was the first (and only) studio he ever built, always before taking over back bedrooms or offices or a TV room. Let's face it, he deserved it. Even though we now live most of the year in New Orleans, it is in Carmel that he does most of his painting today. I guess you could say that it's our Xerox house and, no question, sell-out or not, it was worth it.

Blue Dog in Three Dimensions

It was around 2000 that George started work in earnest on the concept of a Blue Dog sculpture. He dabbled as early as 1992, but those pieces are flat cut-outs made of wood, usually mahogany, about two inches thick, and painted as if on canvas. Occasionally he surrounded these pieces with neon or added other elements such as a moon or hot dog. He tried a few on poles, dogs with two fronts, one side blue and the other side red.

The Blue Dog exists only in two dimensions, a fact presenting the biggest challenge in creating a sculpture. It's not like a dog at all. It doesn't run or bark or chase its tail. It doesn't have a backside. It exists only in a specific pose and within the design of a Rodrigue painting.

The early two-dimensional sculptures were fun; however, other than their wooden structure, they were no

different than had he cut the image from a painting with scissors, attaching it to the wall sans background. The idea of a three-dimensional sculpture haunted George, but an effective design eluded him. In addition to wood, he experimented with bronze and plaster, but still the results were cutout shapes that hung like canvases.

George created numerous bronze sculptures within his Cajun series; however the trees and figures translated well into three dimensions. With the Blue Dog, he sought a sculpture that would stand on its own while retaining its flat, well-defined shape.

By the late 1990s, the idea of a Blue Dog sculpture became almost a daily part of George's creative process. He played with paper and cardboard, bending, pasting, and cropping, with occasional add-ons such as toothpicks and mini-easels, in hopes of creating a model that was more than a shape cut from a painting.

One night in 2003, as we sat talking at a restaurant bar, George played absentmindedly with the cocktail napkins. He stopped suddenly and grinned:

"I've got it!"

"Got what?"

"The sculpture. I know how to do it."

And that was how three cocktail napkins, each balanced on one edge and held together in concave arches between our pinching fingers, became the design for the first true Blue Dog sculpture. Each side would be a dog-front, with the feet matching up at the bottom.

The Other Side of the Painting

George went on to explain that the three-sided piece would be two hundred and fifty feet high, hold a Louisiana Welcome Center and Historical Museum at its base, and sit on a grassy area at the foot of the Luling Bridge, just outside of New Orleans.

"I'll build it like a rig!"

The following week he visited Begneaud's Manufacturing in Lafayette and began work on a four-foot prototype constructed of chrome, aluminum, and steel. There were many challenges during this trial run, including bending the metal, avoiding problems with wind (for the large scale), theft and birds (for the small scale), and how best to apply the color. In the end he mounted the piece on a heavy stand and pole, elevating it three feet from the ground, completing the job at an automotive paint shop where he sealed it like a car.

Within weeks of his "eureka" with the cocktail napkins, George finished a four-foot sculpture and saw endless possibilities for integrating the piece as public art. Within six months he created an eight-foot sculpture, red, yellow, and blue, now installed at the Sydney and Walda Besthoff Sculpture Garden at the New Orleans Museum of Art.

Following the lengthy disruption of Hurricane Katrina in 2005, George built another eight-foot piece (2007) which he covered in automotive flip-flop paint, so that the sculpture alters in color with changes in lighting and vantage point.

And in 2010, Jefferson Parish installed a twenty-eight-foot Blue Dog sculpture on Veterans Boulevard in Metairie, a suburb of New Orleans. This large scale prompted new challenges, including working with and curving enormous sheets of metal, transporting the work more than one hundred miles from the Lafayette fabrication warehouse, arranging landscaping, security, lighting, and parking, planning for hurricane force winds, and most importantly, working with area legislators and citizens to ensure a sculpture and installation that adds in a positive way to the community.

Nearly a year in the making, the piece received its automotive flat colors of red, blue, and yellow before George painted the details, as the sculpture, suspended and lying on its side, turned on a giant rotisserie he designed for this purpose.

In usual George Rodrigue form, these projects were only the beginning. He translated the sculpture into a table base, stacked heads, and other designs.

And what of the two hundred and fifty-foot gateway Blue Dog? Oh, he still talks about it like it's happening next month. Nothing would surprise me.

Swamp Dogs: A Series on Metal

Created between 2011 and 2013, George's *Swamp Dogs* combine print, photography, and varnish on large sheets of metal, resulting in a unique perspective of the Louisiana landscape. Beyond materials, however, the series originates with two stories. George illustrates Louisiana lore including not only the loup-garou, but also, in this case, allusions to the *feux follets*, or swamp gas.

"It comes from the earth and explodes at night into large balls of fire," explains George. "The Cajuns thought it was something magical—a swamp mystery they couldn't explain—when actually it was natural gas ignited by static electricity."

The loup-garou legend, the origin of George's Blue Dog, talks of a crazy wolf-type animal living in the swamp.

"With *Swamp Dogs*, I combine these mysteries, the loup-garou and the feux follets."

Before releasing the series last month, George experimented for more than a year, both in paint and photography, ultimately combining the two mediums within his computer.

"In the minds of the Cajuns, the feux follets was magic, but real, just as the loup-garou was mythical, but true. To inject reality, I started with my photographs of the Atchafalaya Basin and altered them, stretching shapes and changing colors. The loup-garou is in the water, through the water, and part of the water."

Using computer technology, George combines his imagination with reality. He painted several versions of the Blue Dog, scanned them into the computer, over-laying them onto his altered photographs. He manipulated these computer collages, increasing saturation but reducing the colors to only five or six, lending varying levels of transparency.

"I blended the photographs and painted imagery onto metal surfaces, using archival ink on aluminum so that parts of the metal show through, such as the dog's nose and areas of the swamp. They appear as raw metal, as does a two-inch border around the final artwork."

Finally, Rodrigue focuses on scale, with an average size of 3 x 5 feet.

"The larger the scale, the more stretched the photograph. The metal becomes more obvious, as does the color enhancement."

At this time, *Swamp Dogs* includes ten versions, each an edition of ten. The computer screen does the reflective surface little justice, an irony considering the artwork's digital origins. George is so pleased with the series' effects in person, however, that he created other works on chrome, including large mixed medias designed for children's hospitals so that patients and visitors see their reflections alongside the Blue Dog, as well as a new series, *Hollywood Stars*, featuring, in place of the Louisiana swamp, actors within classic roles from the 1940s and 1950s.

Hollywood Stars

Most folks have seen *Casablanca* so many times that, unless one happened to visit a theater in 1942, we don't remember our first encounter with Rick and Ilsa. The film runs together as a nostalgic and romantic constant, a symbol for moviegoers everywhere of why we love the picture show.

In *Hollywood Stars* (2012-2013), George pays tribute to the Golden Age of Hollywood with unique, large-scale works on chrome featuring stars of the Silver Screen. These include Humphrey Bogart, Ingrid Bergman, Marilyn Monroe, Clint Eastwood, and Doris Day.

The Hollywood characters played by these stars are larger than life and impervious to time. I thought of this recently as I read Kent Westmoreland's detective novel *Baronne Street* and slipped unwittingly into a Bogie accent as Burleigh Drummond, PI, hunts the killer of his ex-girlfriend, Coco Robicheaux. The setting is New Orleans, 2000, yet the flavor, regardless of the wheels, is Casablanca, 1940:

"The T-Bird was probably the only thing I really cared

about and definitely the only commitment I've ever made."
–Westmoreland, *Baronne Street*, 2010

Explains George:

"These movie stars were under contract with major Hollywood studios, and their images, in most cases, were managed and promoted as characters associated with their films."

"I use the Blue Dog on either side of the figures, indicating one as their Hollywood image and the other as the real person behind the myth. Just as the dog has two sides, so do these actors, their true self and their screen self.

"As an example, Marilyn Monroe is the Blue Dog screen image, while Norma Jean is her Red Dog real self."

Hollywood Stars is a unique collection of large-scale (41 x 62 inches) artwork on metal, not to be confused with an edition. Although based on the images, George makes each piece individually on chrome, altering the images slightly by hand using silver paint, so that no two are identical. He then signs the finished works with his name and the notation "unique."

After all these years, I should know better than to ask George about his favorite from this or any series. Yet I wasn't willing to accept his standard answer, "the painting I'm working on now," and pushed him.

"Well, I wasn't going to show you this 'til it's finished," he grinned, "but I designed this one just for us."

And with that, he unveiled another Hollywood Star, this one inspired by a classic horror film and a repeated subject on his painted high school t-shirts: *Blue Dog Meets the Creature from the Black Lagoon.*

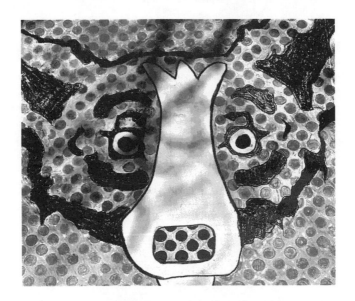

A Life of Its Own

Feel the dignity of a child. Do not feel superior to him, for you are not. –Robert Henri

It was in Hollywood, ironically, that George and I reflected recently on the Blue Dog in a new way. We learned of a school in Southern California that used the styles of art world masters to paint Blue Dogs. Like most school districts in America today, the school operates without any funding for the arts. Thanks to an active P.T.A. and a dynamic, dedicated art teacher, however, these students study great artists from Modigliani to Nevelson and, to our astonishment, use George Rodrigue's Blue Dog to do it.

We receive thousands of class projects annually, piled high for years in our dining room and now uploaded online in our student art gallery for all to enjoy. These come from Japan, New Zealand, Germany, and every state in the U.S.

Yet George winces when I compare him to Picasso, the school-wide artist in my day, the 1970s. We studied Picasso because he was accessible, like George, appealing to students of all ages. Still working in his studio, Picasso wasn't yet mythic like Michelangelo or Monet, and the idea of his existence made the art world real.

"What I would have given," I told students in Valencia, California, "to see Picasso at work. And yet George Rodrigue paints here for you and shares his story."

Admittedly, we visited Southern California on an unrelated personal mission. It was our foundation that suggested, since we would be in the area, that we investigate this school-wide arts program, nearly nine hundred students painting Blue Dogs in the styles of other great artists. They devoted their year to this project, and their preparation and welcome was unprecedented. They knew everything about George Rodrigue, his Landscapes, Cajuns, and Blue Dogs, so that their anticipation fed ours, intensifying as we arrived, greeted by students, teachers, community leaders, journalists, and large-scale class projects constructed on linoleum squares.

The Blue Dog has always had a life of its own. Museums from Memphis to Frankfurt continue to elevate the work beyond kitsch with exhibitions since the 1990s. Yet it was this school visit, our first in California, that impacted George more than any museum.

"I never once considered myself in league with artists like Miró and Mondrian, yet this school saw my art in these terms and spent a year connecting the Blue Dog to other artists and tying it to a higher level.

"After all this time, this idea and connection was a complete shock to me. It took a grammar school teacher and students to show me a new perspective. I think for the first time, I saw where this has gone and how, over the past thirty years, it's affected the art world and others."

We shared with the children during two lectures and

demonstrations, yet it was their questions and enthusiasm that made this school visit, more than others, such a success.

"It was obvious," says George, "that they studied both me and my art in context with these other artists and actually grasped what was going on."

As we shared the images, the young kids laughed with innocence. But during the later session, the older students asked serious questions about line, shape, color, and content. Our speeches are unscripted, and we begin by feeling the energy in the room and the mood of the audience. One child who watched both presentations told his mother,

"But this lecture is different than the other one!"

With only a loose plan, we share the art according to the level of interest. This varies not only among ages, but also among regions. In this Southern California school, for example, I focused on George's years at the Art Center College of Design, just thirty miles from North Park Elementary. I talked about his portrait of President Ronald Reagan, which hung for years in the Reagan Library in nearby Simi Valley. And, I shared the unique role that Californians played in the *Blue Dog* series.

"Up until then," says George, "I thought of it as the loup-garou. It was California that named it the Blue Dog. It was California that gave me the idea to try painting, after twenty-five years of Cajun folk-life, without the oak tree."

George also shared with the students their good fortune in studying the arts, something unavailable and unappreciated in many schools, even today. In 1950s New Iberia, art was non-existent in schools.

"I didn't have the opportunity to study and emulate great artists. I drew things I liked, and the first original painting I saw was my own. Sixty years later I still paint the way I felt as a child. I emphasize to students how important it is to retain that innocence, and that it's okay to create art in this way.

"The only art I saw growing up was what Vincent Price curated for Sears & Roebuck; yet it influenced me and remains with me today."

The school visits and our work with the George Rodrigue Foundation of the Arts (GRFA) represent both a legacy and new direction for George and the Blue Dog. One would think that the growing museum attention would spark this momentum, yet the children are the future, and they are far more important.

"Usually we visit schools to teach," says George. "This time, however, the school taught us. It's the kids who bridge the art. To be studied by a child is the best way to connect with the future and is more important than hanging on the walls with great masters. It took a grammar school teacher and students to help me see this perspective. It gave both me and Wendy a completely different view and impact, and maybe even a new beginning."

Chapter 10

I'm Thinking about the Road

Since 1993, George Rodrigue and I cross the country in our truck once each year. We explore the Gulf South, Texas, and New Mexico, sharing stories, making memories, and getting to know each other better.

Paintin' Shrimp Boats
and Pickin' Crabs

Shrimp boats is a-comin', there's dancin' tonight![x]

After many months indoors, George Rodrigue and I ease cautiously yet eagerly this Fall 2012 into adventure. Here in south Louisiana, diversion awaits in exploring small towns, riding an airboat, or walking on the nearest levee. Our last adventure, some six months ago, took us past Lafayette to the city of Abbeville, where we followed nostalgia, visiting family in New Iberia and photographing shrimp boats in Delcambre.

George longed to revisit the boats he painted as a young man, his first paintings upon his return from art school, now misplaced and mostly forgotten, superseded by the Rodrigue oaks that followed close behind.

"Anytime my mama cooked shrimp, we didn't just visit the grocery store," explains George. "Instead we rode thir-ty minutes from New Iberia to Delcambre. At the time,

347

there were three or four processing plants on the docks, including the Dooley's, friends of our family. My mother refused to buy frozen shrimp. It had to be fresh, straight off of the boat.

"When I returned from California and art school in 1967 and decided to paint Louisiana, my first idea was to paint the shrimp boats. I photographed the docked boats at Delcambre. There were hundreds of them, but today only a handful remain."

"I set up a dark room in a small closet at my mother's house in New Iberia, where I developed the black-and-white film myself, making 8 x 10 photos of the boats. I used the pictures to paint watercolors of the shrimping industry."

Last weekend we again traced old ground, but this time towards the crabbing industry and Pierre Part, Louisiana, now famous as the home of Troy Landry and *Swamp People*. More than twenty years since his last visit, George was curious about any changes brought on by the History Channel's popular show.

Instead we found a tiny town, unchanged except, exclaimed George, "Where are the restaurants?!" as we circled the lake and drove the main drag five times dreaming of fresh seafood. At last we spotted Landry's, its only visible sign . . . well . . . invisible.

While pickin' crabs, George and I exchanged childhood stories. I recalled Granny's step-ins suspended from the clothesline by crab claws during New Orleans family reunions; Dad swimming into Choctawhatchee Bay (Fort Walton Beach, Florida) on a scavenger hunt for his crab trap, tied thirty feet from the dock and loaded with raw chicken and our soon-to-be dinner; and Great Aunt Lois from her trailer on the Tchoutacabouffa River (Biloxi, Mississippi) jumping in fear as I whispered behind her, "Help me, help me" (à la *The Fly*), channeling the squirming crabs as she dropped them into the boiling water.

"Those crabs are confounding!" exclaimed my Memphis friend Jan after seeing our photos. "I never understood how to eat those things."

Surprised by her comments, I thought about the differences between areas of the South, so often lumped together as one stereotype by the national press. I grew up in the Florida Panhandle, and we consider ourselves the Deep South, akin to Alabama and Georgia, as though Disney World and Key West belong to a different state. History favors Virginia as the true South, but any Gulf state local shakes their head with skepticism. I didn't think of New Orleans as the South until I moved here. The accent may be more Brooklyn than drawl, but one ride past the plantations along River Road corrects the illusion. And southwest Louisiana is a different place altogether.

"I only ate crabs once as a kid," explained George. "I went with my aunts to Pecan Island, where we walked in the water, feeling the crabs with our feet."

"Barefoot?!" I exclaimed.

"I wore my tennis shoes. But my old aunts, they were tough, and they walked barefoot, collecting the crabs for that night's feast."

Wendy Rodrigue

At our house today we forego crawfish, not because we don't love them, but because George is allergic. Yet one of my best childhood memories is awaiting the Grela Parade on Mardi Gras Day in Gretna, eating crawfish from a plastic trashcan on the curb by 9:00 a.m.

The old "Help me" scene with Great Aunt Lois still haunts me, so you won't find crabs scratching the underside of my gumbo pot's lid. Boiled shrimp, however, is a staple at our house, as it was during my childhood when my mother, sister, and I visited the boats at the Destin Wharf.

Today George and I buy from area shrimp boats when possible or, in a pinch, from Rouses, a wondrous dream of home-grown Louisiana seafood, sausage, seasonings and, because we southerners simply can't help ourselves, nostalgia.

* Jo Stafford, "Shrimp Boats," 1951.

The American Indian
in Louisiana

As George and I explored ancient Indian mounds in northeast Louisiana, the sun in my eyes and warm, wind-blown hair in my face, I accidentally turned to an old page in my notebook covered with scribbles from an earlier adventure. Unaware of my mistake, I wrote,

"Each ridge 4-6 ft high when built, 50 ft across top, 100 ft in between. Imagine without trees but with huts."

I didn't notice until later that alongside my notes above appear the words, "abstractions of American Modernism," referring to artist Georgia O'Keeffe, and yet somehow fitting regarding these patterned, evenly spaced ridges and oddly shaped, unexplainable man-made hills, the largest spanning seven hundred feet across and seventy-two feet in the air.

Wendy Rodrigue

Our guide explained the area in detail, predicating her information with phrases like, "We think . . . ," "Archeologists surmise . . . ," and "We don't know for sure, but . . . ."

"Poverty Point archaeology," writes anthropologist Jon L. Gibson, "consists of a few facts, lots of interpretations, and much that is not known."

Indeed the site, named for a nineteenth-century nearby farm and spreading one hundred miles on Bayou Macon in the Mississippi River Delta, surprises in a state so flat that in the 1930s the New Orleans Audubon Zoo constructed a large mound of dirt to "show the children of New Orleans what a hill looks like" (from the zoo's website, describing "Monkey Hill.")

Throughout our tour, George recalled his lifelong fascination with the American Indian. In 1960 he won 1st place in the Social Science category at the Catholic High Science Fair in New Iberia. He also won 1st place at the district science rally in Lafayette and 3rd place at the state rally in Alexandria.

His project, "Indian Tribes of 1650," focused on the American Indian culture before the influence of the white man. A large U.S. map shows the location of tribes before any imposed migration caused by European settlers. He illustrated similarities and differences in housing, clothing, and food-gathering between Native Americans within varying parts of the country.

"My skill in drawing and painting had a lot to do with the success of my project," recalls George. "I expanded the display at each level. By the time I reached State, it was four times larger than when I started.

"I was the only student from New Iberia in 1960 to win an award at state level. Along with my popular monster paintings and my achievement of Eagle Scout, it's one of the best moments of my high school years.

"Twenty-five years later I revisited the Native American culture on my canvas when I traveled regularly to New

Mexico. By the mid-1980s the Cajun food craze reached Santa Fe, and I met Rosalea Murphy of the Pink Adobe Restaurant, who was originally from New Orleans. She gave me a show, and I filled it with paintings of the American Indian but in the same style as my paintings of Cajun folk life."

It's easy, I thought to myself as George reminisced, to understand why the Native Americans chose Poverty Point as their home for seven hundred years. Although the modern world, such as it is in rural, mid-state Louisiana, drove out or killed the once-abundant animals, this is indeed God's country, with wildflowers, lush grass, flowing water, shade, sun, and breeze.

"These Indians had it made," commented George, recalling our Grand Canyon camping trip. "Think of the Anasazi living within caves hundreds of feet above the ground and trapped each winter by the snow."

"Use your imagination," urged our Poverty Point guide. So we pictured pyramid-like structures made of earth rather than stone, the stage for ceremonies, and a focal point for people living in semi-circles around the base of the largest mass. Our imagination expanded, as we learned that the oldest mound in this area of Louisiana dates to 3900 B.C., some 1,500 years before the Egyptians built the pyramids at Giza!

According to archaeologists, 23,000 people lived at Poverty Point in 1300 B.C. during the height of its culture, the same period King Tutankhamun ruled Egypt. They hunted animals, wove baskets, and hauled dirt, some mounds requiring the equivalent of 16,000 dump truck loads, or 10-12 million baskets-full. The unnamed American Indian tribe lived atop the concentric ridges, affording drainage and order for their thatched huts. Bayou Macon was a lake at this time, and the Mississippi River flowed only three miles away.

Rich with artifacts, the site boasts arrowheads, pottery shards, tools, jewelry, and evidence of baskets, as well as rocks carved with figures and animal designs, usually birds and foxes. Anthropologists believe the Indians traded baskets for stone with their contemporaries in the West. Unlike the tombs within the Egyptian pyramids, the mounds at Poverty Point reveal no ancient human remains, indicating instead cremation. The larger mounds were probably built for ceremonial use.

Experts claim that this organized and rooted society was highly unusual for the hunter-gatherers (a term I had not heard since grade school). They built their mounds with determination and skill, packing the dirt in layers so that today, 3,500 years of erosion later, we're left with an anomaly: Louisiana's Hill Country.

Eventually these original Americans adopted *us*, fighting for a "new" country, the place they already called home and revered as sacred for thousands of years. They created a legacy not only worth studying, but also worth visiting. On our road trip to northeast Louisiana, the area between Rayville and Tallulah, we gained a new appreciation for America's history and Louisiana's important role in preserving the story of our ancient world.

Sources:

Jon L. Gibson, *The Ancient Mounds of Poverty Point: Place of Rings* (University Press of Florida, 2001).

"Poverty Point: National Monument Louisiana," U.S. National Park Service, http://www.nps.gov.

Remembering Old Biloxi

Most towns have a nearby escape, the place everyone travels on a beautiful weekend. For south Louisiana, Biloxi is our destination.

Plagued by Gulf storms and famous for Hurricane Camille long before Katrina, Biloxi, a Louisiana tourist destination since the eighteenth century, also boasts grand and historic southern homes, a charming old town, and, these days, plenty of high-rise casinos, fine restaurants, and museums.

George's family visited Biloxi, Mississippi, often in the 1950s, usually for a week at the Alamo Plaza Courts, located on the beach. They caravanned to the Mississippi Gulf Coast from New Iberia, Louisiana, along Old Hwy 90, a two lane road sprinkled with cafés and gas stations. The adventures included a lunch stop outside of Gulfport, where on one afternoon they pulled into the parking lot just as a stretch black limousine pulled out. Inside the café, their giddy waitress greeted them with a napkin in hand, the ink still drying on the scrawled signature: "Elvis Presley."

My mother-in-law told a story of one summer when, as she swam at the Biloxi beach, she recognized the Iberia Parish priest on the shore:

"Oh, no!" she exclaimed. "It's Father Richard!" (pronounced "Ree-shard")

Marie Rodrigue remained up to her neck in the Gulf waters for four hours rather than face the clergyman in a bathing suit.

Twenty years later I vacationed several times each year during the 1970s and 1980s with my family on the Tchoutacabouffa River (pronounced "Choo-tu-ku-buff-a," with the u's and a's all short), an inland area of Biloxi, a beautiful city full of bayous and oaks and people epitomizing southern hospitality. Great Aunt Lois cared for the family home, first destroyed by Camille in 1969, then rebuilt in the early 1970s, and replaced around 1980 with a trailer, which was all we really needed, because we lived outside.

We drove from Fort Walton Beach, Florida, meeting our New Orleans relatives for weekends of mischief. From the dock we caught catfish during the day and snakes after dark. One year I even reeled in my baby stroller, which had washed along with the rest of the house into the river during Hurricane Camille.

This was the same water where we swam and innertubed, as though the bayou magically rid itself of garfish and alligators during the hot afternoons. With catfish or moccasins writhing at the ends of our cane poles, we screamed for Aunt Lois, who at age seventy-five ran to the dock with a cleaver and either cleaned the fish or decapitated the snakes, stocking our bait for round two.

We caught dinner in the crab traps, snapped beans and shelled pecans during thunderstorms, collected eggs from the hen house, raced four wheelers and mopeds through the surrounding swamps, and played bourré in the evenings on the back porch.

We stayed in the woods and on the river, already spoiled with the beach back home. But the beaches in Biloxi are beautiful, just as pretty as the Emerald Coast, with white sands and long clean stretches of paradise.

I loved Biloxi so much that I saved my babysitting money for the Greyhound Bus from Fort Walton Beach, a six-hour ride in those days, to spend two nights with Great Aunt Lois in between family vacations. I slept next to her in that trailer, the glowing light of Dürer's praying hands, copied in plastic and holding a nightlight, on one side and of Aunt Lois's cigarette on the other, dangling from her mouth as she snored, until it died in a heap within the ashtray balanced on her chest, all the while my faith placed in those hands, protecting us from a fire.

The closest I got to the beach on those trips was Mr. Glenn's downtown diner, where I bussed tables most mornings. Aunt Lois's old friend flipped omelets and burgers as he spit his chewing tobacco into the empty baked beans can tied around his neck. At age twelve, I understood the resplendence of local characters, I played a mean game of cards, and I had change in my pocket. Life was good.

Today we visit Biloxi at least once every few months. We drive along the coast and marvel at the pristine and empty beaches; we try to remember which historic home stood on which slab before Katrina washed them away in 2005, even though many survived some one hundred fifty years previous, including through the hurricane benchmark, Camille.

We hang out at the bar at Mary Mahoney's and visit with her son Bobby about watermarks, politics, and the good ol' days, before enjoying a fine Creole dinner on par with Antoine's, followed by slot machines and a show at Beau Rivage.

Like everything in life, our experience has changed. But Biloxi is still a wonderful place, a town that jogs memories and makes new ones on every visit. The people remain some of the nicest anywhere, and even today, though they're all long dead, I have no trouble imagining Elvis just leaving the Waffle House, Mr. Glenn wiping his hands on his apron, and Great Aunt Lois ringing the dinner bell for fried okra and cornbread.

Crossing West Texas

You just can't live in Texas unless you've got a lot of soul.
–Waylon Jennings

I believe the hype: Texas is bigger and better than anyplace else. As we drive I-10 and listen to "Willie's Place" on SiriusXM Radio, I enjoy the long stretches of flat land and occasional hills, the seemingly abandoned towns, and the (today) raging dry creek beds. I'm reminded of Texas pride, about people who observe,

"There is no denying that Lubbock is a wonderful town. That's where Buddy Holly went to see Elvis!"*

I've got Texas in my blood. My grandparents are originally from Fort Worth, and Grandma Helen, shocked at my reluctance to attend LSU, reconsidered her support provided I choose a school "in San Antone," which I did.

It's a state of big dreams and even bigger ideas, where my relatives, although dirt poor, named their children after American Presidents: Thomas Jefferson McClanahan, John Adams McClanahan, and George Washington McClanahan. They lie alongside each other in the tiny town of Stephenville, their important names chiseled on their tombstones to impress future generations.

George and I drive across Texas at least once, usually twice, each year, taking one of two routes with occasional detours if time permits. This week we took the southern route, a bit regretful to my mind (although I didn't tell George), knowing we would miss the buried Cadillacs, the Big Texan, and the scent of cattle in Amarillo, along with the junk shops and grain silos west of Wichita Falls in Vernon, Quanah, and Childress, their steel structures standing like a Bernd and Hilla Becher sight-seeing tour, stark and outlined against the moody Texas sky.

Those photos are for another day, however, because today we traveled George's favorite route, from Houston to San Antonio to that pivotal (to his mind) Texas town located deep in the heart of nowhere: Fort Stockton.

In the twenty summers that I've traveled across the country with George Rodrigue, I've probably spent more time than most American adventurers (truckers aside) with Fort Stockton as the long-distance driver's nirvana.

He speaks about it as though it's a desired, dreamy destination, all because it's where two highways meet, where our route turns north (so that we by-pass El Paso and, with as much regret, Van Horn—a frequent stop on our northern route), where the cafes and motels never change, and most of all, because he likes to hear himself say it:

"Tomorrow we'll get to Fort Stockton"; or "Let's stop for gas in Fort Stockton"; or, "Remember that diner across from the old motel in Fort Stockton?"

People in Texas can't imagine why anyone would live outside of "the accommodating high 90s," combined with the wafting smell of cattle. A homegrown Texan makes a person feel silly for preferring Honolulu over Kerrville, and they make fun of their own cities with an endearment reserved for locals:

"It's so dry in Lubbock that the trees were chasing the dogs around."*

George and I tell Texas stories in our truck. I reminisce about chasing tumbleweeds with my college roommate Debbie and her dad on the outskirts of El Paso.

The Other Side of the Painting

"It was the first time I'd ever seen one! We abandoned the car in the middle of the street and ran after a mass of twigs into the desert."

George talks of his long drives on Route 66 back from art school in Los Angeles. He relives the dramatic visual change from Texas's big sky to Louisiana's tiny horizon, an observation that shaped his landscape approach, resulting in the Rodrigue oaks.

We visit Dairy Queen for coconut and pineapple blizzards, which we slurp to the music of our favorite Texan, Waylon Jennings, sending us on another tangent, as we recall the day he died. Distraught at the news, we hid ourselves and our sadness from our houseful of company. And in the laundry room amidst piles of separated clothes, we danced silently and slowly, before returning to our guests as though everything was fine:

"Amanda, light of my life.

Fate should have made you a gentleman's wife."

As we approached Santa Fe early this evening, after twenty hours on the road, the glowing light of our favorite time of day sent long, thin shadows from the short, fat pinon pines, checkering the red and green hills against the bluest sky in America.

We'll stay in Santa Fe for three nights, visiting friends and making memories, followed by a lengthy stay near Four Corners. Tonight, although exhausted, we tune in once again to "Willie's Place" for a riveting special report, one they've touted for the past two days:

"Runaway Truck Ramps: Are They Doing Their Job Correctly?"

Happy Trails.

* Bill Mack, "Willie's Place," SiriusXM Radio.

Rosalea Murphy
and *Evergreen Lake*

"She hates women."

That's the first thing George told me about Rosalea Murphy. He met her thirty years ago in Santa Fe, New Mexico, at a gallery show of his Cajun paintings. They became close friends, and through her he met a slew of artists, actors, and musicians, nearly all of them men. However, she also reluctantly introduced him to the artist Georgia O'Keeffe and by accident, when she left him alone at the bar one afternoon, to a young Indian woman named Evergreen Lake.

Our first Santa Fe visit together was in 1994. We had dated for just over a year, and George shared with me his American haunts on a cross-country drive that summer, the start of an annual tradition. We walked into the

Dragon Room Bar at the Pink Adobe early on a weekday afternoon. The room was empty except for a small woman at a round wooden table painted with dragons, planets, and roosters.

Sitting on the bench on either side of her were two large dogs, Gina Lollobrigida and Don Juan, drinking from blue glass bowls bearing their names. The accomplished flamenco guitarist Ruben Romero serenaded the trio from a barstool a few feet away.

Seeing George, Rosalea swooned. Immediately she was full of questions about his Casanova friend and usual travel companion who, unknown to us, mailed her love letters:

"Where is Romain? Does he ask for me?"

Don Juan moved closer to Gina so that George could sit closer to Rosalea. I stood and waited.

"Rosalea, this is Wendy," said George.

She ignored his introduction, and she ignored me, and I got the feeling that my presence represented Romain's absence and so, before I said hello, I was the enemy.

Fortunately, a lifetime with an eccentric mother prepared me, and I stood mesmerized by this tiny person with the enormous presence. At age eighty-two, her eyes shone and her hair, died jet black, hung around her shoulders. She dressed like a teenage country music star, in black velvet leggings, a hot pink blouse, a four-inch silver *R* hanging from one ear and an *M* from the other and, most impressive, hand-tooled and painted Falconhead cowboy boots.

We walked across the courtyard to the Pink Adobe restaurant housed in a three hundred-year-old adobe structure. In the 1940s Rosalea moved to Santa Fe from her hometown, New Orleans, and sold hamburgers from a vending cart on the street (the Old Santa Fe Trail), using the money she made at lunch to purchase the meat for dinner. Within a few years she bought the building and opened her own restaurant, the Pink Adobe, where she became famous for her gypsy stew, chicken enchiladas, and apple pie.

She also became famous for her paintings, filling the restaurant and bar with her tables and canvases.

When George stepped away, I dared to speak, asking her about the painting hanging above her head. She glanced at the art:

"My friend Larry Hagman (as in *I Dream of Jeannie* and *Dallas*) told me a joke that was so funny, I had to paint it."

"What was the joke?" I asked.

She looked me in the eye for the first time and said, as though testing me,

"What do you get when you cross an owl with a rooster?"

I stared back, knowing we connected as she delivered the punch line,

"A cock that stays up all night."

What looked like a price tag hung from the painting.

"Is it for sale?"

"Yes."

George returned to the table, surprised to find us laughing and exchanging stories like old friends. I almost lost her that same night, however, when I asked about O'Keeffe. Rosalea disliked both the artist and her paintings, never understanding why anyone would care about her flowers and skulls (as opposed to dragons and roosters, I suppose). She, along with other notables, frequented the Dragon Room bar. Rosalea charmed the presidents and male actors, but it's a wonder that women still visited the place. She claimed to have thrown O'Keeffe and others out on numerous occasions for no reason other than that she hated them—or, more likely, because they grabbed a passing man's attention.

George told me later that he too almost lost Rosalea, when he approached Evergreen Lake at the Dragon Room during a visit in 1985, arranging to photograph her the following day. He admired a particular look in this beautiful young Indian woman, and although they never met again (out of respect for Rosalea), he used the photographs from that afternoon in dozens of paintings over the years. She became for him another Evangeline or Jolie Blonde and appears in his work not only as herself, a Native American woman, but also as a Cajun traiteur, or healer. He also incorporated her into the *Blue Dog* series.

As I carried my rooster and owl painting down the street and towards our hotel, I enjoyed delirious success. George, however, barely believed this conquest and tried to reimburse me the $400 for the painting.

Over the years we grew close to Rosalea. Through her we met and became friends with several artists, including Armand Lara and Doug Magnus, as well as Scott Wayne Emmerich of Falconhead boots. It was special for me to witness these creative pow-wows, as Rosalea and her men encouraged each other in the arts. Eventually George and Doug collaborated on a collection of Blue Dog jewelry.

Beginning in 1995 we stayed for a week each summer in Rosalea's apartment above the Pink Adobe, where we awoke to purple bedding, pink walls, and five-foot sunflowers, complementing the view of the Church of San Miguel (1610), the oldest church structure in America, located across the street from the restaurant. If we happened to be in town on a Wednesday, we joined Rosalea and her merry bunch in the apartment for poker. It was then that I learned that I wasn't the only woman in her life. As long as the men fawned on her first and the women understood their place, they were welcome. Her family, namely her daughter and granddaughter, were exceptions to this understanding, and they enjoyed her sustaining devotion and pride regardless of any unstated rules for the rest of us. Rosalea's daughter, Priscilla Hoback, is also an artist. George and I especially enjoy her works in clay and treasure several pieces within our home.

Rosalea Murphy died in 2000. She was buried wearing her "R" and "M" earrings, made by Doug Magnus, along with her custom made Scott Wayne boots. George and I struggle to visit the Pink Adobe, often avoiding it, because the popular restaurant and bar, now run by her grandson and his family, seems empty without Rosalea and her dogs. We pay tribute to her with the paintings in our collection, as well as a prized painted table and large pots of sunflowers.

On those rare occasions that we do stop into the Dragon Room and visit with Rosalea's men, I remember my place, hanging back a bit, watching these talented artists as they visit about old times, current projects, and especially the strong woman who loved them and brought them together.

Cloud Illusions

I watched the sunrise this morning over New Mexico from the window of our adobe hotel room in downtown Santa Fe. The storms skirted us all week, and the clouds enhance the orange light as it stretches from behind the fugacious masses, so unlike the clouds in a Rodrigue painting.

I'm reminded instead of the German romantic artist Caspar David Friedrich (1774-1840) and the large-scale library book that my conscience should have purchased during college. I dog-eared the corners and stained the pages with my inky fingerprints, as I rested between Art History papers, returning to the dreamy paintings repeatedly.

Like this week's atmospheric, transitory skies, the Friedrich paintings awakened my pensiveness, that side of me revealed as a young girl when, unable to sleep, I stood on the balcony off of my room, listened to the Gulf waves, and sang to the air,

> "Bows and flows of angel hair
> And ice cream castles in the air"*

"How do you paint clouds like that? . . ." I asked George, as we drove from Flagstaff, Arizona, to Gallup, New Mexico. Behind us the darkness obscured the sunset so that the light jumped over the thunderclouds, causing an interesting sky in the East.

"It's tricky," he said. "You have to figure out the layers first. You paint the entire canvas with the color of the farthest clouds, so that the sky itself becomes a cloud. That's your foundation."

"Why didn't you paint clouds in your Cajun paintings?" I asked him.

"There was no room," he replied.

I knew immediately what he meant. Once he pushed the oak tree to the front of the canvas, the sky was full, and clouds would have muddied the composition. With the Blue Dog paintings, however, George paints clouds in the same way he paints flowers, with little connection to the real world. His clouds are simple and stylized, so that no element of the painting holds more weight than another.

An homage to Matisse (1869-1954), George's cloud-style is veritable wallpaper, replacing the traditional subject, foreground, and background with a controlled pattern. Nothing is random, and there is no hint of reality. It's as though the clouds are clip-art, cut out and glued onto the sky with perfect spacing. Unlike real clouds, there is no potential for movement or change.

Whether Rodrigue's Blue Dog or Matisse's vase of flowers, the same can be said for every shape in the painting. No element, nor the space between the elements, is more important than any other. Because of the patterns and strong colors, George's clouds are far removed from the ethereal quality of a real sky. As an artist, his canvas changes with his moods, and these cloud paintings, twenty or so images between 1999 and 2001, have an almost child-like joy about them, while at the same time a studied control.

How different from his moody landscapes of the 1970s, the fragmented Blue Dogs of post-Katrina, and the mysticism of *Bodies*, where the control, although still important, is subjugated to the concept or symbolism of the overall work.

We recognize these mood changes within our own lives, and George is not the first artist to associate clouds with our transitory existence and emotions.

"So many things I would have done

But clouds got in my way"*

With this essay in mind, George and I stared at the sky this week. We thought aloud about the wonders of nature and the challenges of painting it. We pulled off of the road and studied the sky's patterns and colors. We thought about the early Spanish settlers crossing these prairies for the first time. We vowed to reread together *Death Comes for the Archbishop* (Willa Cather, 1927) before our return visit this winter.

And we reminisced: George talked about his early years in Santa Fe and the artist friends awaiting his visit. And I recalled my childhood, standing on the balcony on Okaloosa Island, dreaming about my future and, even at a young age, the meaning of life and relationships.

* Joni Mitchell, "Both Sides Now," 1967. (written in March of 1967, the same month and year of my birth, along with many of my Fort Walton Beach High School classmates: "It's life's illusions I recall; I really don't know life at all.")

Turquoise Hill

Crossing America, whether by sky or highway, affords views of mines of many kinds, massive holes in the ground, gigantic pits surrounded by bulldozers and dump trucks, the equipment of the modern mining operation.

Yet this is not the case within Turquoise Hill, the ancient Cerrillos mines near Santa Fe, New Mexico, where over millions of years water trickled downward through the jagged plates or perhaps upward from hot springs. The moisture transformed the copper and iron into the most beautiful blue, a Tiffany blue, a rock and its land sought after more than one thousand years ago by the Anasazi Indians, then by the Spanish, by the American Turquoise Company (since 1880, with connections to Tiffany & Company), by music video and movie producers, and all along by the curious and the enchanted, unable to resist this unique color or the earth that created it.

Wendy Rodrigue

Since 1988 artist-jeweler Douglas Magnus has owned and protected several of these mines. They sit on private property, accessible by his invitation and escort until upon his death and according to his instruction, they pass to the Archeological Conservancy, a non-profit organization "dedicated to acquiring and preserving the best of our nation's remaining archaeological sites." Visiting Santa Fe this week, George and I enjoyed a tour deep within a mine, as well as its blanket-like terrain, hills that disguise the buried treasure so well that most locals remain unaware of its existence, despite the fact that the mines and their stones lie scattered in plain view. We spent hours roaming these hills, occasionally reminding each other of the vista, forcing our gaze from the Tiffany blue rocks crunching beneath our boots.

According to Magnus, the scientists visiting this area know little of its origins. Interested in the exploration of oil and gas, most have but a general knowledge of the land's geological formations, and they wonder, no different than the rest of us, at the colored red, yellow, and blue rocks.

Unsurprisingly, this same veneration attracts Hollywood. Stephen Spielberg and Ron Howard both made movies on this hill, and the mines serve as sets for dozens of actors, including Russell Crowe and Christian Bale for the movie *3:10 to Yuma*, along with Tobey Maguire and Sam Shepard for *Brothers*.

It was the Anasazi Indians, however, that first recognized the magic of Turquoise Hill. Without bulldozers or drills, they smashed the rocks and formed deep mines using hand-made stone mauls. They wove the blue Cerrillos pebbles into animal hides and hair, creating ceremonial clothing, jewelry, and other heirlooms, items so important to their culture that the mines today hold special significance to their descendants, the Pueblo Indians. Sensitive to this heritage, Magnus opens the mines to the Santo Domingo tribe, the Kiua, who honor these sacred hills.

The Other Side of the Painting

Others, too, revere this area, outsiders who encounter it not just in person, but also within their soul. Georgia O'Keeffe (1887-1986) first visited New Mexico in 1929 and, although not a native, made the land her own, a place eventually nicknamed "O'Keeffe Country." It was her paintings of this area that transformed her reputation in New York. She already grasped the increasingly popular abstract shapes of Modern Art, and she adapted these to the New Mexico high desert, painting the doorway of her adobe house or the shape of the sky as seen through the empty eye socket of a cow's skull.

And yet she denied the abstraction. She painted what she saw using her inherent ability to understand the element of shapes. According to Hunter Drohojowska-Philp's O'Keeffe biography *Full Bloom*, as a student O'Keeffe grasped concepts and designs over fundamentals such as figure drawing. Perhaps this was a blessing. By her own account, she struggled with the specific renderings; however, from the beginning she saw the shapes and colors of New Mexico with clarity.

> I like it better here than anyplace I have ever been. I had such a wonderful walk up the arroyo bed of a wide valley lined on both sides with high pink hills—a sort of waving ripple along the tops—a few cedar and pinon trees—earth ranging from pink through red to deep purple with streaks of green in it. At the head of the arroyo, the very high cliffs—fantastic shapes—it is a beautiful world—There is something clean about a world like that—it is like walking across new snow.
> –Georgia O'Keeffe

(Without judgment, I consider the opposite: Norman Rockwell, an artist who missed abstraction because he dealt with the exact reproduction of the scene before him. He filled his canvas with people and objects rather than deal with the shapes left behind.)

We visited the Georgia O'Keeffe Museum, as we have

many times in the past. The current exhibition *O'Keeffiana: Art & Art Materials* focuses on her art supplies, as well as inspirational materials such as the rocks and bones she collected from the hills surrounding her homes at Ghost Ranch and Abiquiu, New Mexico.

For some, O'Keeffe is a hit-or-miss artist. In truth, I enjoy many of her paintings better as reproduced in a book as opposed to in person. Her cloud paintings, in particular, move me, and it is rare that I fly in a plane and not think of her large patterned compositions, so specific within a book and yet seemingly haphazard in person, as though she barely had time or material to cover the raw canvas and paint the (by definition) fleeting shapes.

Artist and restaurateur Rosalea Murphy told me that Georgia O'Keeffe visited her bar, the Dragon Room. The two were not close friends, holding different ideas about art, men, and food. Yet their rivalry was an interesting one, as they watched each other's careers and shared a love for their adopted home.

Similar in its adobe architecture to the Church of Saint Francis of Assisi in Ranchos de Taos, a structure reproduced numerous times by O'Keeffe in paintings, perhaps the San Miguel Mission, the oldest church in America, and directly across the street from the Pink Adobe, lured the famous artist to the bar, a room covered with Murphy's paintings of roosters and dragons. The church and Dragon Room are sirens for many artists, no different than the Turquoise Hills for Doug Magnus and the Anasazi Indians, and no different than the intoxicating New Mexico package for me and George.

Tranquility from Chaos

I tell my generation that we were born during the darkest period in our long history. There is a big challenge and it is very unfortunate. But if there is a challenge then there is an opportunity to face it, an opportunity to demonstrate our will and our determination. So from that viewpoint I think that our generation is fortunate.
—His Holiness the Fourteenth Dalai Lama

This is a chaotic world. We seek solutions to calm us down, to ground us, whether the beach, a cocktail, or a mile-wide meteor crater, formed 50,000 years ago when a small space rock, disintegrating not quite fast enough, sped through our atmosphere at 26,000 mph, slamming into our planet and throwing millions of pounds of earth rock onto the surrounding terrain, twenty-six miles southwest of today's Winslow, Arizona. Somewhere in this story of a sudden and violent occurrence resulting in a tranquil, permanent symbol of our impermanence, lies a lesson.

Last week during a snowstorm, I planned a quiet afternoon in a hotel in Santa Fe, New Mexico, phoning room service for a cup of tea and extra firewood. Within half an hour, the panicked hotel employee, who failed to open the flue before striking the match, stood on a chair waving a towel at the screaming fire alarm; members of security, maintenance, and hotel management evacuated much of the third floor and descended into my no longer quiet space with walkie-talkies, fire extinguishers, and other equipment. Snow flurries and an icy wind joined the dense smoke in the room.

The phone rang.

"Get over here," said George, who explored the city in what we southerners call a blizzard. "It's the most unbelievable thing I've ever seen."

"Impossible!" I shouted between coughs and smoky tears before hanging up the phone.

Familiar with these summons, I assumed that whatever it was—the distant cousin from New Iberia, the killer jalapeño poppers, or the bronze statue of John Wayne— could wait. Nothing compared to the mess before me.

Perhaps the real chaos, the most dangerous discord, lies within our minds. It exists within a panicked room service waiter convinced of his termination, a panicked hotel manager anticipating guest complaints, and a panicked guest (me) taking blame for the accident with hopes of saving a man's job.

At last the room emptied of people. I poured myself a cup of lukewarm tea and awaited the fire department, on its way to replace the alarm.

Within minutes I heard a knock at the door.

"What the . . . ?" said my friend Barbara, openmouthed, as she entered the freezing, smoky room.

"No matter what it is, I'm not going," I groaned, curling up under the comforter. "Besides, I'm waiting for the fire department."

"But George says you have to come. It's Tibetan sand painting!"

A meteor hit my brain and the clutter dissipated. I grabbed my coat, earmuffs, wool hat, scarf, rubber soled boots, gloves, and mittens and headed into the storm, trudging ten blocks to view an ancient tradition.

George met me at the door:

"Listen, in case he asks, I told the guy over there, the one that speaks English, that you met the Dalai Lama."

Drowning once again in mental chaos, I stared at my husband:

"You lied . . . to a monk . . . about the Dalai Lama . . . and me? I can't go in! What will I say? I can't lie, much less to a holy man about the spiritual leader of his people. What possessed you?"

"It was easy," shrugged George. "It made him really happy!"

Hoping to see the painting, I assessed the situation. Barbara agreed to run interference with the monk.

Inside I watched the Drepung Loseling monks, life-long students of Buddhism and the alleviation of suffering, bend their backs over a sand painting five feet in diameter.

Using metal funnels called *chakpur*, the monks tap the sand, grain by grain, onto the intricate design, only to destroy it on New Year's Eve. They pour their picture into the Santa Fe River, where the waters disperse the compassion and love of a symbolic painting's peaceful creators throughout the world.

As I understand it, the bright-colored mandala represents the universe; its creation in sand and its inevitable destruction represent the impermanence of life.

With metaphor and basic teachings, whether we call it Buddhism or not, we have the opportunity to contemplate the impermanence of life through a mandala or a meteor's crater. We could embrace exercises in compassion, perhaps imagining that the thousands of people we pass at the airport or see at the Saints game are our brothers and sisters, all of whom we are pleased to see, with genuine concern for their welfare and happiness. We also could embrace the insults of others as an opportunity to explore kindness in the face of painful personal circumstances.

These methods are difficult. They are the lifelong challenges of Buddhist monks, the goal of their studies, and the reason for the genuine smiles on the faces of a displaced and persecuted people.

I too seek this goal, instructed by the awesomeness of a meteor and the simple example of a monk.

America the Beautiful

All men were made by the Great Spirit Chief. They are all brothers. –Chief Joseph

It was in a college class, "Religion and Social Issues," that I first read Dee Brown's *Bury My Heart at Wounded Knee* (1970), a story that sunk my sheltered self into a depression I had not known since reading half of *The Rise and Fall of the Third Reich* (William L. Shirer, 1960), a book my mother absconded from me at age fifteen when she noticed that I lost my smile.

I revisited *Bury My Heart* ten years ago when George and I viewed a related exhibit at the Buffalo Bill Historical Center in Cody, Wyoming. The book, along with the American crisis, came rushing back. George had never seen me in such a state, unable to grip my emotions for the guilt I felt from what my white-skinned ancestors perpetrated on the Native Americans.

Today I thought about it again as we crossed New

Mexico and northeastern Arizona, including the Navajo Nation and the Hopi Indian Reservation. On SeriusXM Radio's "Willie's Place," Dolly Parton sang "Color Me America: Red, White and Blue," as George and I drank in the colors of this land, iced with the same clouds Georgia O'Keeffe painted from Abiquiu, as she stood in a New Mexico desert.

I imagined the Hopi Chief standing on the edge of a mesa, summoned by a representative sent by the president of the United States:

"As far as you can see, this land is your land."

Indeed, the Hopi land is as far as the eye can see, finally fading into a hazy horizon. It could not be more endless if the pact was made on the coast of California as they stared across the Pacific.

Yet I cry for our Native Americans, the ones from my home area of northwest Florida "relocated" by an American hero, Andrew Jackson. They live in a beautiful, bountiful country, in trailers on either side of bumpy, broken roads, their only consolation the casinos, which may or may not help their plight. It's as though we threw them to the desert and forgot them, gave them land and said, "Now you're on your own," a near impossibility in this government-dependent, money-borrowing land of ours (and I mean *all of ours*).

George and I stopped at the Hubbell Trading Post, a national landmark within the Navajo Nation. A sign encouraged us to barter, but I couldn't bring myself to haggle with the striking merchant, his black hair shining and reaching below his waist, over the price of homemade bread-n-butter pickles, fig preserves, and habanero salsa.

On our drive I thought about the Indians buried in mass graves behind the Mission at San Juan Bautista (built 1797), a church they died building, a popular tourist destination for its architecture, gardens, and California history, a place George and I crash weddings and cart houseguests.

These are the beautiful people, the original American culture. How must it be for them to look at me, descended from a family that stole their land, standing in their Western sun, blonde, fair-skinned, holding a camera, and wearing their jewelry?

Although the buildings on the reservation look abandoned, all are occupied:

"I wonder how many of these people ever leave this place," I mused aloud.

"None of them," said George.

For me, the American West is marked by a mixture of the tragic and the stunning, of land that tells a story, with people in the smallest roles, consumed by the dust, the warm air, the American expanse, the soul of a true American people.

But crossing America, it's not only the Indians on my mind. On every drive, the closer we get to California, the more I recall another book, a story of American dreams and destiny, *The Grapes of Wrath* (John Steinbeck, 1939). I imagine first the pioneers, then the gold-miners, and finally those just seeking a better life picking peaches or tilling a field for garlic or strawberries.

I imagine these folks in their wagons crossing the same ridges we drive in our 70-mph, air-conditioned truck, facing a week within a valley and maybe more rounding a mountain. I imagine them not seeking a vacation home, wine tastings, and backyard barbeques, but rather shelter, a bath, and their next meal.

And this wasn't so long ago! The trading post we visited today within the Navajo Nation began with a couple of out buildings built by a man of Anglo and Spanish descent, John Lorenzo Hubbell in 1878. His descendants lived on the property and operated the business until 1967 when they transferred it to the National Historic Registry, which operates it today as a significant site in United

States history.

For the better part of our drive, George and I rode silent and sentimental, our voices muzzled by "the big picture." To myself, I try to pinpoint my mood. Why am I not happy for these people, the original Americans? I mean, shouldn't they be pleased living on this land that we gave them? At last I uncover the word for this churning in my chest.

Shame.

Yet the shame does not, cannot, overshadow my pride in my country. Nestled in the red rocks above the trailers, we see adobe churches shining like the medieval castles of Hessen. And we see land, more land than a city-dweller comprehends on earth, this thing we must protect, this thing that defines us just as much as our people and history.

And I remember that as the generations pass, we mature as a people. We're more conscious of the environment, of influences on our children, of a global society. Everything changes, maybe for the better and maybe not—but it does change. Here's a small example:

For several years George and I filled our truck on our cross-country drive with clay pots, many formed in the shapes of turtles or frogs, discovered along the way at road stands and junk shops. Finally abandoning this passion, to my horror George confessed his interest in taxidermy, and we traveled with assorted dead animals carefully arranged amidst our luggage.

I specifically recall the year of the Jackson Hole moose, disguised like trash in the bed of our bright red pick-up with hopes of averting thieves, but nevertheless requiring that we trade watch throughout the night at the window of our Motel 6 room (it wouldn't fit through the door). The same moose, now painted blue, was rescued from the burning Café Tee George in 1998 and hangs today over the Blue Dog Café entrance in Lafayette.

The Other Side of the Painting

I was too young and newly married to effectively protest this purchase, something George knows I would frown on today, aside from the occasional and, according to George, irresistible stuffed raccoon (oh, how I wish I were kidding).

But times and sentiments change, even for a near seventy-year-old otherwise stuck-in-his-ways Cajun. This trip, with the help of a good friend, we acquired two racks, both from animals that died in the wild, an elk for George and some sort of African deer-type skull for me—my first. I found it to be delicate and earthy, and I hung it in my office, joining my mother's painting of Stonehenge and a Native American flute, a treasured gift from my dad.

The point is that the animals did not die for these mounts (a fact that finally pleases George as much as it does me), and it is the sculpture of their bones that reminds us of not only the circle of life, but also the inter-relatedness of all beings, that philosophy that makes us not just Americans but members of the world's community.

We celebrate the Fourth of July not just because of a famous document and its resulting independence for all people in this country, but even more so because it is a sign of our swelling compassion and intelligence, superseding tragedies such as the displaced American Indians, the slavery of African Americans, and other horrific indiscretions.

This seed began with our independence, but we must celebrate this forward thinking, this diversity, and this land, not just on the Fourth of July, but every day.

> Listen! Ha! In the Frigid Land you repose, O Blue Dog. O now you have swiftly drawn to hearken. O great [spirit], you never fail in anything. O appear and draw near running, for your prey never escapes. You have settled a very small part of it far off there at the end of the earth.*

*A Cherokee prayer, shared by Edgar Bounds.

Chapter 11

Breathe in "Who" Breathe out "Dat"

The more we travel, the more George and I appreciate the unique city of New Orleans. "We're leaving until we miss it again," we say before every journey. And, whether following a month or a year on the road, we return, always, home.

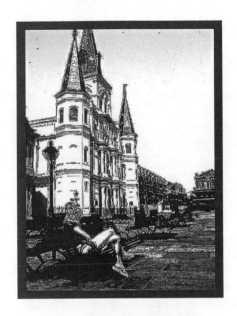

For New Orleans

From the back porch of our Faubourg Marigny home, I see the west bank of the Mississippi River through the branches of our enormous tree, a live oak that Mr. Foche probably nurtured himself when he built this house in 1835.

God only knows what the tree has endured. Nicholas Foche, a free man of color from Jamaica, arrived long before the levees. That means that the Mississippi River rushed periodically through the ground floor, from the back door to the front. The water settled at times, I know it did. It delivered alligators, snakes, and lots and LOTS of rats, and it bred millions of mosquitoes, spreading fever, disease, and death throughout this, a great American city.

As a series, I don't think *Tremé* (based on a neighborhood only a few blocks from ours) is fabulous, but on the other hand, the fact that I find it difficult to watch may be a testament to its insight. I recall the pilot as a misrepresentation, even a joke, on behalf of the *Tremé* writers to suggest restaurants and groceries and water bills and newly painted houses and dumpsters and taxis (and Elvis Costello and a limousine!) and Zapp's potato chips and safe neighborhoods, and people who feel like singing— all just three months after the storm.

And yet right this second, six years to the day after George Rodrigue and I (the oh-so-fortunate) sat in a hotel room in Houston and watched on television as our city drowned, I sit on our 175-year-old porch and watch the tops of the ships go by. I see tourists wave to the shore of the river that made Louisiana the key state in Napoleon's sale of 828,000 square miles of this country, and I watch our oak tree, now held together by steel wires and sprouting strong, near floating, swaying, and shaking its branches to the beat of New Orleans. Three months after or six years after—I guess it doesn't much matter.

We were the lucky ones, out of our house for only nine months, no flooding. But much of the old asbestos roof blew off, leaving our house wet, moldy, uninhabitable, and yet nothing to complain about. I'm ashamed, but nevertheless admit, that as we stayed with our former neighbors in Lafayette, George and I worried about our tree:

"What should we do? How can we save it?"

We couldn't ask for help. It's a tree!

Through the kindness of a police officer we were allowed into New Orleans three days before Hurricane Rita struck. We saw an abandoned city, a twilight zone, not a car, not a person, not a bird, not a sound, nothing. We walked through an empty and immaculate Jackson Square, perhaps the only place in New Orleans devoid of debris, the backdrop of our president's televised speech.

We found our back door wide open and our house remarkably, shockingly, without vandalism. In the 100-degree heat we climbed up and down the Creole townhouse's three flights removing paintings.

You see, we did not evacuate, but rather, by happenstance, were in Houston for an exhibition. Evacuation differs from weekend travel. Weekend travel is cocktail

dresses, bathing suits, and make-up. Evacuation, however, is paintings and photo albums and whatever that last little thing is that one dreams of having on a deserted island.

These are the things we grabbed. Silent and rushing, we observed our tree from a distance. Its roots raised our courtyard in places three, five, and six feet high, so that we couldn't get close. The oak was split but standing, with George's life-size painted fiberglass cow (from the 1999 Chicago Cow Parade) caught upside down, high in its branches. Pained for our entire city, we stared silently at our tree and ignored the complaints of our (later replaced) insurance adjustor:

"I can't work in these conditions! Where can I get a cold drink? Don't you have a better way to pack those paintings? That bathroom is filthy!"

We have pictures of all of this, but I hate looking at them and share only the two in this essay.

Tremé misses a lot. But I think that's okay. The show actually idealizes us in some important ways, too painful, too heady, and too political to detail here. However, I'd be hard-pressed to find anyone who wouldn't fall on their knees to see a Mardi Gras Indian dressed and singing with conviction even now in their street.

And yet our oak, twice each year since Katrina, holds parrots, a whole hierarchy of them, from the top of the tree to the bottom, the macaws to the finches, a migrating flock of freed animals, perhaps the meaningful equivalent of a costumed tradition.

I realize that *Tremé* is a TV show; it's reality-based fiction, not a documentary. It's okay with me that the story is skewed. And it must rouse feelings for everyone here in New Orleans who watches it. Somehow *Tremé* makes us look wonderful and like a third world country, both at the same time. Heck, just three months after Katrina we're downright beguiling! But then, maybe we always were.

I remember the first time I laughed after the storm: My friend Geri described the $200,000 worth of rodent damage to her house as "squirrels gone wild."

I remember the first time I sang: It was Lundi Gras (the day before Fat Tuesday), and the Chee Weez led thousands of us, strangers from the entire Gulf Coast, people from Biloxi, Pass Christian, Slidell, almost all living in FEMA trailers, gathered together at Spanish Plaza and singing *a capella* as though we'd practiced it for months,

"Jeremiah was a bullfrog, Was a good friend of mine . . . "*

Treasure New Orleans. Go to Vaughn's and hear Kermit Ruffins. Eat a po' boy. Take a carriage ride. Visit the New Orleans Museum of Art. Dance at Mulate's. Ride an airboat through the swamp. Drink a hurricane. Take a cemetery tour. Admire the oaks. And if nothing else, walk on a levee.

Remember.

* Hoyt Axton, "Joy to the World," 1971.

Saints Fever

I awoke at 5:30 a.m. to screams of "Who Dat!" hollered from our sidewalk as though I were Stella herself giving up on the half sleep that comes from tumultuous relationships and reignited passion.

I awoke in a city blissfully plagued with hangovers and swollen eyes and strained vocal chords. Maybe you did too? Our New York and Irish friends called after last night's Saints play-off game to report their evening exercise—jumping around the living room, followed by sazeracs at the local pub. It's "Who Dat" insanity, and since I was reminded in Washington, D.C., this week that I shouldn't assume that all the world knows these Louisiana peculiarities (everyone from our cab drivers to the *maître de* at the Old Ebbitt Grill to the director of the Hirshhorn asked me for help), here's the real thing:

"Who dat say dey gonna beat dem Saints? WHO

DAT?! WHO DAT?!"

I had a ticket, but I gave it up. Sounds crazy, right? But not really. I went last week and am still high on the experience of hugging strangers, of screaming like life itself depended on stopping the other team on a third down, of gripping my seat and my chest until the bitter end, terrified something would go wrong ("If only they can get ahead by five touchdowns; then we'll be safe . . . .")

Like last night, I found it impossible to eat or drink as the knots in my stomach took over. It's a game, and yet God's loudspeaker might as well have announced world peace. I've never seen this town so happy.

Douglas, the Rodrigue Gallery's take-care-of-everything person for more than twenty years and pictured with George at the top of this story, passed on his near weekly pilgrimage to Houston's Rothko Chapel and attended his first ever playoff game in my place. He accompanied George to the Superdome, where they high-fived police officers, hot dog vendors, and the governor himself.

Following the game, as I sat on the couch with the phone stuck to my ear and the Kleenex box in my lap, George burst inside and recounted every play for me as though I hadn't seen a thing. When he realized I recorded it, he grabbed a beer and shouted at the television until the wee hours. It was just one of those nights.

Last week I was surprised to learn that, even in New Orleans, football and yoga don't generally mix. Not only was I the only person in my workshop who attended the game, I was the only one who watched it, or in some cases even knew that the Saints won and what it meant.

Okay, so I'm probably putting the words "football" and *namaste* (loosely translated, honoring the spirit within another person) in a sentence together for the first time, but I can't help but see this wonder—this team bringing together a city that struggles with race relations, corruption, poverty, and crime—as cause for a celebration the likes of which even this party town has never known. Furthermore, it all happens inside of the Superdome, a structure that only four years previous held immense suffering.

This victory symbolizes the continued healing of a deep and painful wound, one that remains fresh here long after the rest of the world thinks we moved on or, most distressful, that we'll never recover. It's as if the doctor at long last visited the waiting room and told the New Orleans family,

"I've got great news. She's going to pull through."

It's 2009, and after forty-three years of waiting, the New Orleans Saints are going to the Super Bowl.

A Happiness Epidemic

New Orleans is back. And now the whole world knows it.
–Tom Benson, Owner of the New Orleans Saints,
February 7, 2010

The closest comparison in my life to this, the first Super Bowl win by the New Orleans Saints, is screaming with my sister as she gave birth to her first child. Only then did I feel this sort of exhilaration, where I can't recall what may have stressed me out two days previous, because whatever it was, it's not important. Nothing feels this important. And this time, the joy is not shared with just family and friends, but it's everywhere. This morning I overheard three clerks at the grocery discussing game plays while stocking the dairy section, and I joined my yoga class in breathing in "Who . . ." and breathing out "Dat . . .", confirming that Saints fever is indeed highly contagious.

At Lee Circle this morning, I forgot the cold wind as I admired from the Exxon station the Mardi Gras flags on surrounding balconies, the streetcar rounding the circle,

General Lee standing clear against the sky, the Mississippi River bridge stretching between the buildings, and the Saints jersey on the guy at the gas pump opposite me, who ran over for a quick high five, a stranger sensing my sentimental mood, because he feels the same way about this old city and its new beginning.

It's as though we have a lucky star hanging over not just the Superdome, not just the French Quarter, but every part of New Orleans and Metairie and surrounding areas. Katrina could have, should have, brought us together; instead the storm, corruption, and racially motivated comments and ugliness divided us further. This victory has done the impossible, uniting us in a way that we thought was lost.

I've been proud of this city all of my life for many reasons, especially its history, culture, and people, but I've been ashamed too, particularly when I read about our troubles in the *New York Times* or *USA Today*. Now the Saints are Super Bowl champions, and New Orleans, finally, graces the world's press with something positive.

Today there is a happiness epidemic throughout this city, and it's infiltrated even the smallest parts of our lives. Something as ordinary as answering the telephone is new and exciting. Every person I called today, whether a friend or for business, answered their phone not with "hello," but with "Who dat?"

We flew back from Miami yesterday, landing by chance just ahead of the Saints football team, owners, and other members of the organization. We stood on the tarmac with only a few chosen folks meeting the team as they emerged from the plane's door.

There were thousands of people waiting to greet the Saints' plane outside of security. We watched them from the airplane windows as we landed, crowding the airport and Veterans Boulevard. And yet we found ourselves by accident standing with the governor and his family, the

Archbishop and two nuns, and a few other area notables. As the team descended the stairs, our band of twenty screamed for the Saints, trying to make them feel welcome and appreciated, although we knew that the waiting crowds would do a much better job.

In my excitement I forgot to be intimidated by Archbishop Aymond and instead shouted to him as though he didn't know the big news:

"We have a clean slate, Your Excellency. Mitch Landrieu (after three tries) is our mayor and we won the Super Bowl! It's like we're starting over!"

Immediately and in chorus, Archbishop Aymond and his nuns looked skyward, opened their arms and called out,

"Thank God!"

In Miami we saw friends from all over the Southeast. Together we shouted, "We're here for you!" We knew our Saints would win. I saw grown men cry at a first down or a replay of the last play-off game's tie-breaking field goal. We grew hoarse screaming our "Who Dat's" and singing "When the Saints Go Marching In."

And we tried to show sympathy, albeit half-heartedly, to the one Colts fan in our midst who commented with a sigh between our singing and cheering,

"All we've got is . . . 'Go Colts' . . ."

George and I travel all over America, and we consistently hear these questions, in tones both surprised and pitiful:

"You're from New Orleans? You mean you stayed? How *are* things?"

And because sharing these stories has taught me that everyone doesn't know the things I take for granted, I'm here to tell you:

Things are great—especially if you're a tourist! The French Quarter has never been cleaner; the famous chefs are in their restaurants; the festivals attract the most talented musicians; the people could not be happier to see you; we have a new mayor; and our football team just won the Super Bowl.

We're not only back; we're better.

Hope to see you soon in the Big Easy.

Good, Good, Good Friends

Artists and chefs share a natural bond. Creating unique art or food, they separate themselves from the pack or, as George would say, from the yardstick.

This form of success naturally distinguishes a chef or artist from his peers. The quality of one's own unique, recognizable style is as important as the basic skills or fundamentals. Finding that style, however, is also the biggest obstacle. George admits his good fortune in this regard. Whether his Oak Trees, Cajuns, Blue Dogs, Hurricanes, or Bodies, he paints in a way unique to him.

This is the definition, he says, of self-made, the recipe for success and happiness. Creative types seduce their audience with their confidence, especially when the audience is local and relates to their innovative approach. I saw this happen with a painting of three chefs during *Rodrigue's Louisiana*, a retrospective exhibition at the New

Orleans Museum of Art in 2008.

In a room full of George's notable portraits such as Governor Huey Long, President Ronald Reagan, and jazz great Mahalia Jackson, it was his painting of three Louisiana chefs which caught the locals by surprise.

Together, Chef Warren LeRuth (1929-2001), Chef Chris Kerageorgiou (1927-2007), and Chef Goffredo Fraccaro (b. 1926), spent years raising money for St. Michael's Special School through an annual fundraising event. Their culinary talents, generosity, and on-stage antics endeared them to the people of south Louisiana forever.

"They played off of each other," recalls George, "cutting up like the Three Stooges, especially at this event. On stage they created a chicken dish, each chef with a prop unknown to the others. One year Goffredo pulled a live chicken from a pillowcase, holding the panicked bird up for the crowd.

"The other two got mad, not wanting to pluck a chicken, so Goffredo pushed it back in the bag and pulled out two rubber chickens and a big knife.

"No Goffredo!" they shouted. "We need a dead chicken with meat on it . . . and NO FEATHERS!"

"Somehow one always turned up, and they made their French, Italian, Cajun concoction. It was a great time, especially when they called me on stage to stir the pot."

George first met the chefs in 1983 at the St. Michael's School fundraiser. From the beginning, Warren LeRuth, a New Orleans native of Belgian descent, collected George's paintings. The two became friends, often meeting at LeRuth's restaurant on the New Orleans Westbank.

"LeRuth's was the first five-star restaurant in the city," says George. "There were always limos parked out front. At the table, the *maître de* placed a small pillow beneath the feet of female diners."

Chef Warren's good friends, Chris Kerageorgiou and Goffredo Fraccaro, often joined them. Of Greek descent, Chef Chris grew up in France, eventually settling in New Orleans and opening La Provence Restaurant on the Northshore in 1972. Italian Chef Goffredo opened La Riviera in 1969 in the suburb of Metairie.

For years before moving to New Orleans, George and I enjoyed La Riviera on every visit to the city. We hovered around saucepans in the kitchen with Chef Goffredo as he and George shared jokes and laughed about days past. The boisterous, heavy-accented Italian was a good match for the boisterous, heavy-accented Cajun, and in no time the entire kitchen was laughing. I don't know which I enjoyed more—the entertainment or the crabmeat raviolis.

"As I got to know them, I ate weekly at La Riviera," recalls George. "Goffredo and I became the closest. The restaurant was open only at night, but I would go for lunch if I could wake them. The chefs slept on the floor of the dining room for their afternoon nap. If I arrived before 11:30, I could eat."

It was Chef Warren LeRuth who convinced his friends to commission a portrait. George painted them in his typical Cajun style, their shapes locked into the Louisiana landscape. Instead of shadowed beneath the oak, the figures glow with the white of their chef's attire, as well as the happiness that comes from personal success and years of good times together.

The original painting remained with Chef Warren Le-Ruth until his death in 2001, and Chef Chris enjoyed it until his passing in 2007. It was Chef Goffredo that loaned the canvas to the New Orleans Museum of Art (NOMA) for the two-month Rodrigue exhibition in 2008.

On opening night, Goffredo announced a surprise. The three chefs agreed years ago that the nostalgia belongs to the people of New Orleans, the people that supported their restaurants and embraced their unique talents. Upon his death, NOMA's permanent collection receives this special painting, a lasting gift from good, good, good friends.

MUSEings from a
Mardi Gras Float

If ever there was a reason for Lasik . . . I thought to myself as I struggled with my glasses, barely touching my nose
over enormous feathered hot pink eyelashes and a manda-
tory mask, all negotiated around a plunger-like stocking
cap and a bouffant Big Bird-yellow Fifi Mahony's custom-
designed wig.

For more than twelve hours my head gathered heat
and suspended reality as I posed for pictures, danced and
sang with hundreds of costumed Muses, and tossed beads,
shoes, and blinky trinkets from a papier mache float. It
was exhausting, expensive, and, to some, flippantly insane.
It was, as my nephews would say, totally awesome.

Each year, I join thousands of other float riders and
parade goers in loving Mardi Gras. Throughout the ride

and for weeks preceding, we warn each other, relentlessly: Pace.

We nap between work, parades, and formal balls. We practice yoga and pilates in small, basically ineffectual spurts. We take mini-rests on the parade route as the floats pause for any number of rumored reasons. And we solicit help from our friends, as we juggle jobs, family, and other commitments. In my case, my friends loaded my beads (during a thunderstorm, no less) and shared their decorated shoes. We fluffed each other's wigs, applied glitter and eye make-up, and monitored the port-o-potty door. Somehow, for a few weeks each year, it all seems terribly important.

"Promise me," I begged my friend Tiffa, who reminded me in her wig of Madame Defarge as she bartended from an overturned bucket, "that no matter how intently I eye your vodka-cranberry, your answer remains, 'We're out.'" I knew from experience that my tolerance level no longer includes hard liquor on parade night.

In New Orleans, instead of complaining about parade traffic, we shrug our shoulders, ditch our cars, and throw our hands in the air:

"Throw Me Something, Sister!" screamed the crowds last night during the Krewe of Muses all-female parade. "They're calling your name, Wendy," said my biological sister, Heather, more than once, as we realized the power of social media and the decreasing anonymity of a mask.

Perspective and priorities shift at Mardi Gras, as further evidenced by our parade day lunch: four over-dressed ladies forgoing the usual salads, dressing on the side, in favor of Emeril's Who Dat Burgers with fries.

"Extra cheese, please," said my sister.

"More ketchup," chimed the table.

Although I've ridden with Muses for years, this was my first time on Float Number One. Unlike the themed floats behind us, we donned our own wigs and made up a few of our own rules.

"Always trade a shoe for champagne," explained Tiffa, as I hesitated at an offer.

"But only good champagne," clarified Pam, as she rejected the sickly sweet pink bubbles.

(Note to crowd: worse than cheap champagne are 1) Foul language: "Throw me a f-ing shoe" never works; and 2) Bare male torsos: Good grief guys, keep your shirts on)

On Float Number One, for the first time in a Mardi Gras parade, I felt real pressure to please. We faced thousands of people, most without adornment, all screaming for shoes and beads and blinky rings.

"Pace, Girls!" shouted Tiffa. "There are twenty-five floats behind you!," as Heather and I attempted to satisfy every child with a stuffed animal and every old lady with a shoe bracelet. We're near eye-level with the crowd on this float, as opposed to our usual spot high overhead. "Don't make eye contact," warned Tiffa each time the float paused.

Also on Float Number One, we experienced for the first time the real beauty of the parade. We watched the flambeaux carriers as they lit their enormous torches. We wondered at the giant lighted butterflies. And we danced for six hours on the route to the beat of the O. Perry Walker High School Marching Band, following close behind. At times we lulled, but our adrenaline (and the hamburger) kicked in, and we marveled at our evening, embracing it full force, amidst historic buildings and magnificent oaks, and the heart of New Orleans—its people.

"Vodka and cranberry?" asked Tiffa, forgetting herself as we approached Lee Circle.

"Heck yeah," I shouted, although I was too busy and never paused to drink.

At Home in the Marigny

"The loud frog is back," tweeted my cousin Elizabeth last night from the kitchen of our Marigny home, as she attacked her Loyola senior term papers with delirium. I sat thinking the same thing in the adjoining room, undecided if I welcomed or shunned the long throaty tone.

I spent many dark nights at our pond in summers past, a rare chance to wear my wellies, flashlight in hand, searching without success for the source of the sound, a bit grating after five hours of "Grooooooaaaaaaaaaaatttttttttt!"

As I turned up the volume on *Matlock*, Elizabeth ran through with her headphones.

"Eat a live frog first thing in the morning and nothing worse will happen to you the rest of the day," wrote Mark Twain, who was probably right. And perhaps someone *would* eat the thing, but fried, if I could find it, because surely it is the biggest frog to ever domicile in downtown

New Orleans.

The Faubourg Marigny, I tell visitors, although not technically downtown, basically *is* downtown, within walking distance anyway, although we are a neighborhood without the high rises of the Central Business District. We sit adjacent to the French Quarter, within the original footprint of the city of New Orleans, on the highest ground, as the earth slopes upwards towards the levees or downwards towards the center of the teacup, depending on one's perspective.

As I understand it, the water ran freely through our Creole townhouse for years, breaching the once five-foot levees and racing towards Lake Pontchartrain, carrying animals and debris, and stranding residents on upper floors for days, maybe weeks. When Nicholas Foche built the house in 1835, he planned for this, leaving the street level a dirt-floored bar, which it remained for one hundred years.

The neighborhood attracts writers, musicians, chefs, artists, and creative folks of all kinds. We have hundreds of dogs, street-wise cats, courtyards, fishponds, oak trees, a pot-bellied pig, and at least one frog. We re-tool our motorcycles and bicycles, carefully preserve old bricks in our sidewalks, treat our oak trees with reverence, buy our produce from Mr. Possum, and watch the tops of the ships pass on the Mississippi River.

We also walk into the French Quarter, where we peruse and purchase. I finally ventured past the window and through the door of Fleur de Paris last month and acquired my first hat, a seven-inch rimmed royal blue straw number with peacock feathers. To my surprise, the best part was strolling back to the Marigny along Royal Street and then Chartres, navigating past other strollers with my hatbox.

"You bought a hat!" said one couple, as another took my picture. A passing carriage driver pointed me out like a French Quarter tourist attraction, as bareheaded passengers slurped hand grenades and stared.

The Other Side of the Painting

At last, I thought to myself, I've channeled Grandma Helen, a New Orleans lady from Gretna who wore a hat and gloves as she shopped on Canal Street in the 1950s. She too had loud frogs in her backyard, as I recall.

Chapter 12

Lucky Dog

For months during 2012 and 2013, although I couldn't bring myself to type the word, I wrote about our emotions surrounding George Rodrigue's battle with Stage 4 Lung Cancer.

Hopeful Discomfort

"Medicine is an art, not a science," explained a friend recently, as I struggled with misdiagnoses and conflicting reports.

"Fifteen people looked at my wife's images," he continued, "and only one analyzed them correctly."

I've thought a lot recently about opinions, specifically about how we view others, how our egos guide us into dangerous errors and, without mentioning specifics, how hero-worship precludes not only effective analyses, but also focused concern. After trying for years, I've finally mastered answering well-meaning, impossible questions like "How's George?" or, worse, "How are you?" with a question, lest I drift into overreaction or, worse, reality.

The word "hopeful" haunts me within emails and conversation, losing its meaning in repetition. Articles and websites mention the latest medical procedures as "hopeful," not to mention the word's proliferation within personal health blogs, support groups and, until this realization, my own email updates. As I sat in another hospital waiting room today, author Liza Campbell admitted, "I do not feel at all hopeful," on the pages of *A Charmed Life*, a gift, pre-crisis, from my sister Heather.

I asked George about the word, but he claims not to have noticed.

"Discomfort," he declares. "That's the word of the month. If one more doctor or disclaimer mentions 'discomfort,' I'll lose it. 'Discomfort' means pain for days, especially the promised 'discomfort' as they send you home on the Friday of a holiday weekend. Discomfort, HA!"

I wonder, had I questioned the hopeful doctors and fought with the hopeful nurses, would my mother be alive today? Instead, my ego guided me, as I worried more about interrupting the stressed health care workers than addressing her discomfort, an issue that even I, a medical novice, noted with suspicion.

The oil paints and especially the spray varnishes that assaulted George's body with hepatitis in the mid-1980s returned with a vengeance in recent months, despite his switch years ago to acrylic paint.

"Many nights I fell into bed as the room spun around me. It's the reason I moved my studio from Jefferson Street to Landry's," explains George, referring to Lafayette, Louisiana, and the mid-1980s. "I couldn't breathe anymore in the attic. I don't know if it was those forty paintings or what . . . ."

. . . recalling the paintings from the book *Bayou*, a project for the 1984 World's Fair, including the first Blue Dog painting. Despite the move, however, George continued to poison himself, painting the *Saga of the Acadians*, several presidential portraits, and numerous early Blue Dog works all in oil before a doctor diagnosed the source of his illness.

The Other Side of the Painting

"I don't want to hear about these problems anymore," said George recently. "I only want to make art."

Twenty-five years later those same toxins ate away his L-1 vertebrae, nearly collapsing his spine until a savior, a single doctor, recognized the crisis on an MRI last week after half a dozen others dismissed George's pain as ordinary discomfort. The surgeon filled his vertebrae with cement, securing his spine just days before paralysis.

I asked him before surgery if George would be okay. The doctor replied,

"We have every reason to be hopeful."

"Are you depressed? If yes, explain . . . ," asks the hospital forms. I hesitate, *Of course he's depressed!* I want to scream, *Who wouldn't be?!* But that would be a tirade, so unlike me, and, for better or worse I mark "no."

"He is already well," stated a friend earlier this week. "Remember that, whatever the doctors say and whatever the test results."

He has a good brain . . . I thought to myself as George entered his brain scan the following day.

And I was right.

Dog in a Box

In yoga, I spent years within our bedroom practicing tree pose, standing on one leg, arms stretching skyward until I balanced with ease. Yet at my first attempt outside, at the edge of our patio in Carmel Valley, California, I fell. Breaking my own rule, I donned my glasses, focusing on a distant tree, and tried once more, teetering a few seconds before falling again.

Obviously, although I never touched them, the four walls and ceiling of our house supported me psychologically during hundreds of tree poses, as though imaginary beams pressed and stabilized with energy from every angle. It was easy to reach for Heaven when it extended past the ceiling, buttressed by the walls of a residential box. But outside, the sky left me reeling and unsteady, both on my feet and inside my head, as I struggled for focus within, ironically, the freedom of a wide open space.

The earliest Blue Dog paintings of the late 1980s and

early 1990s referenced, without exception and unlike to-day, the loup-garou, a werewolf or ghost dog that haunted George's childhood memories:

"If you're not good today," warned his mother, "the loup-garou will eat you tonight."

From the first Blue Dog painting, *Watchdog* (1984), Ro-drigue imagined the mythical creature under a dark sky and within cemeteries and sugarcane fields. It ran wild in the humid Louisiana night air, unlike its model, Tiffany, a family pet born and transported in a box.

"Tiffany's first doghouse was a cardboard box," ex-plains George. "We brought her home in it, and she liked it as her house, only venturing into the grass after she out-grew the box. Even as I painted the loup-garou, at times my mind drifted to Tiffany, until eventually I created a se-ries of paintings less about a ghost story and more about my dog."

Although wont to claim claustrophobia, for George, enclosed spaces, unlike my supports and Tiffany's home, are unpleasant and relate to ill health. This began in his childhood when, while suffering from polio in the early 1950s, he witnessed children, those in more advanced stag-es of the disease, confined within iron lungs. He talks of it today with anxiety as he faces medical tests or procedures, opting for an open tube whenever possible.

"First thing they ask you is what kind of music you want to hear—which doesn't help at all when you're trapped for an hour in a pipe."

My advice fails too, as I suggest he close his eyes and imagine wide open spaces.

"All I think about are those iron lungs," he explains. "And my aching arms and back, stuck forever in one posi-tion."

On his canvas, the idea of a box changed over time as much as the dog. In recent years, both the loup-garou and Tiffany remain mere roots of a series that developed beyond Cajun country and family memories. Today the paintings range from the acutely personal to universal, but always carefully planned, using shape, color and design, as though George attacks a puzzle, transferring it from his expansive brain to the space bounded by four sides of a canvas.

"Tiffany outgrew her box; however, as an artist, the box idea never left me. Each painting begins with a problem: a two-dimensional canvas-box that has to be filled and dissected and arranged—eventually becoming a three dimensional illusion."

My yoga practice recedes and grows in the same way. Today I stand half-blind and steady outside, whether overlooking a valley or standing on a pier. It's when I close my eyes, however, that the supports fail again, and I'm falling and flailing as though once more out of my box and new to the world.

Years ago, after four failed MRI attempts, my Grandma Helen, at her doctor's suggestion, endured my voice throughout her test as I recounted family stories. I guess it was my first speech, as she remained captive for thirty minutes or more, trapped and unable to respond, while I rattled on about holiday plans, George's latest paintings, new growth in our garden, and whatnot. She came through it, relieved, no doubt, to escape my soliloquy as much as the tiny tube.

Recently I shared this memory with George and made the same offer.

"That's okay; I'll make it," replied the Blue Dog Man. "Besides, they gave me something for pain."

And I swear he rolled his eyes.

Summer Distractions

"I know what your problem is, Wendy," noted Heather, as she endured, as sisters do, my somewhat minor, but nevertheless ridiculous breakdown over exceedingly minor things. A whiny, determined adolescent wins out occasionally, lurking, pouting, and stewing within my, one-would-hope, adult mind over dumb stuff.

I am not exchanging a three-year-old print purchase for the same print sporting this guy's new lucky number! Doesn't my 'anonymous' cyber stalker know that she can't hide from my stat counter? Where the heck is Downton Abbey, *Season 2 on Net-flix?*

"You're bored," continued Heather, squeezing in a word.

It's not boredom, I've decided, but it is a state of mind. This summer the bigger issues overwhelm my conscience to such a degree that I shove them back, unwilling to face them twenty-four hours a day, filling my mind instead with folly.

George, as far as I know, has never done this. While I worry about explaining the paint splatters on our hotel room coffee table, he ponders, so I thought, the colossal quagmire, the very real situation that landed us in Houston for the next several months. And yet, he counters . . .

"My concerns are primarily art concerns. The Blue Dog never really stops talking to me."

Recently, for both our sakes, I pull a subject from the air, as we sit lost without Maggie Smith, looking through hundreds of paintings and letters from children at Liza Jackson Preparatory School from my hometown of Fort Walton Beach, Florida.

"Did you ever have a pen pal?"

"Of course, everybody did," George shrugged; "it was the thing. Somebody told my mama that her son dropped his pen pal, and so I took him up. He was Turkish, and I could hardly read his writing. Mostly we sent postcards."

"Did you want to go to Turkey?"

"I had no idea what a Turkey was; nor did I really think about it."

I tried again.

"Doesn't sound like much fun."

"No, it wasn't fun!"

And finally, he started . . .

"I was interested in airplanes. I wanted to be a pilot (author's note: news to me). And I liked buying airplane books—military, jet fighters, commercial, all kinds. I wrote to airplane companies—Lockheed, Boeing, and others, requesting photographs of planes. They sent me beautiful 8 x 10 images.

"I worked on an airplane scrapbook. It's still in my attic studio on St. Peter Street.

"The pictures were better than in the magazines, and it was free, just like the internet! It was much more exciting than a Turkish pen pal."

Distracted at last, George remained lost in the fifth grade, 1954, doodling airplanes as I continued reading get-well letters, 2012.

I prefer his diversions to mine, I thought, recalling my earlier complaints to my sister. I focused on the hand-made cards.

"When you paint," reads one, "take a sip of water after every stroke."

"Use Band-aids and eat soup (or, rather, 'soop')," suggest others.

At last, refocused, I dropped the petty worry, apologized to my husband and sister, and recalled the important things in life.

Match Race

The straight sprints raced in heats or in match races where the two riders would balance for long seconds on their machines for the advantage of making the other rider take the lead and then the slow circling and the final plunge into the driving purity of speed.
−Ernest Hemingway*

Because life intended it this way, George and I are with characters in Houston, Texas, for the summer. One couple, Janice and Tom "Slim" Gray, pigeon racers, formerly horse racers, formerly rooster fighters, formerly dairy farmers, join us on Mondays for the baseball cap and banana bread swap. We women nod "Mornin'" while the men forego the salutations in favor of the point:

"Years ago, when I was smokin' and drinkin' and runnin' with wild women . . . " offers Slim, beginning the politically incorrect exchange that flows naturally from a Cajun and a Cowboy trapped in a storytelling match race every week for six hours in a sterilized room.

"Call it like it is, Wendy," says George as I read him this opening. "A Coonass and a Horse's Ass. It was the cowboys that named us Coonasses; so we returned the favor."

For me, the days are full of firsts:

. . . the first time I've heard of rice, when added to gumbo, called "ice cream"; the first time I've heard a heated defense for electing convicted felons to public office; the first time, since my Papa Mac, who died in 1972, that I've heard the word "dago" in casual conversation.

"He kinda looks like Hank Williams," I whispered to George on the day we spied Slim. We eavesdropped as he spoke to his wife.

"Is it next week we'll be in New Iberia with those dagos?" he asked, as she shushed him and crawled under her chair.

I glanced at Janice with sympathy while George, hearing his hometown, jumped in.

"You're going to New Iberia?"

They continued from one subject to the next across the room.

"You remember Moon Mullican?" called George. "You know they say he wrote 'Jambalaya.'"

"We got an ol' boy in Alvin (Texas) plays 'Jambalaya' on the squeeze box," replied Slim.

"Ya' know, Nolan Ryan's from Alvin," he continued.

It was also the first time I've heard of a match race outside of George Rodrigue's paintings and, ironically, an offhand reference within Hemingway's *A Moveable Feast*, which I finished, also this week, as the geriatric crowd slept.

It was Slim's recollection of a match race, in fact, that gave me the idea for this story.

"What's a match race?" I whispered to George.

"All of my paintings of horses running are of match races," he explained, shaking his head, *where has she been?*. "Cajuns race quarter horses, matching one horse and one jockey against the other.

"Many are claiming races—you win the race, you win the other horse. I saw them first as a kid at the track in Abbeville, and when I started painting horses, I went back to the races again.

"It was a lot like the cock fights, betting against some-one else's horse or rooster.

"A lot of inside bettin' on that . . . " he continued.

"I fought roosters," interjected Slim.

"You ever shoot skeet?" asked George.

"Yup, but we use live pigeons."

In this weekly match race, George started on one side of the room and Slim on the other. The first day they flung friendly obscenities. The second day they sat two chairs closer; and by day three they sat side-by-side, exchanging thoughts on today as though they were days gone by. In between lab runs and lunch orders, Janice and I occasion-ally got in a word.

"You're laying black top in Breaux Bridge, Louisiana?" I asked Janice, knowing George was just as curious after over-hearing her phone conversation about work in the Crawfish Capital.

"Yeah, but I'm having trouble getting my delivery. I may have to do it myself."

"You're a true modern woman," I commented, genu-inely impressed. "When I was a young girl we all aspired to be First Lady. It never occurred to us to shoot for the top job."

"When I was a girl," countered Janice, "we all aspired to wear an apron and raise kids. That *was* the top job."

George and I discussed our recent passion for 1960s *Columbo*, before Slim and Janice trumped us with *The Wal-tons*.

"Tell them about the preacher," I urged George.

"Years ago," he began, "as I passed through Alexandria, a preacher and his wife approached me in the parking lot of Landry's Restaurant for a Jolie Blonde print. The preacher peeled $25,000 in one hundred dollar bills from his pocket, and they bought five paintings and a bronze from the trunk of my Lincoln Continental. I threw in the print," he laughed, "*lagniappe*."[†]

"'Everybody thinks we live with hardly nothin' in our shotgun house,' explained the preacher's wife. 'But we sure like our art!'"

With an unprecedented pocketful of cash, George continued his drive from Alexandria to Shreveport, where he delivered paintings to a collector who invited him to the Louisiana Downs Racetrack. There they joined Racing Commissioner Gus Mijalis in his suite, and in less than an hour, betting with the rowdy bunch, George lost $22,000.

Dejected, he moved to the bar, where he struck up a conversation with a small man hunched over a racing form.

"Got any winners?" asked George.

"I got 'em all," mumbled the bookie through his cigar, sharing a glimpse of his form.

"I just need two," said George, holding up his fingers.

Betting his last $3,000, he walked away with $23,000 and a lesson.

"I haven't bet on the ponies since," he says . . . and that's true, as I recall him playing the slots last time we joined friends at the track.

We all laughed, and Slim and George continued their exchange, one-upping each other, pulling stories from memory in anticipation of this weekly match race. As Janice returned to her black top negotiations, I opened my book:

"For a long time," wrote Hemingway, "it was enough just . . . to bet on our own life and work, and on the painters that you knew and not try to make your living gambling and call it by some other name."[*]

The Other Side of the Painting

* Ernest Hemingway, *A Moveable Feast* (Scribner, 1964).

† The word "lagniappe" is a Cajun term meaning "a little something extra."

Lucky Dog

Yesterday morning I sat in the window of a Houston, Texas, café, George's sandwich order in hand, awaiting the counter change from breakfast to lunch. An Ignatius J. Reilly nearby spoke of high water and broken computers into what I first thought was a hand-free phone but turned out to be air.

"Damn this spilled coffee!" he shouted, looking at me. I shrugged, seeing nothing. He repeated his creed until I nodded in agreement, handing him a napkin which he tossed aside, grinding his teeth and abandoning his tray.

"Hot dogs, hot dogs," called the Ignatius in my head. "Savories from the hygienic Paradise kitchens."*

As if on cue, Yusuf Islam, a.k.a. Cat Stevens, began "Don't Be Shy" over the speakers of the now empty restaurant, sending me again into a helpless emotional state.

Adding to this surreal scene is our current situation,

433

too private to share in detail, but real, the source of speculation and concern, the surprising "job training," as my friend Barbara calls it, and the catalyst of a bigger life's picture: family, legacy, and love.

"Let me tell you how you are . . ." started George as I shared my café-encounter. I laughed and grabbed my notebook at this unexpected sign of normalcy.

"What!?" he questioned, a bit too loud.

"I can tell he's feeling better, because he's telling me how I am," I wrote, before tuning out, at feigned attention, for the familiar analysis, my husband's hands chopping the air as he dissects, for my benefit, my personality.

"George," begged my sentimental mood, "tell me what you love. Shout it out."

"What do I love?" he said quietly, and for him, almost shyly.

"Yes! What do you love? Don't get philosophical on me. Just say it fast, all in a row."

"I love Blue Dogs! I love LSU football! I love modern medicine! And more than anything in the whole world, I love to paint!"

"And in one word, George, how do you feel right now?"

"Lucky," he said, without hesitating. "Make that damn lucky!"

"Have you ever painted a Lucky Dog vendor?," I continued, knowing his love of hot dogs.

"No, you giving me that idea?"

"It's yours."

"I'll make him a Blue

The Other Side of the Painting

Dog vendor and have him sell paintings from his cart," he laughed, pulling out his sketchbook.

George and I meet daily this summer with a man whose military reserve unit returned recently from the deserts of Afghanistan, by way of the jungles of Haiti and the Dominican Republic. He serves, protects, and saves lives from one country to the next, including his skillful operation of the TomoTherapy machine that brought us together in Houston, coincidentally nicknamed "Hi-Art."

"I've never met anyone like George . . ." he said last week, explaining the joy and interest of their visits, especially George's stories and philanthropy, both as appealing as his artwork. I listened, touched, to this American hero and made notes for this essay, another chapter in the story of one lucky dog.

"And in one word, how do *you* feel?" asked George, after reading my draft.

"That's easy," I said, although still a bit peevish . . .

"Grateful."

* John Kennedy Toole, *A Confederacy of Dunces* (Louisiana State University Press, 1980).

Courage for our Friends

After ten weeks in Houston, George and I returned today to New Orleans. Our homecoming, however, is bittersweet, as we change our undesired summer's routine while leaving behind the people who shared our experience, the people we grew to love.

"It's weird," I said to George a few weeks into our summer. "It's not like we're in Houston; it's like we're on some medical planet."

We saw some of them weekly, some daily. We held in common personal struggles, each unique and similar at the same time, folks from around the world, some fighting for their lives, some saving lives, but all grounded, as we practiced together the rawness and realness of life outside of the expectations and obligations of normality.

"I'm recycling my life," noted George, mid-summer, as we discussed our situation. "I didn't expect this new experience, and we should make as much of it as we can; because we're all living in the moment, whatever that may be."

For George and me, this was an oddly welcome diversion from society, from fundraisers and dinner parties, from lectures and book signings, from the curiosity and gossip that accompany his fame.

(Note: As if on cue, a tour group on segways pauses just now as I write this, below the window of our Faubourg Marigny home; their guide tells of the great Louisiana artist within.)

Still, George gave impromptu art lessons this summer in the most unlikely of places. Too weak to paint, he embraced these discussions, sharing not because he felt obligated, but because he sincerely missed painting, and because his new friends relate less to the celebrity and more to the man.

"Every great artist has taken a common thing and made people see it in a different way," he explained in a hospital waiting room earlier this week.

There are people, we all know them, who live life on the surface. Maybe pretense is easier; maybe it follows from childhood defenses or a sense of self-preservation. Some seek the cliché and "find themselves," while others drift happily in a contrived and, perhaps safer, existence.

"The closer you are to who you really are—is the best thing," counters George, as we philosophize. "Yet most people can't get past 5:00 p.m."

This summer, George and I experienced for the first time in our lives a Reality Planet, a place immersed in raw emotions, genuine concern, unabated fear, and tenacious courage.

"I've never seen him turn down strawberries and cream," I whispered, distressed, to one new friend. She nodded and smiled, because *she knew*.

"He'll like them again," she said. "I promise."

438

. . . and her empathy, a welcome epidemic on this Reality Planet, comforted me.

Today, I can say with certainty that a healthy and strong George will return soon to his easel. His ordeal began more than twenty years ago, when paint fumes and varnishes poisoned his body, and it culminated this summer with a near collapse of his spine followed by ten weeks of treatment.

"What does that mean?"

. . . he asked his doctor recently, who warned him of the flu-like side effects of one medication. The doctor looked at me, confused.

"He doesn't know the flu," I explained. "He only knows big stuff, like polio and the plague."

George is stalwart in the face of difficult situations, and from the beginning I believed that, one way or another, he would beat his illness.

"A lot of stuff, good and bad, happens to me; but I don't let any of it get attached to me. Once I make myself happy, that's the end of it. I paint a painting; I'm happy; and that's me."

Both of us, as this summer ends, struggle with the good news far more than the bad. We are trapped within our guilt, and many nights George cries, "Why me?," as we think of our new friends. We couldn't bring ourselves to tell them while in Houston of a rare mutation, discovered just last week within his disease, treatable with a simple pill.

Folks talk of grace, karma, luck, fate, what have you— but none of this explains our situation; because George, the oldest in the room, will recover, while these young folks with young families still fight and fight and fight.

"Courage, Merry," whispers the Princess Eowyn to the Hobbit Merry as they charge into battle. "Courage for our friends."*

We are home, and we are changed. How exactly remains to be seen. But something happened . . . something big.

* From the Rohirrim charge, *Lord of the Rings: Return of the King*, 2003.

Painting (and Living?) Again

George and I returned to New Orleans in early August as though our old lives were a dream.

"It's hard to believe we threw parties in this house," I mused, as we settled into our sofa and BBC television.

"I barely remember going out to dinner," countered George.

Meanwhile, artist Glenda Banta asked me online about our home, about sharing snippets of collections and décor within my blog and on Facebook. I dreamed, or rather nightmared, as I thought about it, recalling New Orleans designer Nadine Blake in our Creole townhouse last May for a friend's birthday party the night before we left for three days, which became three months, in Houston. With southern grace she complimented our living room, yet I recall with horror her talented eye scanning our eclectic mess. I also remember that night as the last time I wore a dress, heels, or make-up, the last time I small-talked, the last time I sipped champagne.

George and I have no use for decorators, and I mean that without offense to their profession, but nevertheless literally. If we hired one, it would become full-time work, sort of like our contractor on the payroll for twenty years, currently repairing our roof and garage. The decorator could live in the guestroom, I suppose, on call for shifts between museum exhibitions, as artwork disappears and materializes, sometimes one piece, but more often ten or twenty, on loan for a month, maybe a year, leaving us, as was the case upon our return a few weeks ago, with blank walls and empty nails.

To compound matters, we dissembled my office ad-jacent to our bedroom, creating a temporary studio for George, who sits at his easel for the first time since Febru-ary after months of back and shoulder pain. This return is in his own time, now every day, some for thirty minutes, some for hours, as he heals slowly, at last nourishing his psyche as well as his body.

A decorator in our home faces not only the hodge-podge of our legacy, my parents' Asian and European fur-niture, everything from Thailand to Bavaria, and George's New Iberia treasures, including his boyhood rocker and his father's brick-laying tools, but also our disconnected taste in art: seventeenth-century South America to twen-tieth-century New York, the novice potter at the craft fair to Warhol's *John Wayne*.

Mix in Rodrigue, his student works, his Oaks and Ca-juns, his nudes, his photography, his sculpture, and, com-manding it all with its presence, his Blue Dog, and one realizes our self-induced and, admittedly, enviable chal-lenge.

Although I took photos, I share here, after much re-flection, only one. Tempted to share more, I'm guarded in this privacy despite the personal vignettes within my writing. Several years ago, we ceased opening our home to fundraisers and strangers. Even with photographs, to do so now feels exposed to the point of no return, like, your consolation, admitting to the Shaun Cassidy poster taped for years to the back of my bedroom door.

It so happens that today we hang a new piece of art-work, a seven-foot painting by Mallory Page, an abstract from her series *Tree House*, eventually headed to George's Carmel studio, but today filling the spot in New Orleans left by his historical piece, *Indians, Cajuns, and Cowboys*, currently on loan to a museum.

The purchase was not without adventure. We planned to buy a Page last spring, but George's health distracted us. Still on his mind, he sent me to her gallery immediately upon our New Orleans return, choosing a painting before the frenzy of White Linen Night, an annual celebration of the arts.

For the first time since May, I donned a dress and heels. I tried eye make-up but felt clownish, settling for a lip pencil and a bit of gloss. Wearing a Jergens tan and dull-rooted hair, its only attribute that it now reaches mid-back, I drove, also for the first time since May, venturing towards the Arts District and a life that seems like it now belongs to someone else.

Self-conscious in my world and attune to the vul-nerability in her abstracts, I chose quickly and easily at Page's gallery, rushing back the two blocks to my car. In the street, my 2007 Louboutin wedges caught a NOLA pothole, and as my ankle twisted, my flouncy dress flew to my waist. I sat on the hot asphalt shedding hot tears until a man, a male Jerusha Bailey,* offered me a hand.

"You shore have nice legs," he said.

I watched him walk on, whispered thank you too late, and absorbed the first compliment I'd heard in months.

And I wondered without worrying if, like George's mother, we now live, for better or worse, a bit lost in the past.

* Jerusha Bailey is a chain-smoking, offensive, sometimes redeemable, sometimes homeless New Orleans character in Patty Friedmann's *Secondhand Smoke* (Counterpoint Press, 2002).

Blue Fall in Louisiana

"When they showed me my body, it was blue," explained George to a friend this week. "Nothing dark, no patches, they were all gone."

I overheard him on the phone and my ears picked up, not because I hadn't seen the scan, but because I hadn't thought of his body as blue, and I rather liked this image of the Blue Dog Man. Coincidentally, at that moment I turned the last pages of Christopher Moore's *Sacré Bleu*,* a modern-day fairytale devoted to the color of western royalty and religion, tracing its source in paintings like Van Gogh's *Starry Night* to a muse, a blue nude, who, with the help of The Colorman, sheds the irresistible hue from her body, bewitching artists with the precious color.

Although today his undisputed favorite color, George barely touched the color blue in his early paintings, dark Louisiana landscapes and near black-and-white scenes of Cajun folk-life. By the early 1980s blue appeared occasionally in the eyes or ribbons of Jolie Blonde. And it was his 1984 painting of the loup-garou, a ghost dog set beneath a dark night sky, that eased the color, first as a blue-grey and then growing with intensity, into nearly every painting since.

"You cannot get a grip on blue," writes Moore.

The intense blue of the Virgin Mary's gown in early artworks such as the Limbourg Brother's *Belles Heures* originates with lapis lazuli, mined in the mountains of Afghanistan. Difficult to obtain, its rarity intoxicated both artists and patrons for centuries, oftentimes the painting's expense related directly to its blue requirements:

> The two Michelangelo (1475-1564) paintings . . . hang in the National Gallery in London to this day, but it's likely that they remain unfinished because the painter was unable to obtain the ultramarine he needed and moved on to other commissions, or the patron refused to pay the high price of the color.
> –Moore, Afterword*

Even today, blue, although no more expensive than other colors, remains precious and linked to the intangible.

(There is a painting I found among my mother's things that I'd never seen before. It's only two hands, painted in blue. It hangs in my closet, and sometimes I place my hands on hers and I think she's there.)†

Curious, I counted the tubes of blue within George's paint drawers and discovered ten manufactured shades with titles like cerulean, cobalt, and ultramarine. We spoke about the color and, although intrigued by its lofty history, the appeal for him lies in the richness of the hue, as opposed to the richness (as in rarity and price tag) of perception.

"There is a spiritual quality to blue, however," he continues. "The dark night sky affects my mood and my paintings, replacing the earthy greens and browns of my early works. As I grow older, my mind expands. I suspend reality on my canvas with greater confidence, exploring not just the trees and grass, but also the mysterious and mystical."

In my early twenties, while traveling alone, I fell to unconsciousness during a hike in the Austrian mountains. I awoke in the snow on a steep incline, wedged against a tree. On that black-blue night, I thought about my tiny place on this mountain, on this earth, and in this universe. As my mind expanded into existentialism, I grew smaller and less important, losing all fear and not really caring whether or not I survived the night.

A brush with death spurs unlikely consequences. This mountain experience, I have often thought, gave me the courage to take every leap since, a lesson George experienced three times, first leading him to paint, then to the Blue Dog, and now to some wondrous unknown.

"This is one of the more unique pieces I've ever done . . ." he explained, referencing a painting from *Bodies*, to his doctor, a philosopher as much as scientist, who near cried along with us, as we discussed George's test results. Originally from Vietnam, the doctor shared his thoughts on karma and kindness, as they studied George's artwork, a nude completed in 2005.

"I turned the figure blue and overlaid it with the Blue Dog," said George, "creating something else altogether."

* Christopher Moore, *Sacré Bleu* (William Morrow, 2012).

† From "Mignon's Flowers," pg. 97.

Epilogue

The Big Picture

As a result of last summer's sidetrack, George and I missed our annual time in Carmel, California, returning just this week for a year, maybe two, as we seek something still ill-defined. We have yet to analyze his near-death experience or rather, our second chance, referring often to the excuse, "it's still too new," as our reason for avoiding the harsh reality of cancer events while embracing the happy ease of school visits and student art contests.

George searches for answers in his art, yet in New Orleans, where he's painted feverishly forty canvases since last fall, he reassesses his life *before* reassessing his art, because he can't help it in that city of over-stimulus, because to reach the heart of the matter, again, "it's still too new," and we have to get out of the city and know quiet for a while.

In a lesson perhaps understood by all of us on some level, it's almost impossible to appreciate fully a situation while one lives it. During bliss, we rarely pause long enough to smell deeply, so that we remember the roses. And enduring hardship, we change maybe for better and maybe for worse, but we don't recognize change as it happens, so that only through reflection years later do we acknowledge "before" and "after."

The same is true in art. George describes his years at the Art Center College of Design in Los Angeles as both frustrating and liberating. He learned from professional artists he admired and emulated, yet he noted these champions of the abstracts' rejection of anything new, specifically, during those mid-1960s Pop Art years, a strong denial of the commercial and literal in art, an ironic rebuff given Art Center's focus on advertising design.

Today, in writing these essays, I face the same challenges. I reflect on George's battle with cancer, still too new to discuss in detail, and yet a giant, abstract lesson looming, waiting to change our lives, to change his art. In fact, unable to face the big picture, I managed to write for months about his disease without mentioning the word itself!

I watch him paint, and I recognize something as different, yet I'm too in the middle of it to articulate the changes, and he's too in the middle of it to broach the emotions with anything but a subtle reference in his art or discussion. This is true of not just his illness, but rather of all life experiences. It is only today, for example, that we can look back on an artistic project like the Xerox Campaign or a disaster like Hurricane Katrina and study them as turning points in George's art as much as in life.

"I realize more today than ever," says George, "that Europe had to experience the Dark Ages in order to have the Renaissance. Art reinvents itself by people who go through things that they may not understand at the time. There's always hope that new generations will discover new things that eventually propel society forward.

"For lack of a better word, I feel now a renaissance in the way I look at things and in the way the Blue Dog looks at me."

The Other Side of the Painting

Sometimes it all becomes clearer when we allow others to observe and conclude for us. Author Patty Friedmann wrote the foreword to this book, and her words struck me physically, to where it's agonizing to realize that someone, until recently a stranger, gets me so well, understands my labyrinthine style, and yet actually likes it. It's hard to read her words and not breathe less steady and wonder how she managed from my muddle to get the picture.

Through our foundation, George and I work often with children. The young ones especially see with untainted eyes. Unafraid of mistakes or stupid questions, children are perfect in both their art and observations. I watch them, as I watch George, who somehow retained this freedom throughout his sixty-nine years, and I try to ease open my brain, relieving age-induced cynicism, prying even harder at my heart, that I might contribute in some way towards widespread sincerity.

I've struggled with this my entire adult life.

For about two years in the mid-1990s I played cards with an old Western character actor in the Carmel Highlands. We met through a mutual friend, who arranged a rare introduction to this cowboy-hermit who, by his own admission, had not left his house since the 1970s. I lost forty dollars to him on that first day, as we played cards on a rotting wooden picnic table overlooking the whales and Monterey Bay. Suspecting I might not return, he struck a deal. I wouldn't have to pay, provided we never play cards for money again. He acted in more than one hundred movies and TV Westerns and, although smoking unceasingly the marijuana he grew on his property, he remembered every card, so that my (sober) gin game no longer honored my grandfather's memory.

From time to time, the big name actors stopped by to pay their homage or supply their stash, and I knew that, provided I remain calm and sworn to secrecy about the drugs, stars, and our rendezvous, I could stay. Other than my mother, I kept my word until this essay and continue to keep my word regarding his name, although, honestly, you won't know him, unless, like my mom and my husband, you're a 1950s and 60s cowboy movie buff, in which case you might recognize his face from TV or possibly a big picture.

"Oh, yeah!" said George, when I showed him a photo.

Like many men, the actor fell for Mignon, and during her visits, they danced in the expansive property's crumbling ballroom, as I swapped out waltzes on the turntable.

"I can't believe you never told me," said George this week as I recalled the story.

Although George and I dated during those years, I still kept the actor's secret, because he didn't want to meet my love interest. "Artists!" he exclaimed more than once, eventually forbidding me to speak of mine. He only wanted a card-player and her mother, and we, the three of us, rather liked the intrigue.

I write this week to the "Welcome home!" of two great horned owls. Their lives too were disrupted, as only one owl visited for several years, now partnered again for the sunrise ritual at the edge of our pool, at this point more their pool than ours. I'm sure they noted our return, but I wonder if they noted our absence. And I wonder if they protected the property, keeping at bay the R.O.U.S. es.*

The owls sing in chorus, delivering some message that I'll probably grasp as part of the big picture in the future, because at this moment I'm too swept up in the details: the fire warming the room, the memory of a cowboy who, as I just learned online, died eleven years ago, and the artist snoring softly beside me.

* "R.O.U.S. es: Rodents of Unusual Size," from *The Princess Bride*, 1987.

Images

Chapter 1

George Rodrigue, *Guitar*, 1965. Paper collage on board, 28 x 18 in. Collection the artist.

Wendy Rodrigue, 2009. Photograph of George Rodrigue before a photograph of Claude Monet, Museum of Modern Art, New York. Collection Rodrigue archives.

Salon, Societe des Artistes Francais, Honorable Mention presented to George Rodrigue, 1974. Paris, France. Collection Rodrigue archives.

George Rodrigue, *Loup-garou*, 1991. Oil on canvas, 72 x 48 in. Collection the artist.

George Rodrigue, 2009. Photograph of Wendy Rodrigue and Jackson Pollock's *One: Number 31, 1950*, Museum of Modern Art, New York. Collection the artist.

Unknown, 2008. Photograph of George Rodrigue, New Orleans, Louisiana. Collection Rodrigue archives.

George Rodrigue, *Blue Wendy*, 2000. Acrylic on watercolor paper, 20 x 24 in. Collection the artist.

George Rodrigue, *Untitled*, 2001. Acrylic sketch on canvas, 60 x 24 in. Collection the artist.

Chapter 2

George Rodrigue, *A Basket of Azaleas (Paris Salon)*, 1983. Poster, 30 x 21 in. Collection the artist.

George Rodrigue, 1966. Photograph of the artist's Corvair and art books. Collection Rodrigue archives.

Unknown, 1946. Photograph of the Rodrigue Family, New Iberia, Louisiana. Collection Rodrigue archives.

George Rodrigue, *Portrait of the Artist's Father*, 1962. Oil on canvas, 24 x 20 in. Collection the artist.

Junior Cambre, 1950. Photograph of George Rodrigue, New Iberia, Louisiana. Collection Rodrigue archives.

George Rodrigue, *Turkey*, 1950. Pencil and crayon on paper, 5 x 3 in. Collection the artist.

Unknown, 1966. Photograph of the Rodrigue Family, New Iberia, Louisiana. Collection Rodrigue archives.

George Rodrigue, *The Ragin' Cajun*, 1979. Oil on canvas, 40 x 30 in. Collection the artist.

Unknown, 1971. Photograph of George Rodrigue, Lafayette, Louisiana. Collection Rodrigue archives.

Chapter 3

Rose McKinney, 1975. Photograph of Wendy Wolfe and Kelly McClanahan, New Orleans, Louisiana.

Mignon Wolfe, *Spring Bouquet*, 1979. Oil on canvas, 40 x 30 in. Collection Heather Wolfe Parker.

Unknown, 1968. Photograph of John Wolfe and Wendy Wolfe, Weiterstadt, Germany.

Unknown, 1958. Photograph of John Wolfe and Mignon McClanahan, Baton Rouge, Louisiana.

George Rodrigue, *The Shadows of New Iberia*, 1969. Oil on canvas, 16 x 20 in. Private collection.

George Rodrigue, *Father Avery Dulles*, 1991. Oil on canvas, 40 x 30 in. Collection the artist.

George Rodrigue, *Soul Mates*, 1997. Silkscreen edition 50, 15 x 22 in. Collection the artist.

George Rodrigue, *Untitled*, 2005. Charcoal on paper, 20 x 16 in. Collection the artist.

Unknown, circa 1953. Photograph of Helen McClanahan as Worthy Matron of the Order of the Eastern Star, New Orleans, Louisiana.

Chapter 4

George Rodrigue, 1969-70. Business card. Collection Rodrigue archives.

George Rodrigue, *Where is the Art World?*, 2005. Remastered digital print edition 90, 22 x 16 in. Collection the artist.

George Rodrigue, *A Night at the Opera*, 1985. Oil on canvas, 40 x 30 in. Private collection.

George Rodrigue, 2010. Photograph of Wendy at the Chinati Foundation, Marfa, Texas.

George Rodrigue, *Shu-fly*, 1999. Acrylic on canvas, 78 x 78 in. Collection the artist.

George Rodrigue, *Louisiana Legends*, 1990. Oil on canvas, 40 x 30 in. Private collection.

George Rodrigue, 2010. Photograph of Wendy with Barbara Ricciardi, Atchafalaya Basin, Louisiana.

Unknown, 2008. Photograph of Pete Fountain and George Rodrigue, New Orleans Museum of Art, New Orleans, Louisiana. Collection Rodrigue archives.

George Rodrigue, *Untitled*, 1965. Oil on illustration board, 24 x 18 in. Collection the artist.

Chapter 5

George Rodrigue, *Untitled*, 2010. Ink pen on paper, 5 x 3 in. Collection Rodrigue archives.

Dana Waldon, *Artists Doug Magnus, Armand Lara, George Rodrigue*, 2008. Photograph. Santa Fe, New Mexico.

George Rodrigue, *No More Dukes*, 1996. Acrylic on canvas, 40 x 30 in. Collection the artist.

George Rodrigue, 2007, Photograph of Wendy and artist Hunt Slonem, Albania Plantation, Jeanerette, Louisiana. Collection Rodrigue archives.

George Rodrigue, *Chicken on the Bayou*, 1986. Oil on canvas, 24 x 36 in. Private collection.

Wendy Rodrigue, 2010, Photograph of George Rodrigue, New Orleans, Louisiana. Collection Rodrigue archives.

Jacques Rodrigue, 2013, Photograph, Lecompte, Louisiana.
George Rodrigue, *Saints on the Bayou*, 2009. Oil on linen, 15 x 30 in. Private collection.

Wendy Rodrigue, 2001, Photograph of George Rodrigue, Carmel, California. Collection Rodrigue archives.

George Rodrigue, *The Invitation (Wendy and Me)*, 1997. Oil and acrylic on canvas, 24 x 36 in. Collection the artist.

Chapter 6

Wendy Rodrigue, 2010, Photograph of George with restaurant sign, Marfa, Texas. Collection Rodrigue archives.

George Rodrigue, 2010, Photograph, Marfa, Texas. Collection Rodrigue archives.

George Rodrigue, 2010, Photograph of Wendy with neon installation by Dan Flavin, Chinati Foundation, Marfa, Texas. Collection Rodrigue archives.

Wendy Rodrigue, 2012, Photograph, Guggenheim Museum, New York, New York.

Davide Ghirlandaio (David Bigordi) (Italian, Florence, 1452-1525), *Selvaggia Sassetti (born 1470)*, 1487-88. Accession Number: 32.100.71. Metropolitan Museum of Art, New York.

George Rodrigue, *Untitled*, 1971. Oil on canvas, 1.5 x 3 in. Collection the artist.

George Rodrigue, 2010, Photograph of Douglas Shiell and Eldridge Tervalon with a Rodrigue painting, New Orleans, Louisiana.

George Rodrigue, *Untitled*, 1965. Red charcoal on tissue paper, 18 x 16 in. Collection the artist.

Unknown, 1977, Photograph of the line for *Treasures of Tutankhamun*, City Park, New Orleans, Courtesy New Orleans Museum of Art.

Chapter 7
Unknown, Photograph of Sean Hicks, winner of the 2009 George Rodrigue Foundation of the Arts Scholarship Contest, New Orleans, Louisiana. Rodrigue archives.

George Rodrigue, *Portrait of Funeral Director George Burgess*, 1959. Oil on canvas, 24 x 20 in. Collection the artist.

Unknown, 1977, Photograph of George Rodrigue and Dr. John Straub with Rodrigue's *Bernice's Calf* (1972, oil on canvas, 24 x 36 in., collection of the Hilliard University Art Museum, Lafayette, Louisiana). Collection Rodrigue archives.

Unknown, 1970s, Photograph of Marvin DuBos, Frances Love, and Ivan Boudier of the Lafayette Art Association, Lafayette, Louisiana.

George Rodrigue, *Secret Hideaway*, 1983. Oil on canvas, 30 x 40 in. Private collection.

George Rodrigue, *In Step Together*, 2003-5. Remastered digital print, 41 x 58 in., edition 3. Collection the artist.

Unknown, 1975, Photograph of George Rodrigue, Lafayette, Louisiana. Rodrigue archives.

George Rodrigue, *Landscape with Cabin and Oak*, 1971. Oil on canvas, 31 x 36 in. Collection the artist.

George Rodrigue, *Together Again*, 2003-5. Remastered digital print, 58 x 41 in., edition 3. Collection the artist.

Unknown, 2010, Photograph of George Rodrigue, New Orleans, Louisiana. Rodrigue archives.

George Rodrigue, *Life on Mars*, 2013. Acrylic on canvas with carved, painted frame, 30 x 24 in. Private collection.

George Rodrigue, *John Courregé's Pirogue*, 1973. Oil on canvas, 36 x 42 in. Private collection.

George Rodrigue, *Untitled*, circa 1985. Ink on paper, 8 x 10 in. Collection the artist.

George Rodrigue, 2011, Photograph, New Orleans, Louisiana. Collection Rodrigue archives.

George Rodrigue, *Untitled*, 1999. Ink on airplane bag, 8 x 4 in. Collection the artist.

Unknown, 2011, Photograph, Painting demo and lecture with George and Wendy Rodrigue at the Alexandria Museum of Art, Alexandria, Louisiana.

Chapter 8

George Rodrigue, *Duperier Oaks*, 1970. Oil on canvas, 30 x 40 in. Private collection.

George Rodrigue, 2008, Photograph of Jacques Rodrigue, New Orleans Museum of Art, New Orleans, Louisiana. Rodrigue archives.

George Rodrigue, *Aioli Dinner*, 1971. Oil on canvas, 32 x 46 in. Collection André Rodrigue and Jacques Rodrigue, on long-term loan to the Ogden Museum of Southern Art and the New Orleans Museum of Art.

Unknown, circa 1920, Photograph, New Iberia, Louisiana. Collection Rodrigue archives.

George Rodrigue, *Evangeline*, circa 1980. Oil on canvas, 48 x 24 in. Private collection.

George Rodrigue, *The Beauty of the Moss*, 1977. Oil on canvas, 30 x 40 in. Collection the Hilliard University Art Museum, Lafayette, Louisiana.

George Rodrigue, *Jolie Blonde*, 1974. Oil on canvas, 24 x 18 in. Private collection.

George Rodrigue, *Broussard's Barber Shop*, 1971. Oil on canvas, 30 x 40 in. Private collection.

Unknown, 1982, Photograph of George Rodrigue and André Rodrigue, Lafayette, Louisiana. Collection Rodrigue archives.

George Rodrigue, *The Cajuns of George Rodrigue*, 1976. Oxmoor House Publishing, Birmingham, Alabama.

George Rodrigue, *Iry LeJeune*, 1972. Oil on canvas, 36 x 36 in. Private collection.

George Rodrigue, *The Patchwork Gift*, 1978. Oil on canvas, 60 x 84 in. Private collection.

George Rodrigue, *The Kingfish*, 1980. Oil on canvas, 60 x 36 in. Private collection.

George Rodrigue, *Uncle Earl*, 1989. Oil on canvas, 48 x 36 in. Private collection.

George Rodrigue, *He-bert, Yes – A Bear, No*, 1985-1989. Oil on canvas, 36 x 24 in. Private collection.

Chapter 9
George Rodrigue, *Man's Best Friend*, 1989. Oil on canvas, 30 x 24 in. Private collection.

George Rodrigue, circa 1979. Photograph of Tiffany, Lafayette, Louisiana. Collection Rodrigue archives.

George Rodrigue, *Starry, Starry Eyes*, 1991. Silkscreen, edition 175, 29 x 22 in. Collection the artist.

George Rodrigue, *I See You, You See Me* (detail), 1993. Silkscreen, edition 35, 16 x 23 in. Collection the artist.

Bridget O'Brian, "How Many Dogs Can Fetch Money?" *The Wall Street Journal*, 1992. Collection Rodrigue archives.

George Rodrigue, *PC Blues*, 2000. Acrylic on canvas, 48 x 36 in. Collection the artist.

George Rodrigue, 2010. Photograph, Metairie, Louisiana. Collection Rodrigue archives.

Unknown, 1983. Photograph of George Rodrigue, Pietrasanta, Italy. Collection Rodrigue archives.

George Rodrigue, *Swamp Dogs Series #7*, 2013. Archival ink printed on metal, edition 10, 48 x 58 in. Collection the artist.

George Rodrigue, *Play it again, Sam*, 2013. Archival ink printed on metal, unique, 41 x 62 in. Collection the artist.

Students, Valencia, California, *Lichtenstein Blue Dog*, 2013. Paint on linoleum. Collection North Park Elementary.

Chapter 10

George Rodrigue, *Shrimp Boat*, 1967. Watercolor on paper, 14 x 18 in. Private collection.

George Rodrigue, *Bayou Indian*, 1984. Oil on canvas, 40 x 30 in. Private collection.

George Rodrigue, *Blue Beach*, 2010. Acrylic on canvas, 18 x 46 in. Private collection.

George Rodrigue, Photograph, South of Pecos, Texas, Hwy 285. Collection Rodrigue archives.

George Rodrigue, *Evergreen Lake*, 1985. Oil on canvas, 24 x 20 in. Private collection.

Rosalea Murphy, *The Owl and the Rooster*, 1994. Oil on canvas, 20 x 24 in. Collection George and Wendy Rodrigue.

George Rodrigue, *Pretty Things Follow Me*, 1999. Acrylic on linen, 16 x 20 in. Private collection.

George Rodrigue, Photograph of Wendy at San Miguel Mission (built 1610), 2010, Santa Fe, New Mexico. Collection Rodrigue archives.

George Rodrigue, Photograph of the Drepung Loseling monks, 2011, Santa Fe, New Mexico. Collection Rodrigue archives.

George Rodrigue, Photograph, Hopi Indian Reservation, 2010. Collection Rodrigue archives.

Chapter 11

Tony Bernard, Two Photographs, September 2005, New Orleans. Collection Rodrigue archives.

Unknown, Photograph of Douglas Shiell and George Rodrigue, 2009, New Orleans. Collection Rodrigue archives.

George Rodrigue, Photograph of Don Sanders, Jacques Rodrigue, Jeff Pellegrin, Jason Dore, February 7, 2010, Miami, Florida. Rodrigue archives.

George Rodrigue, *Good, Good, Good Friends*, 1985. Oil on canvas, 40 x 30 in. Private collection.

George Rodrigue, Photograph of Heather Parker and Wendy Rodrigue, 2012, New Orleans. Collection Rodrigue archives.

George Rodrigue, *Kiss a Frog Good Morning* (detail), 1994. Oil on canvas, 36 x 48 in. Private collection.

Chapter 12

George Rodrigue, *Doctor on the Bayou*, 1982. Oil on canvas, 40 x 30 in. Collection Lake Charles Memorial Hospital.

George Rodrigue, *Dog in a Box*, 1990. Oil on canvas, 30 x 40 in. Collection the artist.

Wendy Rodrigue, Photograph of Get Well Cards, 2012. Collection Rodrigue archives.

George Rodrigue, *Racing at Broussard's Farm*, 1982. Oil on canvas, 30 x 40 in. Private collection.

George Rodrigue, *Hot Dog Halo*, 1995. Oil and acrylic on canvas, 30 x 24 in. Collection the artist.

Unknown, Photograph of George Rodrigue, 1995, Lafayette, Louisiana. Collection Rodrigue archives.

Wendy Rodrigue, Photograph of George Rodrigue, 2003, Carmel, California. Collection Rodrigue archives.

Wendy Rodrigue, Photograph of Rodrigue House, 2012, New Orleans. Collection Rodrigue archives.

George Rodrigue, *Blue Fall in Louisiana*, 2006. Acrylic on canvas, 24 x 30 in. Private collection.

George Rodrigue, *The Best of Both Worlds*, 2013. Archival ink printed on metal, edition 5, 32 x 60 in. Collection the artist.

About the Author

Wendy Wolfe Rodrigue grew up in Fort Walton Beach, Florida, where her father was stationed at Eglin Air Force Base. She graduated from Trinity University in San Antonio, Texas, with degrees in Art History and English, followed by graduate studies at Tulane University in New Orleans and one year at the American University in Vienna, Austria. In 1991 Wendy joined the staff of the Rodrigue Gallery in New Orleans and moved later that year to Carmel, California, where she managed George Rodrigue's gallery for six years. Today, Wendy remains involved in Rodrigue Gallery operations and the George Rodrigue Foundation of the Arts; writes occasional guest columns for publications including *Gambit*, *Country Roads Magazine*, and *Louisiana Cultural Vistas*; works on Rodrigue exhibitions and publishing projects; and lectures frequently on Rodrigue art and Louisiana history. Wendy is a past member of the Board of Trustees of the New Orleans Museum of Art and the Louisiana Endowment for the Humanities. George and Wendy married in 1997 and lived in Lafayette, Louisiana, before moving to New Orleans in 2001. Today they divide their time between their homes in New Orleans's Faubourg Marigny and Carmel Valley, California. Wendy's blog Musings of an Artist's Wife can be found at www.wendyrodrigue.com.